Daily Light on the Daily Path

By LOUIS KLOPSCH

THE FAMILY INSPIRATIONAL LIBRARY

PUBLISHERS *Grosset & Dunlap* NEW YORK

Daily Light on the Daily Path

This one thing I do: forgetting those things which are behind, . . . I press toward the mark for the prize of the high calling of God in Christ Jesus.

F<small>ATHER</small>, I will that they . . . whom thou hast given me, be with me where I am; that they may behold my glory which thou hast given me.—I know whom I have believed, and am persuaded that he is able to keep that which I have committed unto him against that day.—He which hath begun a good work in you will perform it until the day of Jesus Christ.

Know ye not that they which run in a race run all, but one receiveth the prize? So run, that ye may obtain.—Let us lay aside every weight, and the sin which doth so easily beset us, and let us run with patience the race that is set before us, looking unto Jesus.

PHILIPPIANS 3: 13, 14. John 17: 24.—II Timothy 1: 12.
—Philippians 1: 16. I Corinthians 9: 24.—Hebrews 12: 1, 2.

JANUARY 2

Sing unto the Lord a new song.

Sing aloud unto God our strength; make a joyful noise unto the God of Jacob. Take a psalm, and bring hither the timbrel, the pleasant harp with the psaltery. —He hath put a new song in my mouth, even praise unto our God: many shall see it, and fear, and shall trust in the Lord.

Be strong and of a good courage; be not afraid, neither be thou dismayed: for the Lord thy God is with thee whithersoever thou goest.—The joy of the Lord is your strength.—Paul . . . thanked God, and took courage.

Knowing the time, that now it is high time to awake out of sleep; for now is our salvation nearer than when we believed. The night is far spent, the day is at hand: let us therefore cast off the works of darkness, and let us put on the armor of light. Let us walk honestly, as in the day; not in rioting and drunkenness, not in chambering and wantonness, not in strife and envying. But put ye on the Lord Jesus Christ, and make not provision for the flesh, to fulfil the lusts thereof.

ISAIAH 42: 10. Psalms 81: 1, 2.—Psalms 40: 3. Joshua 1: 9.—Nehemiah 8: 10.—Acts 28: 15. Romans 13: 11-14.

He led them forth by the right way.

He found (Jacob) in a desert land, and in the waste howling wilderness; he led him about, instructed him, he kept him as the apple of his eye. As an eagle stirreth up her nest, fluttereth over her young, spreadeth abroad her wings, taketh them, beareth them on her wings: so the LORD alone did lead him.—Even to your old age I am he; and even to hoar hairs will I carry you: I have made, and I will bear; even I will carry, and will deliver you.

He restoreth my soul: he leadeth me in the paths of righteousness for his name's sake. Yea, though I walk through the valley of the shadow of death, I will fear no evil: for thou art with me; thy rod and thy staff they comfort me.

The LORD shall guide thee continually, and satisfy thy soul in drought, and make fat thy bones: and thou shalt be like a watered garden, and like a spring of water, whose waters fail not.—For this God is our God for ever and ever: he will be our guide even unto death.—Who teacheth like him?

PSALMS 107: 7. Deuteronomy 32: 10-12.—Isaiah 46: 4.
Psalms 23: 3, 4. Isaiah 58: 11.—Psalms 48: 14.—Job 36: 22.

JANUARY 4

Ye are not as yet come to the rest and to the inheritance, which the Lord your God giveth you.

This is not your rest.—There remaineth therefore a rest to the people of God.—Within the veil; whither the forerunner is for us entered, even Jesus.

In my Father's house are many mansions: if it were not so, I would have told you. I go to prepare a place for you. And if I go and prepare a place for you, I will come again, and receive you unto myself; that where I am, there ye may be also.—With Christ; which is far better.

God shall wipe away all tears from their eyes; and there shall be no more death, neither sorrow, nor crying, neither shall there by any more pain; for the former things are passed away.—There the wicked cease from troubling: and there the weary be at rest.

Lay up for yourselves treasures in heaven. For where your treasure is, there will your heart be also. —Set your affection on things above, not on things on the earth.

DEUTERONOMY 12: 9. Micah 2: 10.—Hebrews 4: 9.— Hebrews 6: 19-20. John 14: 2, 3.—Philippians 1: 23. Revelation 21: 4.—Job 3: 17. Matthew 6: 20, 21.—Colossians 3: 2.

We which have believed do enter into rest.

THEY weary themselves to commit iniquity.—I see another law in my members warring against the law of my mind, and bringing me into captivity to the law of sin which is in my members. O wretched man that I am! who shall deliver me from the body of this death?

Come unto me, all ye that labor and are heavy laden, and I will give you rest.—Being justified by faith, we have peace with God through our Lord Jesus Christ: by whom also we have access by faith into this grace wherein we stand, and rejoice in hope of the glory of God.

He that is entered into his rest, he also hath ceased from his own works.—Not having mine own righteousness, which is of the law, but that which is through the faith of Christ, the righteousness which is of God by faith.—This is the rest wherewith ye may cause the weary to rest; and this is the refreshing.

HEBREWS 4: 8. Jeremiah 9: 5.—Romans 7: 23, 24. Matthew 11: 28.—Romans 5: 1, 2. Hebrews 4: 10.—Philippians 3: 9.—Isaiah 28: 12.

JANUARY 6

Let the beauty of the Lord our God be upon us:
and establish thou the work of our hands.

THEY weary themselves to commit iniquity.—I see
thy beauty: for it was perfect through my comeliness,
which I had put upon thee, saith the Lord God.—We
all, with open face beholding as in a glass the glory
of the Lord, are changed into the same image from
glory to glory, even as by the Spirit of the Lord.

Blessed is every one that feareth the Lord: that
walketh in his ways. For thou shalt eat the labor of
thy hands; happy shalt thou be, and it shall be well
with thee.—Commit thy works unto the LORD, and
thy thoughts shall be established.

Work out your own salvation with fear and trembling. For it is God which worketh in you both to will
and to do his good pleasure.—Our Lord Jesus Christ
himself, and God, even our Father, which hath loved
us, and hath given us everlasting consolation and
good hope through grace, comfort your hearts, and
stablish you in every good word and work.

PSALMS 90: 17. Ezekiel 16: 14.—II Corinthians 3: 18.
Psalms 128: 1, 2.—Proverbs 16: 13. Philippians 2: 12, 13.—
II Thessalonians 2: 16, 17.

Think upon me, my God, for good.

Thus saith the LORD; I remember thee, the kindness of thy youth, the love of thine espousals, when thou wentest after me in the wilderness.—I will remember my covenant with thee in the days of thy youth, and I will establish unto thee an everlasting covenant.—I will visit you, and perform my good word toward you. . . . For I know the thoughts that I think toward you, saith the LORD, thoughts of peace, and not of evil, to give you an expected end.

As the heavens are higher than the earth, so are my ways higher than your ways, and my thoughts than your thoughts.—I would seek unto God, and unto God would I commit my cause: which doeth great things and unsearchable; marvellous things without number.—Many, O Lord my God, are thy wonderful works which thou hast done, and thy thoughts which are to us-ward: they cannot be reckoned up in order unto thee: if I would declare and speak of them they are more than can be numbered.

NEHEMIAH 5: 19. Jeremiah 2: 2.—Ezekiel 16: 60.—Jeremiah 29: 10, 11. Isaiah 55: 9.—Job 5: 8, 9.—Psalms 40: 5.

JANUARY 8

They that know thy name will put their trust in thee: for thou, Lord, hast not forsaken them that seek thee.

THE name of the LORD is a strong tower: the righteous runneth into it, and is safe.—I will trust, and not be afraid: for the LORD JEHOVAH is my strength and my song; he also is become my salvation.

I have been young, and now am old; yet have I not seen the righteous forsaken, nor his seed begging bread.—For the LORD loveth judgment, and forsaketh not his saints; they are preserved for ever: but the seed of the wicked shall be cut off.—The LORD will not forsake his people for his great name's sake: because it hath pleased the LORD to make you his people.—Who delivered us from so great a death, and doth deliver; in whom we trust that he will yet deliver us.

Be content with such things as ye have; for he hath said, I will never leave thee, nor forsake thee. So that we may boldly say, The Lord is my helper, and I will not fear what man shall do unto me.

PSALMS 9: 10. Proverbs 18: 10.—Isaiah 12: 2. Psalms 37: 25.—Psalms 37: 28.—I Samuel 12: 22.—II Corinthians 1: 10. Hebrews 13: 5, 6.

Thou hast given a banner to them that fear thee, that it may be displayed because of the truth.

JEHOVAH NISSI (The Lord my banner).—When the enemy shall come in like a flood, the Spirit of the LORD shall lift up a standard against him.

We will rejoice in thy salvation, and in the name of our God we will set up our banners.—The LORD hath brought forth our righteousness: come, and let us declare in Zion the work of the LORD our God.—We are more than conquerors through him that loved us.—Thanks be to God, which giveth us the victory through our Lord Jesus Christ.

My brethren, be strong in the Lord, and in the power of his might.—Valiant for the truth.—Fight the LORD's battles.—Be strong, all ye people of the land, saith the Lord, and work: . . . fear ye not.—Lift up your eyes, and look on the fields; for they are white already to harvest.—Yet a little while, and he that shall come, will come, and will not tarry.

PSALMS 60: 4. Exodus 17: 15.—Isaiah 59: 19. Psalms 20: 5.—Jeremiah 1: 10.—Romans 8: 37.—I Corinthians 15: 57.—Hebrews 2: 10. Ephesians 6: 10.—Jeremiah 9: 3.—I Samuel 18: 17.—Haggai 2: 4, 5.—John 4: 35.—Hebrews 10: 37.

JANUARY 10

I pray God your whole spirit and soul and body be preserved blameless unto the coming of our Lord Jesus Christ.

CHRIST loved the church, and gave himself for it; that he might present it to himself a glorious church, not having spot, or wrinkle, or any such thing; but that it should be holy and without blemish.—Whom we preach, warning every man, and teaching every man in all wisdom; that we may present every man perfect in Christ Jesus.

The peace of God . . . passeth all understanding. —Let the peace of God rule in your hearts, to the which also ye are called in one body.

Our Lord Jesus Christ himself, and God, even our Father, which hath loved us, and hath given us everlasting consolation and good hope through grace, comfort your hearts, and stablish you in every good word and work.—Who shall also confirm you unto the end, that ye may be blameless in the day of our Lord Jesus Christ.

I THESSALONIANS 5: 23. Ephesians 5: 25, 27.—Colossians 1: 28. Philippians 4: 17.—Colossians 3: 15. II Thessalonians 2: 16, 17.—I Corinthians 1: 8.

Praise waiteth for thee, O God, in Zion.

To us there is but one God, the Father, of whom are all things, and we in him; and one Lord Jesus Christ.—All men should honor the Son, even as they honor the Father. He that honoreth not the Son honoreth not the Father which hath sent him.—By him therefore let us offer the sacrifice of praise to God continually, that is, the fruit of our lips giving thanks to his name.—Whoso offereth praise glorifieth me: and to him that ordereth his conversation aright will I show the salvation of God.

I beheld, and lo, a great multitude, which no man could number, of all nations, and kindreds, and people, and tongues, stood before the throne, and before the Lamb, clothed with white robes, and palms in their hands; and cried with a loud voice, saying, Salvation to our God which sitteth upon the throne, and unto the Lamb. Amen: Blessing, and glory, and wisdom, and thanksgiving, and honor, and power, and might, be unto our God for ever and ever. Amen.

PSALMS 65: 1. I Corinthians 8: 6.—John 5: 23.—Hebrews 13: 15.—Psalms 50: 23. Revelation 7: 9, 10, 12.

JANUARY 12

The only wise God our Saviour.

CHRIST JESUS, who of God is made unto us wisdom, and righteousness, and sanctification, and redemption.—Canst thou by searching find out God? Canst thou find out the Almighty unto perfection? It is as high as heaven; what canst thou do? deeper than hell; what canst thou know?

We speak the wisdom of God in a mystery, even the hidden wisdom, which God ordained before the world unto our glory.—The mystery, which from the beginning of the world hath been hid in God, who created all things by Jesus Christ: to the intent that now unto the principalities and powers in heavenly places might be known, by the church, the manifold wisdom of God.

If any of you lack wisdom, let him ask of God, that giveth to all men liberally, and upbraideth not; and it shall be given him.—The wisdom that is from above is first pure, then peaceable, gentle, and easy to be entreated, full of mercy and good fruits, without partiality, and without hypocrisy.

JUDE 25. I Corinthians 1: 30. Job 11: 7, 8. I Corinthians 2: 7.—Ephesians 3: 9, 10. James 1: 5.—James 3: 17.

12

Thou wilt keep him in perfect peace, whose mind is stayed on thee.

Cast thy burden upon the LORD, and he shall sustain thee; he shall never suffer the righteous to be moved.—I will trust, and not be afraid; for the LORD JEHOVAH is my strength and my song; he also is become my salvation.

Why are ye fearful, O ye of little faith?—Be careful for nothing; but in everything by prayer and supplication with thanksgiving let your requests be made known unto God. And the peace of God, which passeth all understanding, shall keep your hearts and minds through Christ Jesus.—In quietness and in confidence shall be your strength.

The effect of righteousness [shall be] quietness and assurance for ever.—Peace I leave with you, my peace I give unto you: not as the world giveth give I unto you. Let not your heart be troubled, neither let it be afraid.—Peace, from him which is, and which was, and which is to come.

ISAIAH 26: 3. Psalms 55: 22.—Isaiah 12: 2. Matthew 8: 26.—Philippians 4: 6, 7.—Isaiah 30: 15. Isaiah 32: 17.—John 14: 27.—Revelation 1: 4.

JANUARY 14

My Father is greater than I.

WHEN ye pray, say, Our Father which art in heaven.—My Father, and your Father; . . . my God and your God.

As the Father gave me commandment, even so I do.—The words that I speak unto you I speak not of myself: but the Father that dwelleth in me, he doeth the works.

The Father loveth the Son, and hath given all things into his hand.—Thou hast given him power over all flesh, that he should give eternal life to as many as thou hast given him.

LORD, show us the Father, and it sufficeth us. Jesus saith unto him, Have I been so long time with you, and yet hast thou not known me, Philip? he that hath seen me hath seen the Father; and how sayest thou then, Show us the Father? Believest thou not that I am in the Father, and the Father in me?—I and my Father are one.—As the Father hath loved me, so have I loved you: continue ye in my love. If ye keep my commandments, ye shall abide in my love; even as I have kept my Father's commandments, and abide in his love.

JOHN 14: 28. Luke 11: 2.—John 20: 17. John 14: 31.—
John 14: 10. John 3: 35.—John 17: 2. John 14: 8-10.—John
10: 30.—John 15: 9, 10.

My soul cleaveth unto the dust: quicken thou
me according to thy word.

If ye . . . be risen with Christ, seek those things
which are above, where Christ sitteth on the right
hand of God. Set your affection on things above, not
on things on the earth. For . . . your life is hid with
Christ in God.—Our conversation is in heaven; from
whence also we look for the Saviour, the Lord Jesus
Christ: who shall change our vile body, that it may be
fashioned like unto his glorious body, according to
the working whereby he is able even to subdue all
things unto himself.

The flesh lusteth against the Spirit, and the Spirit
against the flesh; and these are contrary the one to
the other; so that ye cannot do the things that ye
would.—Brethren, we are debtors, not to the flesh, to
live after the flesh. For if ye live after the flesh, ye
shall die: but if ye through the Spirit do mortify the
deeds of the body, ye shall live.—Dearly beloved, I
beseech you as strangers and pilgrims, abstain from
fleshly lusts, which war against the soul.

PSALMS 119: 25. Colossians 3: 1-3.—Philippians 3: 20,
21. Galatians 5: 17.—Romans 8: 12, 13.—I Peter 2, 11.

JANUARY 16

It pleased the Father, that in him should all fulness dwell.

THE Father loveth the Son, and hath given all things into his hand.—God hath highly exalted him and given him a name which is above every name: that at the name of Jesus every knee should bow, of things in heaven, and things in earth, and things under the earth; and that every tongue should confess that Jesus Christ is Lord, to the glory of God the Father.—Far above all principality, and power, and might, and dominion, and every name that is named, not only in this world, but also in that which is to come.—By him were all things created, that are in heaven, and that are in earth, visible and invisible, whether they be thrones, or dominions, or principalities, or powers: all things were created by him and for him.

Christ both died, and rose, and revived, that he might be Lord both of the dead and living.—And ye are complete in him, which is the head of all principality and power.—Of his fulness have all we received.

COLOSSIANS 1: 19. John 3: 35.—Philippians 2: 9-11.—Ephesians 1: 21.—Colossians 1: 16. Romans 14: 9.—Colossians 2: 10.—John 1: 16.

Thou hast in love to my soul delivered it from the pit of corruption.

Gᴏᴅ sent his only begotten son into the world, that we might live through him.—Herein is love, not that we loved God, but that he loved us, and sent his Son to be the propitiation for our sins.

Who is a God like unto thee, that pardoneth iniquity, and passeth by the transgression of the remnant of his heritage? he retaineth not his anger for ever, because he delighteth in mercy. He will turn again, he will have compassion upon us; he will subdue our iniquities; and thou wilt cast all their sins into the depths of the sea.—O Lᴏʀᴅ my God, I cried unto thee, and thou hast healed me. O Lᴏʀᴅ, thou hast brought up my soul from the grave: thou hast kept me alive, that I should not go down to the pit.—When my soul fainted within me I remembered the Lᴏʀᴅ; and my prayer came in unto thee, into thy holy temple.—I waited patiently for the Lᴏʀᴅ. He brought me up . . . out of a horrible pit, out of the miry clay, and set my feet upon a rock.

ISAIAH 38: 12. I John 4: 9, 10. Micah 7: 18, 19.—Psalms 30: 2, 3.—Jonah 2: 7.—Psalms 40: 1, 2.

JANUARY 18

Him that was to come.

JESUS . . . made a little lower than the angels for the suffering of death, . . . that he by the grace of God should taste death for every man.—One died for all.—As by one man's disobedience many were made sinners, so by the obedience of one shall many be made righteous.

The first man Adam was made a living soul; the last Adam was made a quickening spirit. . . . That was not first which is spiritual, but that which is natural; and afterward that which is spiritual.—God said, Let us make man in our image, after our likeness. So God created man in his own image, in the image of God created he him.—God . . . hath in these last days spoken unto us by his Son, . . . the brightness of his glory, and the express image of his person.—Thou hast given him power over all flesh.

The first man is of the earth, earthy: the second man is the Lord from heaven. As is the earthy, such are they also that are earthy, and as is the heavenly, such are they also that are heavenly.

ROMANS 5: 14. Hebrews 2: 9.—II Corinthians 5: 14.—
Romans 5: 19. I Corinthians 15: 45, 46.—Genesis 1: 26, 27.—
Hebrews 1: 1-3.—John 17: 2. I Corinthians 15: 47, 48.

Serving the Lord with all humility of mind.

Whosoever will be great among you, let him be your minister; and whosoever will be chief among you, let him be your servant: even as the Son of man came not to be ministered unto, but to minister, and to give his life a ransom for many.

If a man think himself to be something, when he is nothing, he deceiveth himself.—I say, through the grace given unto me, to every man, . . . not to think of himself more highly than he ought to think; but to think soberly, according as God hath dealt to every man the measure of faith.—When ye shall have done all those things which are commanded you, say, We are unprofitable servants: we have done that which was our duty to do.

Our rejoicing is this, . . . that in simplicity and godly sincerity, not with fleshly wisdom, but by the grace of God, we have had our conversation in the world.—We have this treasure in earthen vessels, that the excellency of the power may be of God, and not of us.

ACTS 20: 19. Matthew 20: 26-28. Galatians 6: 3.—Romans 12: 3.—Luke 17: 10. II Corinthians 1: 12.—II Corinthians 4: 7.

JANUARY 20

His name shall be called Wonderful.

THE WORD was made flesh, and dwelt among us, (and we beheld his glory, the glory as of the only begotten of the Father,) full of grace and truth.— Thou hast magnified thy word above all thy name.

They shall call his name Emmanuel, which being interpreted is, God with us.—JESUS: for he shall save his people from their sins.

All men should honor the Son, even as they honor the Father.—God . . . hath highly exalted him, and given him a name which is above every name.—Far above all principality, and power, and might, and dominion, and every name that is named, not only in this world, but also in that which is to come; and hath put all things under his feet.—He had a name written, that no man knew, but he himself. . . . KING OF KINGS, AND LORD OF LORDS.

Touching the Almighty, we cannot find him out.— What is his name, and what is his son's name, if thou canst tell?

ISAIAH 9: 6. John 1: 14.—Psalms 138: 2. Matthew 1: 23. —Matthew 1: 21. John 5: 23.—Philippians 2: 9.—Ephesians 1: 21, 22.—Revelation 19: 16. Job 37: 23.—Proverbs 30: 4.

Every branch that beareth fruit, he purgeth it.

HE is like a refiner's fire, and like fuller's soap: and he shall sit as a refiner and purifier of silver; and he shall purify the sons of Levi, and purge them as gold and silver, that they may offer unto the LORD an offering in righteousness.

We glory in tribulations: knowing that tribulation worketh patience; and patience, experience; and experience, hope: and hope maketh not ashamed; because the love of God is shed abroad in our hearts by the Holy Ghost which is given unto us.—If ye endure chastening, God dealeth with you as with sons; for what son is he whom the father chasteneth not? But if ye be without chastisement, whereof all are partakers, then are ye bastards, and not sons. Now no chastening for the present seemeth to be joyous, but grievous: nevertheless afterward it yieldeth the peaceable fruit of righteousness unto them which are exercised thereby. Wherefore lift up the hands which hang down, and the feeble knees.

JOHN 15: 2. Malachi 3: 2, 3. Romans 5: 3-5.—Hebrews 12: 7, 8, 11, 12.

JANUARY 22

This God is our God for ever and ever: he will be our guide even unto death.

O Lord, thou art my God; I will exalt thee, I will praise thy name; for thou hast done wonderful things; thy counsels of old are faithfulness and truth. —The Lord is the portion of mine inheritance, and of my cup.

He leadeth me in the paths of righteousness, for his name's sake. Yea, though I walk through the valley of the shadow of death, I will fear no evil: for thou art with me; thy rod and thy staff they comfort me. —Thou hast holden me by my right hand. Thou shalt guide me with thy counsel, and afterward receive me to glory. Whom have I in heaven but thee? and there is none upon earth that I desire beside thee. My flesh and my heart faileth: but God is the strength of my heart, and my portion for ever.—Our heart shall rejoice in him, because we have trusted in his holy name.—The Lord will perfect that which concerneth me: thy mercy, O Lord, endureth for ever: forsake not the works of thine own hands.

PSALMS 48: 14. Isaiah 25: 1.—Psalms 16: 5. Psalms 23: 3, 4.—Psalms 73: 23-26.—Psalms 33: 21.—Psalms 138: 8.

Hope maketh not ashamed.

I AM the LORD: . . . they shall not be ashamed that wait for me.—Blessed is the man that trusteth in the LORD, and whose hope the LORD is.—Thou wilt keep him in perfect peace, whose mind is stayed on thee: because he trusteth in thee. Trust ye in the LORD for ever: for in the LORD JEHOVAH is everlasting strength.—My soul, wait thou only upon God; for my expectation is from him. He only is my rock and my salvation: he is my defence; I shall not be moved.—I am not ashamed, for I know whom I have believed.

God, willing more abundantly to show unto the heirs of promise the immutability of his counsel, confirmed it by an oath: that by two immutable things, in which it was impossible for God to lie, we might have a strong consolation, who have fled for refuge to lay hold upon the hope set before us: which hope we have as an anchor of the soul, both sure and steadfast, and which entereth into that within the veil; whither the forerunner is for us entered, even Jesus.

ROMANS 5: 5. Isaiah 49: 23.—Jeremiah 17: 7.—Isaiah 26: 3, 4.—Psalms 62: 5, 6.—II Timothy 1: 12. Hebrews 6: 17-20.

JANUARY 24

The Lord is at hand.

THE LORD himself shall descend from heaven with a shout, with the voice of the archangel, and with the trump of God: and the dead in Christ shall rise first: then we which are alive and remain, shall be caught up together with them in the clouds, to meet the Lord in the air: and so shall we ever be with the Lord. Wherefore comfort one another with these words.—He which testifieth these things saith, Surely I come quickly. Amen. Even so, come, Lord Jesus.

Wherefore, beloved, seeing that ye look for such things, be diligent that ye may be found of him in peace, without spot, and blameless.—Abstain from all appearance of evil. And the very God of peace sanctify you wholly; and I pray God your whole spirit and soul and body be preserved blameless unto the coming of our Lord Jesus Christ. Faithful is he that calleth you, who also will do it.

Be ye also patient; stablish your hearts; for the coming of the Lord draweth nigh.

PHILIPPIANS 4: 5. I Thessalonians 4: 16-18.—Revelation 22: 20. II Peter 3: 14.—I Thessalonians 5: 22-24. James 5: 8.

The righteousness of God which is by faith of
Jesus Christ unto all and upon all them that
believe.

H E hath made him to be sin for us, who knew no
sin; that we might be made the righteousness of God
in him.—Christ hath redeemed us from the curse of
the law, being made a curse for us.—Who of God is
made unto us wisdom, and righteousness, and sanctification, and redemption.—Not by works of righteousness which we have done, but according to his
mercy he saved us, by the washing of regeneration,
and renewing of the Holy Ghost; which he shed on
us abundantly through Jesus Christ our Saviour.

I count all things but loss for the excellency of the
knowledge of Christ Jesus my Lord: for whom I have
suffered the loss of all things, and do count them but
dung, that I may win Christ, and be found in him,
not having mine own righteousness, which is of the
law, but that which is through the faith of Christ,
the righteousness which is of God by faith.

ROMANS 3: 22. II Corinthians 5: 2.—Galatians 3: 13.—
I Corinthians 1: 30.—Titus 3: 5, 6. Philippians 3: 8, 9.

JANUARY 26

Let us go forth unto him without the camp, bearing his reproach. For here have we no continuing city, but we seek one to come.

Beloved, think it not strange concerning the fiery trial which is to try you, as though some strange thing happened unto you: but rejoice, inasmuch as ye are partakers of Christ's sufferings; that, when his glory shall be revealed, ye may be glad also with exceeding joy.—As ye are partakers of the sufferings, so shall ye be also of the consolation.

If ye be reproached for the name of Christ, happy are ye; for the Spirit of glory and of God resteth upon you: on their part he is evil spoken of, but on your part he is glorified.

They departed from the presence of the council, rejoicing that they were counted worthy to suffer shame for his name.—Choosing rather to suffer affliction with the people of God, than to enjoy the pleasures of sin for a season; esteeming the reproach of Christ greater riches than the treasures in Egypt: for he had respect unto the recompense of the reward.

HEBREWS 13: 13, 14. I Peter 4: 12, 13.—II Corinthians 1: 7. I Peter 4: 14. Acts 5: 41.—Hebrews 11: 25, 26.

Ye know that he was manifested to take away our sins; and in him is no sin.

G<small>OD</small>, . . . hath in these last days spoken unto us by his Son, . . . who being the brightness of his glory, and the express image of his person, and upholding all things by the word of his power, when he had by himself purged our sins, sat down on the right hand of the Majesty on high.—He hath made him to be sin for us, who knew no sin.

Pass the time of your sojourning here in fear: forasmuch as ye know that ye were not redeemed with corruptible things, as silver and gold; . . . but with the precious blood of Christ, as of a lamb without blemish and without spot: who verily was foreordained before the foundation of the world, but was manifest in these last times for you.—The love of Christ constraineth us; because we thus judge, that if one died for all, then were all dead: and that he died for all, that they which live should not henceforth live unto themselves, but unto him which died for them, and rose again.

I JOHN 3: 5. Hebrews 1: 1-3.—II Corinthians 5: 21. I Peter 1: 17-20.—II Corinthians 5: 14, 15.

JANUARY 28

As thy days, so shall thy strength be.

WHEN they shall lead you, and deliver you up, take no thought beforehand what ye shall speak, neither do ye premeditate; but whatsoever shall be given you in that hour, that speak ye: for it is not ye that speak, but the Holy Ghost.—Take no thought for the morrow: for the morrow shall take thought for the things of itself. Sufficient unto the day is the evil thereof.

The God of Israel is he that giveth strength and power unto his people. Blessed be God.—He giveth power to the faint; and to them that have no might he increaseth strength.

My grace is sufficient for thee: for my strength is made perfect in weakness. Most gladly therefore will I rather glory in my infirmities, that the power of Christ may rest upon me. Therefore I take pleasure in infirmities, in reproaches, in necessities, in persecutions, in distresses for Christ's sake: for when I am weak, then am I strong.—I can do all things through Christ which strengtheneth me.—O my soul, thou hast trodden down strength.

DEUTERONOMY 33: 25. Mark 13: 11.—Matthew 6: 34. Psalms 68: 35.—Isaiah 40: 29. II Corinthians 12: 9, 10.— Philippians 4: 13.—Judges 5: 21.

Thou God seest me.

O LORD, thou hast searched me, and known me.
Thou knowest my down-sitting amd mine uprising,
thou understandest my thought afar off. Thou com-
passest my path and my lying down, and art acquainted with all my ways. For there is not a word
in my tongue, but lo, O Lord, thou knowest it altogether. . . . Such knowledge is too wonderful for me:
it is high, I cannot attain unto it.

The eyes of the Lord are in every place, beholding
the evil and the good.—The ways of man are before
the eyes of the Lord, and he pondereth all his goings.
—God knoweth your hearts: for that which is highly
esteemed among men is abomination in the sight of
God.—The eyes of the Lord run to and fro throughout the whole earth, to show himself strong in the
behalf of them whose heart is perfect toward him.

Jesus . . . knew all men, and needed not that any
should testify of man: for he knew what was in man.
—Lord, thou knowest all things; thou knowest that
I love thee.

GENESIS 16: 13. Psalms 139: 1-4, 6. Proverbs 15: 3.—
Proverbs 5: 21.—Luke 16: 15.—II Chronicles 16: 9. John 2:
24, 25.—John 21: 17.

JANUARY 30

Let us run with patience the race that is set before us, looking unto Jesus the author and finisher of our faith.

IF any man will come after me, let him deny himself, and take up his cross daily, and follow me.—Whosoever he be of you that forsaketh not all that he hath, he cannot be my disciple.—Let us therefore cast off the works of darkness.

Every man that striveth for the mastery is temperate in all things. Now they do it to obtain a corruptible crown; but we an incorruptible. I therefore so run, not as uncertainly; so fight I, not as one that beateth the air: but I keep under my body, and bring it into subjection: lest that by any means, when I have preached to others, I myself should be a castaway.—Brethren, I count not myself to have apprehended: but this one thing I do, forgetting those things which are behind, and reaching forth unto those things which are before, I press toward the mark for the prize of the high calling of God in Christ Jesus.—Then shall we know, if we follow on to know the Lord.

HEBREWS 12: 1, 2. Luke 9: 23.—Luke 14: 33.—Romans 13: 12. I Corinthians 9: 25-27.—Philippians 3: 13, 14.—Hosea 6: 3.

If ye will not drive out the inhabitants of the
land from before you; those which ye let remain
of them shall be pricks in your eyes, and thorns
in your sides, and shall vex you in the land
wherein ye dwell.

FIGHT the good fight of faith.—The weapons of our
warfare are not carnal, but mighty through God to
the pulling down of strongholds; casting down
imaginations, . . . and bringing into capitivity every
thought to the obedience of Christ.

Brethren, we are debtors, not to the flesh, to live
after the flesh. For if ye live after the flesh, ye shall
die: but if ye through the Spirit do mortify the deeds
of the body, ye shall live.—The flesh lusteth against
the Spirit, and the Spirit against the flesh; and these
are contrary the one to the other: so that ye cannot
do the things that ye would.—I see another law in
my members, warring against the law of the mind,
and bringing me into captivity to the law of sin which
is in my members.—We are more than conquerors
through him that loved us.

NUMBERS 33: 35. I Timothy 6: 12.—II Corinthians 10:
4, 5. Romans 8: 12, 13.—Galatians 5: 17.—Romans 7: 23.—
Romans 8: 37.

FEBRUARY 1

Whom having not seen, ye love.

WE walk by faith, not by sight.—We love him, because he first loved us.—And we have known and believed the love that God hath to us. God is love; and he that dwelleth in love dwelleth in God, and God in him.—In whom ye trusted, after that ye heard the word of truth, the gospel of your salvation: in whom also, after that ye believed, ye were sealed with that Holy Spirit of promise.—God would make known what is the riches of the glory of this mystery among the Gentiles; which is Christ in you, the hope of glory.

If a man say, I love God, and hateth his brother, he is a liar: for he that loveth not his brother whom he hath seen, how can he love God whom he hath not seen?

Jesus saith unto him, Thomas, because thou hast seen me, thou hast believed: blessed are they that have not seen, and yet have believed.—Blessed are all they that put their trust in him.

I PETER 1: 8. II Corinthians 5: 7.—I John 4: 19.—I John 4: 16.—Ephesians 1: 13.—Colossians 1: 27.—I John 4: 20. John 20: 29.—Psalms 2: 12.

Oh that thou wouldest keep me from evil.

WHY sleep ye? rise and pray, lest ye enter into temptation.—The spirit is willing, but the flesh is weak.

Two things have I required of thee; deny me them not before I die: remove far from me vanity and lies; give me neither poverty nor riches; feed me with food convenient for me: lest I be full and deny thee, and say, Who is the LORD? or lest I be poor, and steal, and take the name of my God in vain.

The LORD shall preserve thee from all evil; he shall preserve thy soul.—I will deliver thee out of the hand of the wicked, and I will redeem thee out of the hand of the terrible.—He that is begotten of God keepeth himself, and that wicked one toucheth him not.

Because thou hast kept the word of my patience, I also will keep thee from the hour of temptation, which shall come upon all the world, to try them that dwell upon the earth.—The LORD knoweth how to deliver the godly out of temptations.

I CHRONICLES 4: 10. Luke 22: 46.—Matthew 26: 41. Proverbs 30: 7, 9. Psalms 121: 7.—Jeremiah 15: 21.—I John 5: 18. Revelation 3: 10.—II Peter 2: 9.

FEBRUARY 3

Be strong, and work: for I am with you, saith the Lord of hosts.

I AM the vine, ye are the branches: he that abideth in me, and I in him, the same bringeth forth much fruit: for without me ye can do nothing.—I can do all things through Christ which strengtheneth me.—Strong in the Lord, and in the power of his might.—The joy of the LORD is your strength.

Thus saith the LORD of hosts: Let your hands be strong, ye that hear in these days these words by the mouth of the prophets.—Strengthen ye the weak hands, and confirm the feeble knees. Say to them that are of a fearful heart, Be strong, fear not.—The LORD looked upon him, and said, Go in this thy might.

If God be for us, who can be against us?—Therefore seeing we have this ministry, as we have received mercy, we faint not.

Let us not be weary in well doing: for in due season we shall reap, if we faint not.—Thanks be to God, which giveth us the victory through our Lord Jesus Christ.

HAGGAI 2: 4. John 15: 5.—Philippians 4: 13.—Ephesians 6: 10.—Nehemiah 8: 10. Zechariah 8: 9.—Isaiah 35: 3, 4. —Judges 6: 14. Romans 8: 31.—II Corinthians 4: 1. Galatians 6: 9.—I Corinthians 15: 57.

The Lord hath said unto you, Ye shall henceforth return no more that way.

TRULY if they had been mindful of that country from whence they came out, they might have had opportunity to have returned. But now they desire a better country, that is, a heavenly. Choosing rather to suffer affliction with the people of God, than to enjoy the pleasures of sin for a season; esteeming the reproach of Christ greater riches than the treasures in Egypt.—The just shall live by faith: but if any man draw back, my soul shall shall have no pleasure in him.—No man, having put his hand to the plough, and looking back, is fit for the kingdom of God.

God forbid that I should glory, save in the cross of our Lord Jesus Christ, by whom the world is crucified unto me, and I unto the world.—Come out from among them, and be ye separate, saith the Lord, . . . and I will receive you.

He which hath begun a good work in you, will perform it until the day of Jesus Christ.

DEUTERONOMY 17: 16. Hebrews 11: 15, 16, 25, 26.— Hebrews 10: 38, 39.—Luke 9: 62. Galatians 6: 14.—II Corinthians 6: 17. Philippians 1: 6.

FEBRUARY 5

I am come that they might have life, and that
they might have it more abundantly.

In the day that thou eatest thereof thou shalt surely
die.—She took of the fruit thereof, and gave also
unto her husband with her; and he did eat.

The wages of sin is death; but the gift of God is
eternal life through Jesus Christ our Lord.—If by one
man's offence death reigned by one; much more they
which receive abundance of grace and of the gift of
righteousness shall reign in life by one, Jesus Christ.
—Since by man came death, by man came also the
resurrection of the dead. For as in Adam all die, even
so in Christ shall all be made alive.—Our Saviour
Jesus Christ . . . hath abolished death, and hath
brought life and immortality to light through the
gospel.

God hath given to us eternal life, and this life is
in his Son. He that . . . hath not the Son of God
hath not life.—For God sent not his Son into the
world to condemn the world; but that the world
through him might be saved.

JOHN 10: 10. Genesis 2: 17.—Genesis 3: 6. Romans 6: 23.
—Romans 5: 17.—I Corinthians 15: 21, 22.—II Timothy 1:
10. I John 5: 11, 12.—John 3: 17.

36

The grace of our Lord was exceeding abundant
with faith and love which is in Christ Jesus.

Ye know the grace of our Lord Jesus Christ, that,
though he was rich, yet for your sakes he became
poor, that ye through his poverty might be rich.—
Where sin abounded, grace did much more abound.

That in the ages to come he might show the exceeding riches of his grace in his kindness toward
us through Christ Jesus. For by grace are ye saved
through faith; and that not of yourselves: it is the
gift of God: not of works, lest any man should boast.
—Knowing that a man is not justified by the works of
the law, but by the faith of Jesus Christ, even we
have believed in Jesus Christ, that we might be justified by the faith of Christ, and not by the works of
the law: for by the works of the law shall no flesh
be justified. According to his mercy he saved us, by
the washing of regeneration, and renewing of the
Holy Ghost; which he shed on us abundantly through
Jesus Christ our Saviour.

I TIMOTHY 1: 14. II Corinthians 8: 9.—Romans 5: 20.
Ephesians 2: 7-9.—Galatians 2: 16.—Titus 3: 5, 6.

FEBRUARY 7

> When thou hast eaten and art full, . . . thou
> shalt bless the Lord thy God for the good land
> which he hath given thee.

BEWARE that thou forget not the LORD thy God.—
One of them, when he saw that he was healed, turned
back, and with a loud voice glorified God, and fell
down on his face at his feet, giving him thanks: and
he was a Samaritan. And Jesus answering said, Were
there not ten cleansed? but where are the nine? There
are not found that returned to give glory to God,
save this stranger.

Every creature of God is good, and nothing to be
refused, if it be received with thanksgiving: for it is
sanctified by the word of God and prayer.—He that
eateth, eateth to the Lord, for he giveth God thanks.
—The blessing of the LORD, it maketh rich, and he
addeth no sorrow with it.

Bless the LORD, O my soul: and all that is within
me, bless his holy name. Bless the LORD, O my soul,
. . . who forgiveth all thine iniquities; . . . who
crowneth thee with loving kindness and tender mercies.

DEUTERONOMY 8: 10. Deuteronomy 8: 11.—Luke 17: 15-
18. I Timothy 4: 4, 5.—Romans 14: 6.—Proverbs 10: 22.
Psalms 103: 1-4.

Henceforth I call you not servants; for the servant knoweth not what his lord doeth: but I have called you friends.

THE LORD said, Shall I hide from Abraham that thing which I do?—It is given unto you to know the mysteries of the kingdom of heaven.—God hath revealed them unto us by his Spirit: for the Spirit searcheth all things, yea, the deep things of God.—Even the hidden wisdom, which God ordained before the world unto our glory.

Blessed is the man whom thou choosest, and causest to approach unto thee, that he may dwell in thy courts: we shall be satisfied with the goodness of thy house, even of thy holy temple.—The secret of the LORD is with them that fear him; and he will show them his covenant.—I have given unto them the words which thou gavest me; and they have received them, and have known surely that I came out from thee, and they have believed that thou didst send me.

Ye are my friends, if ye do whatsoever I command you.

JOHN 15: 15. Genesis 18: 17.—Matthew 13: 11.—I Corinthians 2: 10.—I Corinthians 2: 7. Psalms 65: 4.—Psalms 25: 14.—John 17: 8. John 15: 14.

FEBRUARY 9

Now he is comforted.

THY sun shall no more go down; neither shall thy
moon withdraw itself: for the LORD shall be thine
everlasting light, and the days of thy mourning shall
be ended.—He will swallow up death in victory; and
the LORD God will wipe away tears from off all faces;
and the rebuke of his people shall he take away
from off all the earth.—These are they which came
out of great tribulation, and have washed their robes,
and made them white in the blood of the Lamb.
Therefore are they before the throne of God, and
serve him day and night in his temple: and he that
sitteth on the throne shall dwell among them. They
shall hunger no more, neither thirst any more; neither
shall the sun light on them, nor any heat. For the
Lamb which is in the midst of the throne shall feed
them, and shall lead them unto living fountains of
waters.—God shall wipe away all tears from their
eyes; and there shall be no more death, neither sorrow,
nor crying, neither shall there be any more pain: for
the former things are passed away.

LUKE 16: 25. Isaiah 60: 20.—Isaiah 25: 8.—Revelation 7:
14-17.—Revelation 21: 4.

The light of the body is the eye: therefore when thine eye is single, thy whole body also is full of light.

THE natural man receiveth not the things of the Spirit of God: for they are foolishness unto him: neither can he know them, because they are spiritually discerned.—Open thou mine eyes, that I may behold wondrous things out of thy law.

I am the light of the world: he that followeth me shall not walk in darkness, but shall have the light of life.—We all, with open face beholding as in a glass the glory of the Lord, are changed into the same image . . . even as by the Spirit of the Lord.—God, who commanded the light to shine out of darkness, hath shined in our hearts, to give the light of the knowledge of the glory of God in the face of Jesus Christ.

The God of our Lord Jesus Christ, the Father of glory, . . . give unto you the spirit of wisdom and revelation in the knowledge of him: . . . that ye may know what is the hope of his calling, and what the riches of the glory of his inheritance in the saints.

LUKE 11: 34. I Corinthians 2: 14.—Psalms 119: 18. John 8: 12.—II Corinthians 3: 18.—II Corinthians 4: 6 Ephesians 1: 17, 18.

FEBRUARY 11

They that feared the Lord spake often one to
another: and the Lord hearkened, and heard it,
and a book of remembrance was written before
him for them that feared the Lord and that
thought upon his name.

It came to pass, that, while they communed together
and reasoned, Jesus himself drew near and went with
them.—Where two or three are gathered together in
my name, there am I in the midst of them.—My fellow-
laborers, whose names are in the book of life.

Let the word of Christ dwell in you richly in all
wisdom; teaching and admonishing one another in
psalms and hymns and spiritual songs, singing with
grace in your hearts to the Lord.—Exhort one another
daily, while it is called to-day; lest any of you be
hardened through the deceitfulness of sin.

Every idle word that men shall speak, they shall
give account thereof in the day of judgment: for by
thy words thou shalt be justified, and by thy words
thou shalt be condemned.

MALACHI 3: 16. Luke 24: 15.—Matthew 18: 20.—
Philippians 4: 3. Colossians 3: 16.—Hebrews 3: 13. Matthew
12: 36, 37.

They shall be mine, saith the Lord of hosts, in
that day when I make up my jewels.

I HAVE manifested thy name unto the men which
thou gavest me out of the world: thine they were,
and thou gavest them me; and they have kept thy
word. I pray for them: I pray not for the world, but
for them which thou hast given me; for they are
thine. And all mine are thine, and thine are mine;
and I am glorified in them. Father, I will that they
also whom thou hast given me be with me where I
am: that they may behold my glory which thou hast
given me; for thou lovedst me before the foundation
of the world.

I will come again, and receive you unto myself.—
He shall come to be glorified in his saints, and to be
admired in all them that believe . . . in that day.—
We which are alive and remain shall be caught up
together with them in the clouds, to meet the Lord
in the air: and so shall we ever be with the Lord.—
Thou shalt also be a crown of glory in the hand of
the LORD, and a royal diadem in the hand of thy God.

MALACHI 3: 17. John 17: 6, 9, 10, 24. John 14: 3.—II
Thessalonians 1: 10.—I Thessalonians 4: 17.—Isaiah 62: 3.

FEBRUARY 13

Upon the likeness of the throne was the likeness
as the appearance of a man above upon it.

THE man Christ Jesus.—Made in the likeness of men
. . . found in fashion as a man.—Forasmuch . . . as
the children are partakers of flesh and blood, he also
himself likewise took part of the same; that through
death he might destroy him that had the power of
death.

I am he that liveth and was dead; and, behold, I
am alive for evermore.—Christ being raised from the
dead dieth no more; death hath no more dominion
over him. For in that he died, he died unto sin once;
but in that he liveth, he liveth unto God.—What and
if ye shall see the Son of Man ascend up where he was
before?—He raised him from the dead, and set him
at his own right hand in the heavenly places.—In him
dwelleth all the fulness of the Godhead bodily.

Though he was crucified through weakness, yet he
liveth by the power of God. For we also are weak
in him, but we shall live with him by the power of
God.

EZEKIEL 1: 26. I Timothy 2: 5.—Philippians 2: 7, 8.—
Hebrews 2: 14. Revelation 1: 18.—Romans 6: 9, 10.—John
6: 62.—Ephesians 1: 20.—Colossians 2: 9. II Corinthians
13: 4.

Suffer it to be so now: for thus it becometh us to fulfil all righteousness.

I DELIGHT to do thy will, O my God: yea, thy law is within my heart.

Think not that I am come to destroy the law, or the prophets; I am not come to destroy, but to fulfil. For verily I say unto you, Till heaven and earth pass, one jot or one tittle shall in no wise pass from the law, till all be fulfilled.—The LORD is well pleased for his righteousness' sake; he will magnify the law and make it honorable.—Except your righteousness shall exceed the righteousness of the scribes and Pharisees, ye shall in no case enter into the kingdom of heaven.

What the law could not do, in that it was weak through the flesh, God sending his own Son in the likeness of sinful flesh, and for sin, condemned sin in the flesh: that the righteousness of the law might be fulfilled in us, who walk not after the flesh but after the Spirit.—Christ is the end of the law for righteousness to every one that believeth.

MATTHEW 3: 15. Psalms 40: 8. Matthew 5: 17, 18.— Isaiah 42: 21.—Matthew 5: 20. Romans 8: 3, 4.—Romans 10: 4.

FEBRUARY 15

Who can say, I have made my heart clean?

THE LORD looked down from heaven upon the children of men, to see if there were any that did understand, and seek God. They are all gone aside, they are all together become filthy: there is none that doeth good, no, not one.—They that are in the flesh cannot please God.

To will is present with me; but how to perform that which is good I find not. For the good that I would I do not: but the evil which I would not, that I do.—We are all as an unclean thing, and all our righteousnesses are as filthy rags; and we all do fade as a leaf; and our iniquities, like the wind, have taken us away.

The Scripture hath concluded all under sin, that the promise by faith of Jesus Christ might be given to them that believe.—God was in Christ, reconciling the world unto himself, not imputing their trespasses unto them.—If we say that we have no sin, we deceive ourselves, and the truth is not in us. If we confess our sins, he is faithful and just to forgive us our sins, and to cleanse us from all unrighteousness.

PROVERBS 20: 9. Psalms 14: 2, 3.—Romans 8: 8. Romans 7: 18, 19.—Isaiah 64: 6. Galatians 3: 22.—II Corinthians 5: 19.—I John 1: 8, 9.

Thy name is as ointment poured forth.

CHRIST . . . hath loved us, and hath given himself for us, an offering and a sacrifice to God for a sweet-smelling savor.—Unto you therefore which believe he is precious.—God also hath highly exalted him, and given him a name which is above every name: that at the name of Jesus every knee should bow.—In him dwelleth all the fulness of the Godhead bodily.

The love of God is shed abroad in our hearts by the Holy Ghost which is given unto us.—The house was filled with the odor of the ointment.—They took knowledge of them, that they had been with Jesus.

O LORD our Lord, how excellent is thy name in all the earth! who hast set thy glory above the heavens.—Emmanuel . . . God with us. His name shall be called Wonderful, Counsellor, The mighty God, the everlasting Father, The Prince of Peace.—The name of the LORD is a strong tower: the righteous runneth into it, and is safe.

CANTICLES 1: 3. Ephesians 5: 2.—I Peter 2: 7.—Philippians 2: 9, 10.—Colossians 2: 9. John 14: 15.—Romans 5: 5.—John 12: 3.—Acts 4: 13. Psalms 8: 1.—Matthew 1: 23.—Isaiah 9: 6.—Proverbs 18: 10.

FEBRUARY 17

The whole bullock shall he carry forth without
the camp unto a clean place, where the ashes are
poured out, and burn him on the wood with fire.

THEY took Jesus, and led him away. And he bearing
his cross went forth into a place called the place of
a skull, which is called in the Hebrew Golgotha:
where they crucified him.—The bodies of those beasts,
whose blood is brought into the sanctuary by the
high priest for sin, are burned without the camp.
Wherefore Jesus also, that he might sanctify the people with his own blood, suffered without the gate.
Let us go forth therefore unto him without the camp,
bearing his reproach.—The fellowship of his sufferings.

Rejoice, inasmuch as ye are partakers of Christ's
sufferings: that, when his glory shall be revealed,
ye may be glad also with exceeding joy.—Our light
affliction, which is but for a moment, worketh for us
a far more exceeding and eternal weight of glory.

LEVITICUS 4: 12. John 19: 16-18.—Hebrews 13: 11-13.—
Philippians 3: 10. I Peter 4: 13.—II Corinthians 4: 17.

Thou art my hope in the day of evil.

THERE be many that say, Who will show us any good? Lord, lift thou up the light of thy countenance upon us.—I will sing of thy power, yea, I will sing aloud of thy mercy in the morning: for thou hast been my defence and refuge in the day of my trouble.

In my prosperity I said, I shall never be moved. Thou didst hide thy face, and I was troubled. I cried to thee, O LORD: and unto the LORD I made supplication. What profit is there in my blood, when I go down to the pit? Shall the dust praise thee? shall it declare thy truth? Hear, O LORD, and have mercy upon me: LORD, be thou my helper.

For a small moment have I forsaken thee; but with great mercies will I gather thee. In a little wrath I hid my face from thee for a moment; but with everlasting kindness will I have mercy on thee, saith the LORD thy Redeemer.—Sorrow shall be turned into joy. —Weeping may endure for a night, but joy cometh in the morning.

JEREMIAH 17: 17. Psalms 4: 6.—Psalms 59: 16. Psalms 30: 6, 8-10. Isaiah 54: 7, 8.—John 16: 20.—Psalms 30: 5.

FEBRUARY 19

The Lord giveth wisdom: out of his mouth cometh knowledge and understanding.

TRUST in the LORD with all thy heart; and lean not unto thine own understanding.—If any of you lack wisdom, let him ask of God, that giveth to all men liberally, and upbraideth not; and it shall be given him.—The foolishness of God is wiser than men; and the weakness of God is stronger than men.—I will give you a mouth and wisdom, which all your adversaries shall not be able to gainsay nor resist.—God hath chosen the foolish things of the world to confound the wise.

The entrance of thy words giveth light; it giveth understanding unto the simple.—Thy word have I hid in my heart, that I might not sin against thee.

All bare him witness, and wondered at the gracious words which proceeded out of his mouth.—Never man spake like this man.—Christ Jesus, who of God is made unto us wisdom, and righteousness, and sanctification, and redemption.

PROVERBS 2: 6. Proverbs 3: 5.—James 1: 5.—I Corinthians 1: 25.—Luke 21: 15.—I Corinthians 1: 27. Psalms 119: 130.—Psalms 119: 11. Luke 4: 22.—John 7: 46.—I Corinthians 1: 30.

He shall see of the travail of his soul, and shall be satisfied.

Jesus . . . said, It is finished: and he bowed his head, and gave up the ghost.—He hath made him to be sin for us, who knew no sin; that we might be made the righteousness of God in him.

That now unto the principalities and powers in heavenly places might be known by the church the manifold wisdom of God, according to the eternal purpose which he purposed in Christ Jesus our Lord. —That in the ages to come he might show the exceeding riches of his grace in his kindness toward us through Christ Jesus.

After that ye believed, ye were sealed with that holy Spirit of promise, which is the earnest of our inheritance until the redemption of the purchased possession, unto the praise of his glory.—Ye are a chosen generation, a royal priesthood, a holy nation, a peculiar people: that ye should show forth the praises of Him who hath called you out of darkness into his marvellous light.

ISAIAH 53: 11. John 19: 30.—II Corinthians 5: 21. Isaiah 43: 21.—Ephesians 3: 10, 11.—Ephesians 2: 7. Ephesians 1: 13, 14.—I Peter 2: 9.

FEBRUARY 21

I am the Lord which sanctify you.

I AM the LORD your God, which have separated you from other people. Ye shall be holy unto me: for I the Lord am holy, and have severed you from other people, that ye should be mine.

Sanctified by God the Father.—Sanctify them through thy truth: thy word is truth.—The very God of peace sanctify you wholly and I pray God your whole spirit and soul and body be preserved blameless unto the coming of our Lord Jesus Christ.

Jesus . . . that he might sanctify the people with his own blood, suffered without the gate.—Our Saviour Jesus Christ . . . gave himself for us, that he might redeem us from all iniquity, and purify unto himself a peculiar people, zealous of good works.—Both he that sanctifieth and they who are sanctified are all of one: for which cause he is not ashamed to call them brethren.—For their sakes I sanctify myself, that they also might be sanctified through the truth. —Through sanctification of the Spirit, unto obedience, and sprinkling of the blood of Jesus Christ.

LEVITICUS 20: 8. Leviticus 20: 24, 26. Jude 1.—John 17: 17.—I Thessalonians 5: 23. Hebrews 13: 12.—Titus 2: 13, 14.—Hebrews 2: 11.—John 17: 19.—I Peter 1: 2.

What man is he that feareth the Lord? him shall
He teach in the way that He shall choose.

THE light of the body is the eye: if therefore thine
eye be single, thy whole body shall be full of light.

Thy word is a lamp unto my feet, and a light
unto my path.—Thine ears shall hear a word behind
thee, saying, This is the way, walk ye in it, when ye
turn to the right hand, and when ye turn to the
left.—I will instruct thee and teach thee in the way
which thou shalt go: I will guide thee with mine
eye. Be ye not as the horse, or as the mule,
which have no understanding: whose mouth must
be held in with bit and bridle, lest they come
near unto thee. Many sorrows shall be to the wicked,
but he that trusteth in the LORD, mercy shall
compass him about. Be glad in the LORD, and rejoice,
ye righteous: and shout for joy, all ye that are upright in heart.

O LORD, I know that the way of man is not in
himself: it is not in man that walketh to direct his
steps.

PSALMS 25: 12. Matthew 6: 22. Psalms 119: 105.—Isaiah
30: 21.—Psalms 32: 8-11. Jeremiah 10: 23.

FEBRUARY 23

The blood of sprinkling speaketh better things than that of Abel.

BEHOLD the Lamb of God, which taketh away the sin of the world.—The lamb slain from the foundation of the world.—It is not possible that the blood of bulls and of goats should take away sins. Wherefore when he cometh into the world, he saith, Sacrifice and offering thou wouldest not, but a body hast thou prepared me. By the which will we are sanctified through the offering of the body of Jesus Christ once for all.

Abel . . . brought of the firstlings of his flock and of the fat thereof. And the LORD had respect unto Abel and to his offering.—Christ . . . hath loved us, and hath given himself for us, an offering and a sacrifice to God for a sweet-smelling savor.

Let us draw near with a true heart in full assurance of faith, having our hearts sprinkled from an evil conscience, and our bodies washed with pure water.—Having . . . boldness to enter into the holiest by the blood of Jesus.

HEBREWS 12: 24. John 1: 20.—Revelation 13: 8.—Hebrews 10: 4, 5, 10. Genesis 4: 4.—Ephesians 5: 2. Hebrews 10: 22.—Hebrews 10: 19.

Thus saith the Lord God, I will yet for this be inquired of.

Yᴇ have not, because ye ask not.

Ask, and it shall be given you; seek, and ye shall find; knock, and it shall be opened unto you: for every one that asketh receiveth; and he that seeketh findeth; and to him that knocketh it shall be opened. —This is the confidence that we have in him, that, if we ask anything according to his will he heareth us: and if we know that he hear us, whatsoever we ask, we know that we have the petitions that we desired of him.—If any of you lack wisdom, let him ask of God, that giveth to all men liberally, and upbraideth not; and it shall be given him.—Open thy mouth wide, and I will fill it.—Men ought always to pray, and not to faint.

The eyes of the Lord are upon the righteous, and his ears are open unto their cry. The Lᴏʀᴅ heareth, and delivereth them out of all their troubles.—Ye shall ask in my name; and I say not unto you, that I will pray the Father for you: for the Father himself loveth you, because ye have loved me.

EZEKIEL 36: 37. James 4: 2. Matthew 7: 7, 8.—I John 5: 14, 15.—James 1: 5.—Psalms 81: 10.—Luke 18: 1. Psalms 34: 15, 17.—John 16: 26, 27.

FEBRUARY 25

Resist the devil, and he will flee from you.

Wʜᴇɴ the enemy shall come in like a flood the Spirit of the Lᴏʀᴅ shall lift up a standard against him. —Get thee hence, Satan: for it is written, Thou shalt worship the Lord thy God, and him only shalt thou serve. Then the devil leaveth him, and, behold, angels came and ministered unto him.

Be strong in the Lord, and in the power of his might. Put on the whole armor of God, that ye may be able to stand against the wiles of the devil.—And have no fellowship with the unfruitful works of darkness, but rather reprove them.—Lest Satan should get an advantage of us: for we are not ignorant of his devices.—Be sober, be vigilant; because your adversary the devil, as a roaring lion, walketh about, seeking whom he may devour; whom resist steadfast in the faith, knowing that the same afflictions are accomplished in your brethren that are in the world.

Who shall lay anything to the charge of God's elect? It is God that justifieth.

JAMES 4: 7. Isaiah 59: 19.—Matthew 4: 10, 11. Ephesians 6: 10, 11.—Ephesians 5: 11.—II Corinthians 2: 11.—I Peter 5: 8, 9. Romans 8: 33.

Let us search and try our ways, and turn again
to the Lord.

Examine me, O Lord, and prove me: try my reins
and my heart.—Behold, thou desirest truth in the inward parts: and in the hidden part thou shalt make
me to know wisdom.—I thought on my ways, and
turned my feet unto thy testimonies.—I made haste,
and delayed not to keep thy commandments.—Let a
man examine himself, and so let him eat of that
bread, and drink of that cup.

If we confess our sins, he is faithful and just to
forgive us our sins, and to cleanse us from all unrighteousness.—We have an advocate with the Father,
Jesus Christ the righteous: and he is the propitiation
for our sins.—Having therefore, brethren, boldness to
enter into the holiest by the blood of Jesus, by a new
and living way which he hath consecrated for us,
through the veil, that is to say, his flesh: and having
a high priest over the house of God; let us draw
near with a true heart, in full assurance of faith,
having our hearts sprinkled from an evil conscience,
and our bodies washed with pure water.

LAMENTATIONS 3: 40. Psalms 26: 2.—Psalms 51: 6.—
Psalms 119: 59, 60.—I Corinthians 11: 28. I John 1: 9.—I
John 2: 1.—Hebrews 10: 19-22.

Reckon ye yourselves to be dead indeed unto sin, but alive unto God through Jesus Christ our Lord.

H<small>E</small> that heareth my word, and believeth on him that sent me, hath everlasting life, and shall not come into condemnation; but is passed from death unto life.—I through the law am dead to the law, that I might live unto God. I am crucified with Christ; nevertheless I live; yet not I, but Christ liveth in me: and the life which I now live in the flesh I live by the faith of the Son of God, who loved me, and gave himself for me.

Because I live, ye shall live also.—I give unto them eternal life: and they shall never perish, neither shall any man pluck them out of my hand. My Father which gave them me, is greater than all; and no man is able to pluck them out of my Father's hand. I and my Father are one.

If ye then be risen with Christ, seek those things which are above, where Christ sitteth on the right hand of God. . . . For ye are dead, and your life is hid with Christ in God.

ROMANS 6: 11. John 5: 24.—Galatians 2: 19, 20. John 14: 19.—John 10: 28-30. Colossians 3: 1, 3.

God so loved the world, that he gave his only-begotten Son, that whosoever believeth in him should not perish, but have everlasting life.

G<small>OD</small> . . . hath reconciled us to himself by Jesus Christ, and hath given to us the ministry of reconciliation: to wit, that God was in Christ, reconciling the world unto himself, not imputing their trespasses unto them; and hath committed unto us the word of reconciliation. Now then we are ambassadors for Christ, as though God did beseech you by us: we pray you in Christ's stead be ye reconciled to God. For he hath made him to be sin for us, who knew no sin; that we might be made the righteousness of God in him.

God is love. In this was manifested the love of God toward us, because that God sent his only-begotten Son into the world, that we might live through him. Herein is love, not that we loved God, but that he loved us, and sent his Son to be the propitiation for our sins. Beloved, if God so loved us, we ought also to love one another.

JOHN 3: 16. II Corinthians 5: 18-21. I John 4: 8-11.

FEBRUARY 29

Boast not thyself of to-morrow; for thou knowest not what a day may bring forth.

Behold, now is the accepted time; behold, now is the day of salvation.—Yet a little while is the light with you. Walk while ye have the light, lest darkness come upon you: for he that walketh in darkness knoweth not whither he goeth. While ye have light, believe in the light, that ye may be the children of light.

Whatsoever thy hand findeth to do, do it with thy might; for there is no work, nor device, nor knowledge, nor wisdom, in the grave, whither thou goest.

Soul, thou hast much goods laid up for many years; take thine ease, eat, drink and be merry. Thou fool, this night thy soul shall be required of thee: then whose shall those things be, which thou hast provided? So is he that layeth up treasure for himself, and is not rich toward God.

The world passeth away, and the lust thereof; but he that doeth the will of God abideth for ever.

PROVERBS 27: 1. II Corinthians 6: 2.—John 12: 35, 36.
Ecclesiastes 9: 10. Luke 12: 19-21. I John 2: 17.

The fruit of the Spirit is love.

GOD is love: and he that dwelleth in love dwelleth in God, and God in him.—The love of God is shed abroad in our hearts by the Holy Ghost which is given unto us.

Unto you who believe he is precious.—We love him, because he first loved us.

The love of Christ constraineth us; because we thus judge, that if one died for all, then were all dead: and that he died for all, that they which live should not henceforth live unto themselves, but unto him which died for them, and rose again.

Ye yourselves are taught of God to love one another.—This is my commandment, That ye love one another, as I have loved you.—Above all things have fervent charity among yourselves: for charity shall cover the multitude of sins.—Walk in love, as Christ also hath loved us, and hath given himself for us, an offering and a sacrifice to God for a sweet-smelling savor.

GALATIANS 5: 22. I John 4: 16.—Romans 5: 5. I Peter 2: 7.—John 4: 19. II Corinthians 5: 14, 15. I Thessalonians 4: 9.—John 15: 12.—I Peter 4: 8.—Ephesians 5: 2.

MARCH 2

God hath caused me to be fruitful in the land of my affliction.

Blessed be God, even the Father of our Lord Jesus Christ, the Father of mercies, and the God of all comfort; who comforteth us in all our tribulation, that we may be able to comfort them which are in any trouble, by the comfort wherewith we ourselves are comforted of God. For as the sufferings of Christ abound in us, so our consolation also aboundeth by Christ.

He shall sit as a refiner and purifier of silver: and he shall purify the sons of Levi.—Now for a season, if need be, ye are in heaviness through manifold temptations; that the trial of your faith, being much more precious than of gold that perisheth, though it be tried with fire, might be found unto praise and honor and glory at the appearing of Jesus Christ.—The Lord stood with me, and strengthened me.

Let them that suffer according to the will of God commit the keeping of their souls to him in well doing, as unto a faithful Creator.

GENESIS 41: 52. II Corinthians 1: 3-5. Malachi 3: 3.—I Peter 1: 6, 7.—II Timothy 4: 17. I Peter 4: 19.

Trust in the Lord with all thy heart; and lean not unto thine own understanding. In all thy ways acknowledge him, and he shall direct thy paths.

Trust in him at all times; ye people, pour out your heart before him: God is a refuge for us.

O our God, wilt thou not judge them? for we have no might against this great company that cometh against us, neither know we what to do; but our eyes are upon thee.—I will lift up mine eyes unto the hills from whence cometh my help: my help cometh from the LORD, which made heaven and earth.—But mine eyes are unto thee, O God the Lord; in thee is my trust; leave not my soul destitute.

If thy presence go not with me, carry us not up hence. For wherein shall it be known here that I and thy people have found grace in thy sight? is it not in that thou goest with us? so shall we be separated, I and thy people, from all the people that are upon the face of the earth.

PROVERBS 3: 5, 6. Psalms 62: 8. II Chronicles 20: 12.—
Psalms 121: 1, 2.—Psalms 141: 8. Exodus 33: 15, 16.

MARCH 4

Set your affection on things above, not on things on the earth.

Love not the world, neither the things that are in the world. If any man love the world, the love of the Father is not in him.—Lay not up for yourselves treasures upon earth, where moth and rust doth corrupt, and where thieves break through and steal: but lay up for yourselves treasures in heaven, where neither moth nor rust doth corrupt, and where thieves do not break through nor steal: for where your treasure is, there will your heart be also.

We walk by faith, not by sight.—We faint not; but though our outward man perish, yet the inward man is renewed day by day. For our light affliction, which is but for a moment, worketh for us a far more exceeding and eternal weight of glory: while we look not at the things which are seen, but at the things which are not seen: for the things which are seen are temporal; but the things which are not seen are eternal. —An inheritance incorruptible, and undefiled, and that fadeth not away, reserved in heaven for you.

COLOSSIANS 3: 2. I John 2: 15.—Matthew 6: 19-21. II Corinthians 5: 7.—II Corinthians 4: 16-18.—I Peter 1: 4.

O Lord, I am oppressed; undertake for me.

UNTO thee lift I up mine eyes, O thou that dwellest in the heavens. Behold, as the eyes of servants look unto the hand of their masters, and as the eyes of a maiden unto the hand of her mistress; so our eyes wait upon the LORD our God.—Hear my cry, O God; attend unto my prayer. From the end of the earth will I cry unto thee, when my heart is overwhelmed: lead me to the rock that is higher than I. For thou hast been a shelter for me, and a strong tower from the enemy. I will abide in thy tabernacle for ever: I will trust in the covert of thy wings.—Thou hast been a strength to the poor, a strength to the needy in his distress, a refuge from the storm.

Christ . . . suffered for us, leaving us an example, that ye should follow his steps: who did no sin, neither was guile found in his mouth: who, when he was reviled, reviled not again; when he suffered, he threatened not; but committed himself to him that judgeth righteously.

ISAIAH 38: 14. Psalms 123: 1, 2.—Psalms 61: 1-4.—Isaiah 25: 4. I Peter 2: 21-23.

MARCH 6

He preserveth the way of his saints.

THE LORD your God . . . went in the way before you, to search you out a place to pitch your tents in, in fire by night, to show you by what way ye should go, and in a cloud by day.—As an eagle stirreth up her nest, fluttereth over her young, spreadeth abroad her wings, taketh them, beareth them on her wings: so the LORD alone did lead him.—The steps of a good man are ordered by the Lord: and he delighteth in his way. Though he fall, he shall not be utterly cast down: for the LORD upholdeth him with his hand.—Many are the afflictions of the righteous: but the Lord delivereth him out of them all.—For the Lord knoweth the way of the righeous; but the way of the ungodly shall perish.—We know that all things work together for good to them that love God, to them who are the called according to his purpose.—With us is the Lord our God to help us, and to fight our battles.

The LORD thy God in the midst of thee is mighty; he will save, he will rejoice over thee with joy.

PROVERBS 2: 8. Deuteronomy 1: 32, 33.—Deuteronomy 32: 11, 12.—Psalms 17: 23, 24.—Psalms 34: 19.—Psalms 1: 6.—Romans 8: 28.—II Chronicles 32: 8. Zephaniah 3: 17.

Thy Maker is thy husband; the Lord of hosts is his name.

This is a great mystery: but I speak concerning Christ and the church.

Thou shalt no more be termed Forsaken . . . but thou shalt be called Hephzi-bah, . . . for the LORD delighteth in thee. And as the bridegroom rejoiceth over the bride, so shall thy God rejoice over thee.— He hath sent me . . . to comfort all that mourn; to appoint unto them that mourn in Zion, to give unto them beauty for ashes, the oil of joy for mourning, the garment of praise for the spirit of heaviness.

I will greatly rejoice in the LORD, my soul shall be joyful in my God; for he hath clothed me with the garments of salvation, . . . as a bridegroom decketh himself with ornaments, and as a bride adorneth herself with her jewels.

I will betroth thee unto me for ever; yea, I will betroth thee unto me in righteousness, and in judgment, and in loving-kindness, and in mercies.

Who shall separate us from the love of Christ.

ISAIAH 54: 5. Ephesians 5: 32. Isaiah 62: 4, 5.—Isaiah 61: 1-3. Isaiah 61: 10. Hosea 2: 19. Romans 8: 35.

MARCH 8

Thou hast cast all my sins behind thy back.

Wʜᴏ is a God like unto thee, that pardoneth iniquity, and passeth by the transgression of the remnant of his heritage? he retaineth not his anger for ever, because he delighteth in mercy. He will turn again, he will have compassion upon us; he will subdue our iniquities: and thou wilt cast all their sins into the depths of the sea.

I will forgive their iniquity, and I will remember their sin no more.

For a small moment have I forsaken thee; but with great mercies will I gather thee. In a little wrath I hid my face from thee for a moment; but with everlasting kindness will I have mercy on thee, saith the Lord thy Redeemer.

Blessed is he whose transgression is forgiven, whose sin is covered. Blessed is the man unto whom the Lord imputeth not iniquity, and in whose spirit there is no guile. The blood of Jesus Christ his Son cleanseth us from all sin.

ISAIAH 38: 17. Micah 7: 18, 19. Jeremiah 31: 34. Isaiah 54: 7, 8. Psalms 32: 1, 2.—I John 1: 7.

The living God giveth us richly all things to enjoy.

Beware that thou forget not the Lord thy God, in not keeping his commandments, and his judgments, and his statutes, which I command thee this day: lest when thou hast eaten and art full, and hast built goodly houses, and dwelt therein; . . . then thy heart be lifted up, and thou forget the Lord thy God: . . . for it is he that giveth thee power to get wealth.

Except the Lord build the house, they labor in vain that build it: except the Lord keep the city, the watchman waketh but in vain. It is vain for you to rise up early, to sit up late, to eat the bread of sorrows: for so he giveth his beloved sleep.—They got not the land in possession by their own sword, neither did their own arm save them: but thy right hand, and thine arm, and the light of thy countenance, because thou hadst a favor unto them.—There be many that say, Who will show us any good? Lord, lift thou up the light of thy countenance upon us.

I TIMOTHY 6: 17. Deuteronomy 8: 11, 12, 14, 18. Psalms 127: 1, 2.—Psalms 44: 3.—Psalms 4: 6.

MARCH 10

The Lord will provide.

GOD will provide himself a lamb for a burnt offering.

Behold, the LORD's hand is not shortened, that it cannot save; neither his ear heavy, that it cannot hear.—There shall come out of Zion the Deliverer, and shall turn away ungodliness from Jacob.

Happy is he that hath the God of Jacob for his help, whose hope is in the LORD his God.—Behold, the eye of the Lord is upon them that fear him, upon them that hope in his mercy; to deliver their soul from death.

My God shall supply all your need, according to his riches in glory by Christ Jesus.—He hath said, I will never leave thee, nor forsake thee. So that we may boldly say, the Lord is my helper, and I will not fear what man shall do unto me.—The LORD is my strength and my shield; my heart trusted in him, and I am helped: therefore my heart greatly rejoiceth: and with my song will I praise him.

GENESIS 22: 14 (marg). Genesis 22: 8. Isaiah 59: 1.—Romans 11: 26. Psalms 146: 5.—Psalms 33: 18, 19. Philippians 4: 19.—Hebrews 13: 5, 6.—Psalms 28: 7.

The Lord bless thee, and keep thee.

THE blessing of the LORD, it maketh rich, and he addeth no sorrow with it.—Thou, LORD, wilt bless the righteous; with favor wilt thou compass him as with a shield.

He will not suffer thy foot to be moved: he that keepeth thee will not slumber. Behold, he that keepeth Israel shall neither slumber nor sleep. The LORD is thy keeper: the LORD is thy shade upon thy right hand. . . . The LORD shall preserve thee from all evil: he shall preserve thy soul. The LORD shall preserve thy going out and thy coming in from this time forth, and even for evermore.—I the LORD do keep it; I will water it every moment: lest any hurt it, I will keep it night and day.

Holy Father, keep through thine own name those whom thou hast given me. While I was with them in the world, I kept them in thy name: those that thou gavest me I have kept.

The Lord shall deliver me from every evil work, and will preserve me unto his heavenly kingdom: to whom be glory for ever and ever. Amen.

NUMBERS 6: 24. Proverbs 10: 22.—Psalms 5: 12. Psalms 121: 3-5, 7, 8.—Isaiah 27: 3. John 17: 11, 12. II Timothy 4: 18.

MARCH 12

The Lord make his face shine upon thee, and be gracious unto thee. The Lord lift up his countenance upon thee, and give thee peace.

No man hath seen God at any time; the only begotten Son, which is in the bosom of the Father, he hath declared him.—The brightness of his glory, and the express image of his person.—The god of this world hath blinded the minds of them which believe not, lest the light of the glorious gospel of Christ, who is the image of God, should shine unto them.

Make thy face to shine upon thy servant: save me for thy mercies' sake. Let me not be ashamed, O Lord; for I have called upon thee.—Lord, by thy favor thou hast made my mountain to stand strong: thou didst hide thy face, and I was troubled.—Blessed is the people that know the joyful sound: they shall walk, O Lord, in the light of thy countenance.

The Lord will give strength unto his people; the Lord will bless his people with peace.—Be of good cheer; it is I; be not afraid.

NUMBERS 6: 25, 26. John 1: 18.—Hebrews 1: 3.—II Corinthians 4: 4. Psalms 31: 16, 17.—Psalms 30: 7.—Psalms 89: 15. Psalms 29: 11.—Matthew 14: 27.

There is one God, and one mediator between God and men, the man Christ Jesus.

FORASMUCH . . . as the children are partakers of flesh and blood, he also himself likewise took part of the same.

Look unto me, and be ye saved, all the ends of the earth: for I am God, and there is none else.

We have an advocate with the Father, Jesus Christ the righteous.—In Christ Jesus, ye who sometime were far off, are made nigh by the blood of Christ. For he is our peace.

By his own blood he entered in once into the holy place, having obtained eternal redemption for us. . . . And for this cause he is the mediator of the new testament, that by means of death, for the redemption of the transgressions that were under the first testament, they which are called might receive the promise of eternal inheritance.—He is able also to save them to the uttermost that come unto God by him, seeing he ever liveth to make intercession for them.

I TIMOTHY 2: 5. Hebrews 2: 14. Isaiah 45: 22. I John 2: 1.—Ephesians 2: 13, 14. Hebrews 9: 12, 15.—Hebrews 7: 25.

MARCH 14

Adorn the doctrine of God our Saviour in all things.

LET your conversation be as it becometh the gospel of Christ.—If ye be reproached for the name of Christ, happy are ye. But let none of you suffer as a murderer, or as a thief, or as an evildoer, or as a busybody in other men's matters.—Be blameless and harmless, the sons of God, without rebuke, in the midst of a crooked and perverse nation, among whom ye shine as lights in the world. Let your light so shine before men, that they may see your good works, and glorify your Father which is in heaven.

Let not mercy and truth forsake thee: bind them about thy neck; write them upon the table of thy heart; so shalt thou find favor and good understanding in the sight of God and man.—Brethren, whatsoever things are true, whatsoever things are honest, whatever things are just, whatsoever things are pure, whatsoever things are lovely, whatsoever things are of good report; if there be any virtue, and if there be any praise, think on these things.

TITUS 2: 10. Philippians 1: 27.—I Peter 4: 14, 15.—Philippians 2: 15.—Matthew 5: 16. Proverbs 3: 3, 4.—Philippians 4: 8.

Perfect through sufferings.

M Y soul is exceeding sorrowful, even unto death: tarry ye here, and watch with me. And he went a little farther, and fell on his face, and prayed, saying, O my Father, if it be possible, let this cup pass from me: nevertheless, not as I will, but as thou wilt.—And being in an agony he prayed more earnestly, and his sweat was as it were great drops of blood falling down to the ground.

The sorrows of death compassed me, and the pains of hell gat hold upon me: I found trouble and sorrow.—Reproach hath broken my heart; and I am full of heaviness: and I looked for some to take pity, but there was none; and for comforters, but I found none.—I looked on my right hand, and beheld, but there was no man that would know me: refuge failed me; no man cared for my soul.

He is despised and rejected of men; a man of sorrows, and acquainted with grief: and we hid as it were our faces from him; he was despised, and we esteemed him not.

HEBREWS 2: 10. Matthew 26: 38, 39.—Luke 22: 44.
Psalms 116: 3.—Psalms 69: 20.—Psalms 142: 4. Isaiah 53: 8.

What is your life? It is even a vapor, that appeareth for a little time, and then vanisheth
away.

My days are swifter than a post, they flee away,
they see no good. They are passed away as the swift
ships: as the eagle that hasteth to the prey.—Thou
carriest them away as with a flood; they are as a sleep:
in the morning they are like grass which groweth up.
In the morning it flourisheth, and groweth up; in the
evening it is cut down, and withereth.—Man that is
born of a woman is of few days, and full of trouble.
He cometh forth like a flower, and is cut down.

The world passeth away, and the lust thereof: but
he that doeth the will of God abideth for ever.

They shall perish, but thou shalt endure: yea, all
of them shall wax old like a garment; as a vesture
shalt thou change them, and they shall be changed:
but thou art the same, and thy years shall have no
end.—Jesus Christ, the same yesterday, and to-day, and
for ever.

JAMES 4: 14. Job 9: 25, 26.—Psalms 90: 5, 6.—Job 14:
2. I John 2: 17. Psalms 102: 26, 27.—Hebrews 13: 8.

He shall put his hand upon the head of the burnt offering; and it shall be accepted for him to make atonement for him.

YE know that ye were not redeemed with corruptible things, as silver and gold, from your vain conversation received by tradition from your fathers; but with the precious blood of Christ, as of a lamb without blemish and without spot.—Who his own self bare our sins in his own body.

He hath made us accepted in the Beloved.

As lively stones, . . . built up a spiritual house, a holy priesthood, to offer up spiritual sacrifices, acceptable to God by Jesus Christ.—I beseech you therefore, brethren, by the mercies of God, that ye present your bodies a living sacrifice, holy, acceptable unto God, which is your reasonable service.

Now unto Him that is able to keep you from falling, and to present you faultless before the presence of his glory with exceeding joy to the only wise God our Saviour, be glory and majesty, dominion and power, both now and ever.

LEVITICUS 1: 4. I Peter 1: 18, 19.—I Peter 2: 24. Ephesians 1: 6. I Peter 2: 5.—Romans 12: 1. Jude 24, 25.

MARCH 18

Mine eyes fail with looking upward.

HAVE mercy upon me, O LORD; for I am weak: O LORD, heal me; for my bones are vexed. My soul is also sore vexed: but thou, O LORD, how long? Return, O LORD, deliver my soul: oh save me for thy mercies' sake.—My heart is sore pained within me: and the terrors of death are fallen upon me. Fearfulness and trembling are come upon me, and horror hath overwhelmed me. And I said, Oh that I had wings, like a dove! for then would I fly away, and be at rest.

Ye have need of patience.

While they looked steadfastly towards heaven as he went up, behold, two men stood by them in white apparel; which also said, Ye men of Galilee, why stand ye gazing up into heaven? this same Jesus, which is taken up from you into heaven, shall so come in like manner as ye have seen him go into heaven.—Our conversation is in heaven; from whence also we look for the Saviour, the Lord Jesus Christ.—That blessed hope, . . . the glorious appearing of the great God and our Saviour Jesus Christ.

ISAIAH 38: 14. Psalms 6: 2-4.—Psalms 55: 4-6. Hebrews 10: 36. Acts 1: 10, 11.—Philippians 3: 20.—Titus 2: 13.

God, having raised up his Son Jesus, sent him to
bless you, in turning away every one of you from
his iniquities.

Blessed be the God and Father of our Lord Jesus
Christ, which according to his abundant mercy hath
begotten us again unto a lively hope by the resurrection of Jesus Christ from the dead.

Our Saviour Jesus Christ, who gave himself for us
that he might redeem us from all iniquity, and purify
unto himself a peculiar people, zealous of good works.
—As he which hath called you is holy, so be ye holy
in all manner of conversation; because it is written,
Be ye holy; for I am holy.

The God and Father of our Lord Jesus Christ, . . .
hath blessed us with all spiritual blessings in heavenly
places in Christ.—In him dwelleth all the fulness of
the Godhead bodily. And ye are complete in him.—
Of his fulness have all we received, and grace for
grace.

He that spared not his own Son, but delivered him
up for us all, how shall he not with him also freely
give us all things?

ACTS 3: 26. I Peter 1: 3. Titus 2: 13, 14.—I Peter 1: 15,
16. Ephesians 1: 3.—Colossians 2: 9, 10.—John 1: 16.
Romans 8: 32.

MARCH 20

The entrance of thy words giveth light.

THIS . . . is the message which we have heard of him, and declare unto you, that God is light, and in him is no darkness at all.—God, who commanded the light to shine out of darkness, hath shined in our hearts, to give the light of the knowledge of the glory of God in the face of Jesus Christ.—The Word was God. . . . In him was life; and the life was the light of men.—If we walk in the light, as he is in the light, we have fellowship one with another, and the blood of Jesus Christ his Son cleanseth us from all sin.

Thy word have I hid in my heart, that I might not sin against thee.—Ye are clean through the word which I have spoken unto you.

Ye were sometime darkness, but now are ye light in the Lord: walk as children of light.—Ye are a chosen generation, a royal priesthood, a holy nation, a peculiar people; that ye should show forth the praises of him who hath called you out of darkness into his marvellous light.

PSALMS 119: 130. I John 1: 5.—II Corinthians 4: 6.—
John 1: 1, 4.—I John 1: 7. Psalms 119: 11.—John 15: 3.
Ephesians 5: 8 — I Peter 2: 9.

Be watchful, and strengthen the things which remain, that are ready to die.

THE end of all things is at hand: be ye therefore sober, and watch unto prayer.—Be sober, be vigilant: because your adversary the devil, as a roaring lion, walketh about, seeking whom he may devour.

Take heed to thyself, and keep thy soul diligently, lest thou forget the things which thine eyes have seen, and lest they depart from thy heart all the days of thy life.—The just shall live by faith: but if any man draw back, my soul shall have no pleasure in him. But we are not of them who draw back unto perdition; but of them that believe to the saving of the soul.

What I say unto you I say unto all. Watch.

Fear thou not; for I am with thee: be not dismayed; for I am thy God; I will strengthen thee; yea, I will help thee; yea, I will uphold thee with the right hand of my righteousness. . . . I the LORD thy God will hold thy right hand.

REVELATION 3: 2. I Peter 4: 7.—I Peter 5: 8. Deuteronomy 4: 9.—Hebrews 10: 38, 39. Mark 13: 37. Isaiah 41: 10, 13.

MARCH 22

Lot lifted up his eyes, and beheld all the plain
of Jordan, that it was well watered everywhere,
before the Lord destroyed Sodom and Gomor-
rah, even as the garden of the Lord. Then Lot
chose him all the plain of Jordan.

JUST Lot . . . that righteous man.

Be not deceived; God is not mocked: for whatsoever a man soweth, that shall he also reap.—Remember Lot's wife.

Be ye not unequally yoked together with un-
believers: for what fellowship hath righteousness with
unrighteousness? and what communion hath light
with darkness? Wherefore come out from among
them, and be ye separate, saith the Lord, and touch
not the unclean thing.

Be not ye . . . partakers with them. For ye were
sometime darkness, but now are ye light in the Lord:
walk as children of light: . . . proving what is acceptable unto the Lord. And have no fellowship with
the unfruitful works of darkness, but rather reprove
them.

GENESIS 13: 10, 11. II Peter 2: 7, 8. Galatians 6: 7.—
Luke 17: 32. II Corinthians 6: 14, 17. Ephesians 5: 7, 8,
10, 11.

Holy, holy, holy, Lord God Almighty.

Thou art holy, O thou that inhabitest the praises of Israel.—Draw not nigh hither: put off thy shoes from off thy feet, for the place whereon thou standest is holy ground. . . . I am the God of thy Father, the God of Abraham, the God of Isaac, and the God of Jacob. And Moses hid his face; for he was afraid to look upon God.—To whom then will ye liken me, or shall I be equal? saith the Holy One.—I am the LORD thy God, the Holy One of Israel, thy Saviour . . . I, even I, am the LORD; and beside me there is no saviour.

As he which hath called you is holy, so be ye holy in all manner of conversation; because it is written, Be ye holy; for I am holy.—Know ye not that your body is the temple of the Holy Ghost which is in you, which ye have of God, and ye are not your own?—Ye are the temple of the living God; as God hath said, I will dwell in them, and walk in them; and I will be their God, and they shall be my people.—Can two walk together, except they be agreed?

REVELATION 4: 8. Psalms 22: 3.—Exodus 3: 5, 6.—Isaiah 40: 25.—Isaiah 43: 3, 11. I Peter 1: 15, 16.—I Corinthians 6: 19.—II Corinthians 6: 16.—Amos 3: 3.

Abraham believed in the Lord; and He counted
it to him for righteousness.

He staggered not at the promise of God through
unbelief; but was strong in faith, giving glory to
God; and being fully persuaded that, what He had
promised, He was able also to perform. And therefore
it was imputed to him for righteousness. Now it was
not written for his sake alone, that it was imputed
to him: but for us also, to whom it shall be imputed,
if we believe on Him that raised up Jesus our Lord
from the dead.

The promise, that he should be the heir of the
world, was not to Abraham, or to his seed, through the
law, but through the righteousness of faith.

The just shall live by faith.—Let us hold fast the
profession of our faith without wavering (for He is
faithful that promised). Our God is in the heavens;
he hath done whatsoever he hath pleased.—With God
nothing shall be impossible. . . . And blessed is she
that believed: for there shall be a performance of
those things which were told her from the Lord.

GENESIS 15: 6. Romans 4: 20-24. Romans 4: 13. Romans
1: 17.—Hebrews 10: 23.—Psalms 115: 3.—Luke 1: 37, 45.

I will never leave thee, nor forsake thee.

So that we may boldly say, The Lord is my helper, and I will not fear what man shall do unto me.

Behold, I am with thee, and will keep thee in all places whither thou goest, and will bring thee again into this land; for I will not leave thee, until I have done that which I have spoken to thee of.—Be strong and of a good courage, fear not, nor be afraid of them: for the LORD thy God, he it is that doth go with thee; he will not fail thee, nor forsake thee.

Demas hath forsaken me, having loved this present world. . . . At my first answer no man stood with me, but all men forsook me. Notwithstanding the Lord stood with me, and strengthened me.—When my father and my mother forsake me, then the LORD will take me up.

Lo, I am with you alway, even unto the end of the world.—I am he that liveth, and was dead; and, behold, I am alive for evermore.—I will not leave you comfortless: I will come to you.

HEBREWS 13: 5. Hebrews 13: 6. Genesis 28: 15.—Deuteronomy 31: 6. II Timothy 4: 10, 16, 17.—Psalms 27: 10. Matthew 28: 20.—Revelation 1: 18.—John 14: 18.

MARCH 26

The kingdom of heaven is as a man travelling
into a far country, who called his own servants,
and delivered unto them his goods . . . to every
man according to his several ability.

Know ye not, that to whom ye yield yourselves
servants to obey, his servants ye are to whom ye obey?

All these worketh that one and the selfsame Spirit,
dividing to every man severally as he will. . . . The
manifestation of the Spirit is given to every man to
profit withal.—As every man hath received the gift,
even so minister the same one to another, as good
stewards of the manifold grace of God.—It is required
in stewards, that a man be found faithful.

Unto whomsoever much is given, of him shall be
much required: and to whom men have committed
much, of him they will ask the more.

Who is sufficient for these things?—I can do all
things through Christ which strengtheneth me.

MATTHEW 25: 14, 15. Romans 6: 16. I Corinthians 12:
11, 7.—I Peter 4: 10.—I Corinthians 4: 2. Luke 12: 48. II
Corinthians 2: 16.—Philippians 4: 13.

To him that soweth righteousness shall be a
sure reward.

AFTER a long time the lord of those servants cometh,
and reckoneth with them. And so he that had received
five talents came and brought other five talents: saying, Lord, thou deliveredst unto me five talents: behold, I have gained beside them five talents more.
His lord said unto him, Well done, thou good and
faithful servant: thou hast been faithful over a few
things, I will make thee ruler over many things: enter
thou into the joy of thy Lord.

We must all appear before the judgment seat of
Christ; that every one may receive the things done in
his body, according to that he hath done, whether
it be good or bad.

I have fought a good fight, I have finished my
course, I have kept the faith: henceforth there is laid
up for me a crown of righteousness, which the Lord,
the righteous judge, shall give me at that day.

Behold, I come quickly: hold that fast which thou
hast, that no man take thy crown.

PROVERBS 11: 18. Matthew 25: 19-21. II Corinthians 5:
10. II Timothy 4: 7, 8. Revelation 3: 11.

MARCH 28

Be strong and of a good courage.

THE LORD is my light and my salvation: whom shall I fear? the LORD is the strength of my life: of whom shall I be afraid?—He giveth power to the faint; and to them that have no might he increaseth strength. Even the youths shall faint and be weary, and the young men shall utterly fall: but they that wait upon the LORD shall renew their strength; they shall mount up with wings as eagles; they shall run, and not be weary; and they shall walk and not faint.—My flesh and my heart faileth: But God is the strength of my heart, and my portion for ever.

If God be for us, who can be against us?—The LORD is on my side; I will not fear; what can man do unto me?

Through thee will we push down our enemies: through thy name will we tread them under that rise up against us.—We are more than conquerors through Him that loved us.

Arise therefore, and be doing, and the LORD be with thee.

JOSHUA 1: 18. Psalms 27: 1.—Isaiah 40: 29-31.—Psalms 73: 26. Romans 8: 31.—Psalms 118: 6. Psalms 44: 5.— Romans 8: 37. I Chronicles 22: 16.

Come, ye blessed of my Father, inherit the kingdom prepared for you from the foundation of the world.

FEAR not, little flock; for it is your Father's good pleasure to give you the kingdom—Hath not God chosen the poor of this world rich in faith, and heirs of the kingdom which he hath promised to them that love him?—Heirs of God, and joint heirs with Christ; if so be that we suffer with him, that we may be also glorified together.

The Father himself loveth you, because ye have loved me.—God is not ashamed to be called their God: for he hath prepared for them a city.

He that overcometh shall inherit all things; and I will be his God, and he shall be my son.—There is laid up for me a crown of righteousness, which the Lord, the righteous judge, shall give me at that day: and not to me only, but unto all them also that love his appearing.

He which hath begun a good work in you will perform it until the day of Jesus Christ.

MATTHEW 25: 34. Luke 12: 32.—James 2: 5.—Romans 8: 17. John 16: 27.—Hebrews 11: 16. Revelation 21: 7.—II Timothy 4: 8. Philippians 1: 6.

> Isaac went out to meditate in the field at the eventide.

LET the words of my mouth, and the meditation of my heart, be acceptable in thy sight, O LORD, my strength, and my redeemer.

When I consider thy heavens, the work of thy fingers, the moon and the stars, which thou hast ordained; what is man, that thou art mindful of him? and the son of man, that thou visitest him?—The works of the LORD are great, sought out of all them that have pleasure therein.

Blessed is the man that walketh not in the counsel of the ungodly, nor standeth in the way of sinners, nor sitteth in the seat of the scornful. But his delight is in the law of the LORD; and in his law doth he meditate day and night.—This book of the law shall not depart out of thy mouth; but thou shalt meditate therein day and night.—My soul shall be satisfied as with marrow and fatness; and my mouth shall praise thee with joyful lips: when I remember thee upon my bed, and meditate on thee in the night watches.

GENESIS 24: 63. Psalms 19: 14. Psalms 8: 3, 4.—Psalms 111: 2 Psalms 1: 1, 2.—Joshua 1: 8.—Psalms 63: 5, 6.

My God shall supply all your need according to his riches in glory by Christ Jesus.

SEEK ye first the kingdom of God, and his righteousness; and all . . . things shall be added unto you.—He that spared not his own Son, but delivered him up for us all, how shall he not with him also freely give us all things?

All things are yours: whether Paul or Apollos, or Cephas, or the world, or life, or death, or things present, or things to come; all are yours; and ye are Christ's; and Christ is God's.—As having nothing, and yet possessing all things.

The LORD is my shepherd; I shall not want.—The LORD God is a sun and shield: the Lord will give grace and glory: no good thing will he withhold from them that walk uprightly.—The living God, . . . giveth us richly all things to enjoy.—God is able to make all grace abound toward you; that ye, always having all sufficiency in all things, may abound to every good work.

PHILIPPIANS 4: 19. Matthew 6: 33.—Romans 8: 32. I Corinthians 3: 21-23.—II Corinthians 6: 10. Psalms 23: 1.—Psalms 84: 11.—I Timothy 6: 17.—II Corinthians 9: 8.

APRIL 1

The fruit of the Spirit is joy.

J OY in the Holy Ghost.—Unspeakable and full of glory.

As sorrowful, yet alway rejoicing; . . . exceeding joyful in all our tribulation.

Jesus the author and finisher of our faith; . . . for the joy that was set before him, endured the cross, despising the shame.—These things have I spoken unto you, that my joy might remain in you, and that your joy might be full.—As the sufferings of Christ abound in us, so our consolation also aboundeth by Christ.

Rejoice in the Lord alway: and again I say, Rejoice. —The joy of the LORD is your strength.

In thy presence is fulness of joy: at thy right hand there are pleasures for evermore.—For the Lamb which is in the midst of the throne shall feed them, and shall lead them unto living fountains of waters: and God shall wipe away all tears from their eyes.

GALATIANS 5: 22. Romans 14: 17.—I Peter 1: 8. II Corinthians 6: 10; 7, 4.—Romans 5: 3. Hebrews 12: 2.—John 15: 11.—II Corinthians 1: 5. Philippians 4: 4.—Nehemiah 8: 10. Psalms 16: 11.—Revelation 7: 17.

If ye do return unto the Lord with all your hearts, then put away the strange gods and Ashtaroth from among you, and prepare your hearts unto the Lord, and serve him only.

LITTLE children, keep yourselves from idols.—Come out from among them, and be ye separate, saith the Lord, and touch not the unclean thing; and I will receive you, and will be a Father unto you, and ye shall be my sons and daughters, saith the Lord Almighty.

Ye cannot serve God and Mammon.

Thou shalt worship no other god: for the LORD, whose name is Jealous, is a jealous God.—Serve him with a perfect heart and with a willing mind: for the LORD searcheth all hearts, and understandeth all the imaginations of the thoughts.

Man looketh on the outward appearance, but the LORD looketh on the heart.—Beloved, if our heart condemn us not, then have we confidence toward God.

I SAMUEL 7: 3. I John 5: 21.—II Corinthians 6: 17, 18. Matthew 6: 24. Exodus 34: 14.—I Chronicles 28: 9. I Samuel 16: 7.—I John 3: 21.

APRIL 3

Beloved, be not ignorant of this one thing, that one day is with the Lord as a thousand years, and a thousand years as one day. The Lord is not slack concerning his promise, as some men count slackness.

M Y thoughts are not your thoughts, neither are your ways my ways, saith the LORD. For as the heavens are higher than the earth, so are my ways higher than your ways, and my thoughts than your thoughts. For as the rain cometh down, and the snow from heaven, and returneth not thither, but watereth the earth, . . . so shall my word be that goeth forth out of my mouth: it shall not return unto me void, but it shall accomplish that which I please, and it shall prosper in the thing whereto I sent it.

God hath concluded them all in unbelief, that he might have mercy upon all. O the depth of the riches both of the wisdom and knowledge of God! how unsearchable are his judgments, and his ways past finding out!

III PETER 3: 8, 9. Isaiah 55: 8-11. Romans 11: 32, 33.

Fear not; I am the first and the last.

Yᴇ are not come unto the mount that might be touched, and that burned with fire, nor unto blackness, and darkness, and tempest, . . . but ye are come unto mount Sion, . . . to God the Judge of all, and to the spirits of just men made perfect, and to Jesus the mediator of the new covenant.—Jesus the author and finisher of our faith.—We have not a high priest which cannot be touched with the feeling of our infirmities; but was in all points tempted like as we are, yet without sin. Let us therefore come boldly unto the throne of grace, that we may obtain mercy, and find grace to help in time of need.

Thus saith the Lᴏʀᴅ the King of Israel, and his Redeemer the Lᴏʀᴅ of hosts; I am the first, and I am the last; and beside me there is no God.—The mighty God, The everlasting Father, The Prince of Peace.

Art thou not from everlasting, O Lᴏʀᴅ my God, my Holy One?—Who is God, save the Lᴏʀᴅ? and who is a rock, save our God?

REVELATION 1: 17. Hebrews 12: 18, 22-24.—Hebrews 12: 2.—Hebrews 4: 15, 16. Isaiah 44: 6.—Isaiah 9: 6. Habakkuk 1-12.—II Samuel 22: 32.

APRIL 5

I will not let thee go, except thou bless me.

L ET him take hold of my strength, that he may make peace with me; and he shall make peace with me.

O woman, great is thy faith: be it unto thee even as thou wilt.—According to your faith be it unto you.— Let him ask in faith, nothing wavering. For he that wavereth is like a wave of the sea driven with the wind and tossed. For let not that man think that he shall receive anything of the Lord.

They drew nigh unto the village, whither they went: and [Jesus] made as though he would have gone farther. But they constrained him, saying, Abide with us: . . . he vanished out of their sight. And they said one to another, Did not our heart burn within us, while he talked with us by the way, and while he opened to us the Scriptures?—I pray thee, if I have found grace in thy sight, show me now thy way, that I may know thee that I may find grace in thy sight. . . . My presence shall go with thee, and I will give thee rest.

GENESIS 32: 26. Isaiah 27: 5. Matthew 15: 28.—Matthew 9: 29.—James 1: 6, 7. Luke 24: 28, 29, 31, 32.—Exodus 33: 13, 14.

96

He ever liveth to make intercession.

W<small>HO</small> is he that condemneth? It is Christ that died . . . who also maketh intercession for us.—Christ is not entered into the holy places made with hands, which are the figures of the true; but into heaven itself, now to appear in the presence of God for us.

If any man sin, we have an advocate with the Father, Jesus Christ the righteous.—There is one God, and one mediator between God and men, the man Christ Jesus.

Seeing . . . that we have a great high priest, that is passed into the heavens, Jesus the Son of God, let us hold fast our profession. For we have not a high priest which cannot be touched with the feeling of our infirmities; but was in all points tempted like as we are, yet without sin. Let us therefore come boldly unto the throne of grace, that we may obtain mercy, and find grace to help in time of need.

Through him we . . . have access by one Spirit unto the Father.

HEBREWS 7: 25. Romans 8: 34.—Hebrews 9: 24. I John 2: 1. I Timothy 2: 5. Hebrews 4: 14-16. Ephesians 2: 18.

APRIL 7

> As sorrowful, yet alway rejoicing; as poor, yet
> making many rich; as having nothing, and yet
> possessing all things.

WE . . . rejoice in hope of the glory of God. And
not only so, but we glory in tribulations also.—I am
filled with comfort, I am exceeding joyful in all our
tribulation.—Believing, ye rejoice with joy unspeakable and full of glory.

In a great trial of affliction the abundance of their
joy and their deep poverty abounded unto the riches
of Christ; and to make all men see what is the fellow-
least of all saints, is this grace given, that I should
preach among the Gentiles the unsearchable riches
of Christ; and to make all men see what is the fellowship of the mystery, which from the beginning of the
world hath been hid in God.

Hath not God chosen the poor of this world rich
in faith, and heirs of the kingdom which he hath
promised to them that love him?—God is able to make
all grace abound toward you; that ye, always having
all sufficiency in all things, may abound to every good
work.

II CORINTHIANS 6: 10. Romans 5: 2, 3.—II Corinthians
7: 4.—I Peter 1: 8. II Corinthians 8: 2.—Ephesians 3: 8, 9.
James 2: 5.—II Corinthians 9: 8.

In everything ye are enriched by Him.

W<small>HEN</small> we were yet without strength, in due time Christ died for the ungodly.—He that spared not his own Son, but delivered him up for us all, how shall he not with him also freely give us all things?

In him dwelleth all the fulness of the Godhead bodily. And ye are complete in him, which is the head of all principality and power.

Abide in me, and I in you. As the branch cannot bear fruit of itself, except it abide in the vine; no more can ye, except ye abide in me. I am the vine, ye are the branches: he that abideth in me, and I in him, the same bringeth forth much fruit: for without me ye can do nothing.—To will is present with me; but how to perform that which is good I find not.— Unto every one of us is given grace according to the measure of the gift of Christ.

If ye abide in me, and my words abide in you, ye shall ask what ye will, and it shall be done unto you. —Let the word of Christ dwell in you richly in all wisdom.

I CORINTHIANS 1: 5. Romans 5: 6.—Romans 8: 32. Colossians 2: 9, 10. John 15: 4, 5.—Romans 7: 18.—Ephesians 4: 2. John 15: 7.—Colossians 3: 16.

APRIL 9

Fear not; for I have redeemed thee.

FEAR not; for thou shalt not be ashamed: neither be thou confounded; for thou shalt not be put to shame: for thou shalt forget the shame of thy youth, and shalt not remember the reproach of thy widowhood any more. For thy Maker is thy husband; the LORD of hosts is his name; and thy Redeemer the Holy One of Israel.—I have blotted out, as a thick cloud, thy transgressions, and, as a cloud, thy sins: return unto me; for I have redeemed thee.—With the precious blood of Christ, as of a lamb without blemish and without spot.

Their Redeemer is strong; the LORD of hosts is his name: he shall thoroughly plead their cause.—My Father, which gave them me, is greater than all; and no man is able to pluck them out of my Father's hand.

Grace be to you and peace from God the Father, and from our Lord Jesus Christ, who gave himself for our sins, that he might deliver us from this present evil world, according to the will of God and our Father: to whom be glory for ever and ever. Amen.

ISAIAH 43: 1. Isaiah 54: 4, 5.—Isaiah 44: 22.—I Peter 1: 19. Jeremiah 50: 34.—John 10: 29. Galatians 1: 3-5.

I am black, but comely.

BEHOLD, I was shapen in iniquity; and in sin did my mother conceive me.—Thy renown went forth among the heathen for thy beauty: for it was perfect through my comeliness which I had put upon thee, saith the Lord God.

I am a sinful man, O Lord.—Behold, thou art fair, my love; behold, thou art fair.

I abhor myself, and repent in dust and ashes.—Thou art all fair, my love; there is no spot in thee.

When I would do good, evil is present with me.—Be of good cheer; thy sins be forgiven thee.

I know that in me (that is, in my flesh) dwelleth no good thing.—Ye are complete in him.—Perfect in Christ Jesus.

YE are washed, . . . ye are sanctified, . . . ye are justified in the name of the Lord Jesus, and by the spirit of our God.—That ye should show forth the praises of him who hath called you out of darkness into his marvellous light.

CANTICLES 1: 5. Psalms 51: 5.—Ezekiel 16: 14. Luke 5: 8.—Canticles 4: 1. Job 42: 6.—Canticles 4: 7. Romans 7: 21. —Matthew 9: 2. Romans 7: 18.—Colossians 2: 10; 1: 28. I Corinthians 6: 11.—I Peter 2: 9.

APRIL 11

In the multitude of words there wanteth not sin: but he that refraineth his lips is wise.

My beloved brethren, let every man be swift to hear, slow to speak, slow to wrath.—He that is slow to anger is better than the mighty: and he that ruleth his spirit than he that taketh a city.—If any man offend not in word, the same is a perfect man, and able also to bridle the whole body.—By thy words thou shalt be justified, and by thy words thou shalt be condemned.—Set a watch, O Lord, before my mouth; keep the door of my lips.

Christ . . . suffered for us, leaving us an example, that ye should follow his steps: who did no sin, neither was guile found in his mouth: who when he was reviled, reviled not again; when he suffered, he threatened not; but committed himself to him that judgeth righteously.—Consider him that endured such contradiction of sinners against himself, lest ye be wearied and faint in your minds.

In their mouth was found no guile: for they are without fault before the throne of God.

PROVERBS 10: 19. James 1: 19.—Proverbs 16: 32.—James 3: 2.—Matthew 12: 37.—Psalms 141: 3. I Peter 2: 21-23.—Hebrews 12: 3. Revelation 14: 5.

What the law could not do, in that it was weak through the flesh, God sending his own Son in the likeness of sinful flesh, and for sin, condemned sin in the flesh.

THE law having a shadow of good things to come, and not the very image of the things, can never with those sacrifices which they offered year by year continually make the comers thereunto perfect. For then would they not have ceased to be offered?—By him all that believe are justified from all things, from which ye could not be justified by the law of Moses.

Forasmuch . . . as the children are partakers of flesh and blood, he also himself likewise took part of the same; that through death he might destroy him that had the power of death, that is the devil; and deliver them who through fear of death were all their lifetime subject to bondage. For verily he took not on him the nature of angels; but he took on him the seed of Abraham. Wherefore in all things it behooved him to be made like unto his brethren.

ROMANS 8: 3. Hebrews 10: 1, 2.—Acts 13: 39. Hebrews 2: 14-17.

Honor the Lord with thy substance, and with the first fruits of all thine increase.

He which soweth sparingly shall reap also sparingly; and he which soweth bountifully shall reap also bountifully.—Upon the first day of the week let every one of you lay by him in store, as God hath prospered him.

God is not unrighteous to forget your work and labor of love, which ye have showed toward his name, in that ye have ministered to the saints and do minister.

I beseech you . . . brethren, by the mercies of God, that ye present your bodies a living sacrifice, holy, acceptable unto God, which is your reasonable service.

The love of Christ constraineth us; because we thus judge, that if one died for all, then were all dead: and that he died for all, that they which live should not henceforth live unto themselves, but unto him which died for them, and rose again.—Whether therefore ye eat, or drink, or whatsoever ye do, do all to the glory of God.

PROVERBS 3: 9. II Corinthians 9: 6.—I Corinthians 16: 2. Hebrews 6: 10. Romans 12: 1. II Corinthians 5: 14, 15. —I Corinthians 10: 31.

My soul shall be satisfied as with marrow and fatness; and my mouth shall praise thee with joyful lips; when I remember thee upon my bed, and meditate on thee in the night watches.

How precious . . . are thy thoughts unto me, O God! how great is the sum of them! If I should count them, they are more in number than the sand: when I awake, I am still with thee.—How sweet are thy words unto my taste! yea, sweeter than honey to my mouth!

Whom have I in heaven but thee? and there is none upon earth that I desire beside thee.

As the apple-tree among the trees of the wood, so is my beloved among the sons. I sat down under his shadow with great delight, and his fruit was sweet to my taste. He brought me to the banqueting house, and his banner over me was love.—His countenance is as Lebanon, excellent as the cedars. His mouth is most sweet: yea, he is altogether lovely. This is my beloved and this is my friend.

PSALMS 63: 5, 6. Psalms 139: 17, 18.—Psalms 119: 103. Psalms 73: 25. Canticles 2: 3, 4.—Canticles 5: 15, 16.

APRIL 15

Their redeemer is strong.

I KNOW your manifold transgressions and your mighty sins.—I have laid help upon one that is mighty.—The LORD . . . thy Saviour and thy Redeemer, the mighty one of Jacob.—Mighty to save.—Able to keep you from falling.—Where sin abounded, grace did much more abound.

He that believeth on him is not condemned: but he that believeth not is condemned already, because he hath not believed in the name of the only begotten Son of God.—He is able . . . to save them to the uttermost that come unto God by him.

Is my hand shortened at all, that it cannot redeem?

Who shall separate us from the love of Christ? . . . I am persuaded, that neither death, nor life, nor angels, nor principalities, nor powers, nor things present, nor things to come, nor height, nor depth, nor any other creature, shall be able to separate us from the love of God which is in Christ Jesus our Lord.

JEREMIAH 50: 34. Amos 5: 12.—Psalms 89: 19.—Isaiah 49: 26.—Isaiah 63: 1.—Jude 24.—Romans 5: 20. John 3: 18. —Hebrews 7: 25. Isaiah 50: 2. Romans 8: 35, 38, 39.

I said in my haste, I am cut off from before thine eyes: nevertheless thou heardest the voice of my supplications when I cried unto thee.

I SINK in deep mire, where there is no standing: I am come into deep waters, where the floods overflow me.—Waters flowed over my head; then I said, I am cut off. I called upon thy name, O LORD, out of the low dungeon. Thou hast heard my voice: hide not thine ear at my breathing, at my cry. Thou drewest near in the day that I called upon thee: thou saidst, Fear not.

Will the LORD cast off for ever? and will he be favorable no more? Is his mercy clean gone for ever? doth his promise fail for evermore? Hath God forgotten to be gracious? hath he in anger shut up his tender mercies? And I said, This is my infirmity: but I will remember the years of the right hand of the Most High. I will remember the works of the Lord: surely I will remember thy wonders of old.—I had fainted, unless I had believed to see the goodness of the Lord in the land of the living.

PSALMS 31: 22. Psalms 69: 2.—Lamentations 3: 54-57. Psalms 77: 7-11.—Psalms 27: 13.

APRIL 17

Whoso offereth praise glorifieth me.

Let the word of Christ dwell in you richly in all wisdom; teaching and admonishing one another in psalms and hymns and spiritual songs singing with grace in your hearts to the Lord. And whatsoever ye do in word or deed, do all in the name of the Lord Jesus, giving thanks to God and the Father by him.

Glorify God in your body, and in your spirit, which are God's.

Ye are a royal priesthood, . . . that ye should show forth the praises of him who hath called you out of darkness into his marvellous light.—Ye . . . as lively stones, are built up a spiritual house, a holy priesthood, to offer up spiritual sacrifices, aceptable to God by Jesus Christ.—By him . . . let us offer the sacrifice of praise to God continually, that is, the fruit of our lips, giving thanks to his name.

My soul shall make her boast in the Lord: the humble shall hear thereof, and be glad. O magnify the Lord with me, and let us exalt his name together.

PSALMS 50: 23. Colossians 3: 16, 17. I Corinthians 6: 20. I Peter 2: 9.—I Peter 2: 5.—Hebrews 13: 15. Psalms 34: 2, 3.

I will raise them up a prophet from among their brethren, like unto thee.

[Moses] stood between the Lord and you at that time, to show you the word of the Lord: for ye were afraid.—There is one God, and one mediator between God and men, the man Christ Jesus.

Now the man Moses was very meek, above all the men which were upon the face of the earth.—Take my yoke upon you and learn of me; for I am meek and lowly in heart: and ye shall find rest unto your souls.—Let this mind be in you, which was also in Christ Jesus: who, being in the form of God, thought it not robbery to be equal with God; but made himself of no reputation, and took upon him the form of a servant, and was made in the likeness of men.

Moses verily was faithful in all his house, as a servant, for a testimony of those things which were to be spoken after; but Christ as a son over his own house; whose house are we, if we hold fast the confidence and the rejoicing of the hope firm unto the end.

DEUTERONOMY 18: 18. Deuteronomy 5: 5.—I Timothy 2: 5. Numbers 12: 3.—Matthew 11: 29.—Philippians 2: 5-7. Hebrews 3: 5, 6.

APRIL 19

> Verily, verily, I say unto you, I am the door of
> the sheep.

THE veil of the temple was rent in twain from the
top to the bottom.—Christ . . . hath once suffered for
sins, the just for the unjust, that he might bring us
to God.—The way into the holiest of all was not yet
made manifest, while as the first tabernacle was yet
standing.

I am the door: by me if any man enter in, he shall
be saved, and shall go in and out, and find pasture.

No man cometh unto the Father, but by me.—
Through him we . . . have access by one Spirit unto
the Father. Now therefore ye are no more strangers
and foreigners, but fellow-citizens with the saints, and
of the household of God.—Having . . . boldness to
enter into the holiest by the blood of Jesus, by a new
and living way, which he hath consecrated for us,
through the veil, that is to say, his flesh.—We . . .
have peace with God through our Lord Jesus Christ:
by whom also we have access by faith into this grace
wherein we stand.

JOHN 10: 7. Matthew 27: 51.—I Peter 3: 18.—Hebrews
9: 8. John 10: 9. John 14: 6.—Ephesians 2: 18, 19.—Hebrews 10: 19, 20.—Romans 5: 1, 2.

There shall cleave naught of the cursed thing
to thy hand.

COME out from among them, and be ye separate,
saith the LORD, and touch not the unclean thing.—
Dearly beloved, I beseech you as strangers and pilgrims, abstain from fleshly lusts, which war against
the soul.—Hating even the garment spotted by the
flesh.

Beloved, now are we the sons of God: and it doth
not yet appear what we shall be; but we know that,
when he shall appear, we shall be like him: for we
shall see him as he is. And every man that hath this
hope in him purifieth himself, even as he is pure.
—The grace of God that bringeth salvation hath
appeared to all men, teaching us that, denying ungodliness and worldly lusts, we should live soberly, righteously, and godly, in this present world; looking for
that blessed hope, and the glorious appearing of the
great God and our Saviour Jesus Christ: who gave
himself for us, that he might redeem us from all
iniquity, and purify unto himself a peculiar people,
zealous of good works.

DEUTERONOMY 13: 17. II Corinthians 6: 17.—I Peter
2: 11.—Jude 23. I John 3: 2, 3.—Titus 2: 11-14.

APRIL 21

Stand fast in the Lord.

M Y foot hath held his steps, his way have I kept, and not declined.—The LORD loveth judgment, and forsaketh not his saints; they are preserved for ever.—The LORD shall preserve thee from all evil: he shall preserve thy soul.

The just shall live by faith: but if any man draw back, my soul shall have no pleasure in him. But we are not of them who draw back unto perdition; but of them that believe to the saving of the soul.—If they had been of us, they would no doubt have continued with us: but they went out, that they might be made manifest that they were not all of us.

If ye continue in my word, then are ye my disciples indeed.—He that shall endure unto the end, the same shall be saved.—Watch ye, stand fast in the faith, quit you like men, be strong.—Hold that fast which thou hast, that no man take thy crown.—He that over-cometh, the same shall be clothed in white raiment; and I will not blot out his name out of the book of life.

PHILIPPIANS 4: 1. Job 23: 11.—Psalms 37: 28.—Psalms 121: 7. Hebrews 10: 38, 39.—I John 2: 19. John 8: 31.—Matthew 24: 13.—I Corinthians 16: 13.—Revelation 3: 11.—Revelation 3: 5.

If his offering be a burnt sacrifice of the herd, let him offer a male without blemish: he shall offer it of his own voluntary will. And he shall put his hand upon the head of the burnt offering; and it shall be accepted for him to make atonement for him.

God will provide himself a lamb for a burnt offering.—Behold the Lamb of God which taketh away the sin of the world.—We are sanctified through the offering of the body of Jesus Christ once for all.—A ransom for many.

No man taketh it from me, but I lay it down of myself. I have power to lay it down, and I have power to take it again.

I will love them freely.—The Son of God . . . loved me, and gave himself for me.

He hath made him to be sin for us, who knew no sin; that we might be made the righteousness of God in him.—He hath made us accepted in the beloved.

LEVITICUS 1: 3, 4. Genesis 22: 8.—John 1: 29.—Hebrews 10: 10.—Matthew 20: 28. John 10: 18. Hosea 14: 4. —Galatians 2: 20. II Corinthians 5: 21.—Ephesians 1: 6.

113

APRIL 23

The Lord was my stay.

Truly in vain is salvation hoped for from the hills, and from the multitude of mountains: truly in the Lord our God is the salvation of Israel.—The Lord is my rock, and my fortress, and my deliverer; my God, my strength, in whom I will trust; my buckler, and the horn of my salvation, and my high tower.

Cry out and shout, thou inhabitant of Zion; for great is the Holy One of Israel in the midst of thee.

The angel of the Lord encampeth round about them that fear Him, and delivereth them. The righteous cry, and the Lord heareth, and delivereth them out of all their troubles.—The eternal God is thy refuge, and underneath are the everlasting arms.—So that we may boldly say, The Lord is my helper, and I will not fear what man shall do unto me.—For who is God save the Lord? or who is a rock save our God? It is God that girdeth me with strength, and maketh my way perfect.

By the grace of God I am what I am.

PSALMS 18: 18. Jeremiah 3: 23.—Psalms 18: 2. Isaiah 12: 6. Psalms 34: 7, 17.—Deuteronomy 33: 27.—Hebrews 13: 6.—Psalms 18: 31, 32. I Corinthians 15: 10.

The Lord visited Sarah as he had said, and the Lord did unto Sarah as he had spoken.

Trust in him at all times; ye people, pour out your heart before him: God is a refuge for us.—David encouraged himself in the LORD his God.—God will surely visit you, and bring you out of this land unto the land which he sware to Abraham, to Isaac, and to Jacob.—I have seen, I have seen the affliction of my people which is in Egypt, and I have heard their groaning and am come down to deliver them. He brought them out, after that he had showed wonders and signs in the land of Egypt, and in the Red sea, and in the wilderness forty years.—There failed not aught of any good thing which the LORD had spoken . . . ; all came to pass.

He is faithful that promised.—Hath he said, and shall he not do it? or hath he spoken, and shall he not make it good?—Heaven and earth shall pass away, but my words shall not pass away.—The grass withereth, the flower fadeth; but the word of our God shall stand for ever.

GENESIS 21: 1. Psalms 62: 8.—I Samuel 30: 6.—Genesis 50: 24.—Acts 7: 34, 36.—Joshua 21: 45. Hebrews 10: 23.—Numbers 23: 19.—Matthew 24: 35.—Isaiah 40: 8.

APRIL 25

Thou shalt call his name Jesus: for he shall save his people from their sins.

YE know that he was manifested to take away our sins.—That we, being dead to sins, should live unto righteousness.—He is able also to save them to the uttermost that come unto God by him.

He was wounded for our transgressions, he was bruised for our iniquities: the chastisement of our peace was upon him; and with his stripes we are healed. The LORD hath laid on him the iniquity of us all.—Thus it behooved Christ to suffer, . . . that repentance and remission of sins should be preached in his name among all nations.—He appeared to put away sin by the sacrifice of himself.

Him hath God exalted with his right hand to be a Prince and a Saviour, . . . to give repentance.— Through this man is preached unto you the forgiveness of sins: and by him all that believe are justified from all things, from which ye could not be justified by the law of Moses.—Your sins are forgiven you for his name's sake.

MATTHEW 1: 21. I John 3: 5.—I Peter 2: 24.—Hebrews 7: 25. Isaiah 53: 5, 6.—Luke 24: 46, 47.—Hebrews 9: 26. Acts 5: 31.—Acts 13: 38, 39.—I John 2: 12.

His left hand is under my head, and his right hand doth embrace me.

Underneath are the everlasting arms.—When [Peter] saw the wind boisterous, he was afraid; and beginning to sink, he cried, saying, Lord, save me. And immediately Jesus stretched forth his hand, and caught him, and said unto him, O thou of little faith, wherefore didst thou doubt?

The steps of a good man are ordered by the Lord: and He delighteth in his way. Though he fall, he shall not be utterly cast down: for the Lord upholdeth him with his hand.

The beloved of the Lord shall dwell in safety by him, and the Lord shall cover him all the day long, and he shall dwell between his shoulders.—Casting all your care upon Him, for he careth for you.—He that toucheth you, toucheth the apple of his eye.

They shall never perish, neither shall any man pluck them out of my hand. My Father, which gave them me, is greater than all.

CANTICLES 2: 6. Deuteronomy 33: 27.—Matthew 14: 30, 31. Psalms 17: 23, 24. Deuteronomy 33: 2.—I Peter 5: 7.— Zechariah 2: 8. John 10: 28, 29.

APRIL 27

Brethren, the time is short.

MAN that is born of a woman is of few days and full of trouble. He cometh forth like a flower, and is cut down: he fleeth also as a shadow, and continueth not.—The world passeth away, and the lust thereof: but he that doeth the will of God abideth for ever.— As in Adam all die, even so in Christ shall all be made alive. Death is swallowed up in victory.— Whether we live, we live unto the Lord; and whether we die, we die unto the Lord: whether we live therefore, or die, we are the Lord's.

To live is Christ, and to die is gain.

Cast not away . . . your confidence, which hath great recompense of reward. For ye have need of patience, that, after ye have done the will of God, ye might receive the promise. For yet a little while, and he that shall come will come and will not tarry. —The night is far spent, the day is at hand: let us therefore cast off the works of darkness, and let us put on the armor of light.—The end of all things is at hand: be ye therefore sober, and watch unto prayer.

I CORINTHIANS 7: 29. Job 14: 1, 2.—I John 2: 17.— I Corinthians 15: 22, 54.—Romans 14: 8. Philippians 1: 21. Hebrews 10: 35-37.—Romans 13: 12.—I Peter 4: 7.

Behold the Lamb of God.

IT is not possible that the blood of bulls and of goats should take away sins. Wherefore when he cometh into the world, he saith, Sacrifice and offering thou wouldest not, but a body hast thou prepared me; in burnt offerings and sacrifices for sin thou hast had no pleasure. Then said I, Lo, I come (in the volume of the book it is written of me) to do thy will, O God.—He was oppressed, and he was afflicted, yet he opened not his mouth: he is brought as a lamb to the slaughter, and as a sheep before her shearers is dumb, so he openeth not his mouth.

Ye were not redeemed with corruptible things, as silver and gold, . . . but with the precious blood of Christ, as of a lamb without blemish and without spot: . . . manifest in these last times for you who by him do believe in God . . . that your faith and hope might be in God.

Worthy is the Lamb that was slain to receive power, and riches, and wisdom, and strength, and honor, and glory, and blessing.

JOHN 1: 29. Hebrews 10: 4-7.—Isaiah 53: 7. I Peter 1: 18-21. Revelation 5: 12.

APRIL 29

Consider how great things He hath done for you.

THOU shalt remember all the way which the LORD thy God led thee these forty years in the wilderness, to humble thee, and to prove thee, to know what was in thy heart, whether thou wouldest keep his commandments, or no. Thou shalt also consider in thy heart, that, as a man chasteneth his son, so the LORD thy God chasteneth thee.

I know, O LORD, that thy judgments are right, and that thou in faithfulness hast afflicted me. It is good for me that I have been afflicted; that I might learn thy statutes. Before I was afflicted I went astray: but now have I kept thy word.—The Lord hath chastened me sore: but he hath not given me over unto death.

He hath not dealt with us after our sins, nor rewarded us according to our iniquities. For as the heaven is high above the earth, so great is his mercy toward them that fear him. He knoweth our frame; he remembereth that we are dust.

I SAMUEL 12: 24. Deuteronomy 8: 2, 5. Psalms 119: 75, 71, 67.—Psalms 118: 18. Psalms 103: 10, 11, 14.

Whoso keepeth his word, in him verily is the love of God perfected.

THE God of peace, that brought again from the dead our Lord Jesus, that great shepherd of the sheep, through the blood of the everlasting covenant, make you perfect in every good work to do his will, working in you that which is well pleasing in his sight, through Jesus Christ; to whom be glory for ever and ever. Amen.

Hereby we do know that we know him, if we keep his commandments.—If a man love me, he will keep my words: and my Father will love him, and we will come unto him, and make our abode with him.— Whosoever abideth in him sinneth not: whosoever sinneth hath not seen him, neither known him. Little children, let no man deceive you: he that doeth right-eousness is righteous, even as He is righteous.

Herein is our love made perfect, that we may have boldness in the day of judgment: because as he is, so are we in this world.

I JOHN 2: 5. Hebrews 13: 20, 21. I John 2: 3.—John 14: 23.—I John 3: 6, 7. I John 4: 17.

MAY 1

The fruit of the Spirit is peace.

To be spiritually minded is life and peace.

God hath called us to peace.—Peace I leave with you, my peace I give unto you: not as the world giveth, give I unto you. Let not your heart be troubled, neither let it be afraid.—The God of hope fill you with all joy and peace in believing.

I know whom I have believed, and am persuaded that he is able to keep that which I have committed unto him against that day.—Thou wilt keep him in perfect peace, whose mind is stayed on thee: because he trusteth in thee.

The work of righteousness shall be peace; and the effect of righteousness quietness and assurance for ever. And my people shall dwell in a peaceable habitation, and in sure dwellings, and in quiet resting-places.— Whoso hearkeneth unto me shall dwell safely, and shall be quiet from fear of evil.

Great peace have they who love thy law.

GALATIANS 5: 22. Romans 8: 6. I Corinthians 7: 15.— John 14: 27.—Romans 15: 13. II Timothy 1: 12.—Isaiah 26: 3. Isaiah 32: 17-18.—Proverbs 1: 33. Psalms 119: 165.

Surely the Lord is in this place; and I knew it not.

Where two or three are gathered together in my name, there am I in the midst of them.—Lo, I am with you alway, even unto the end of the world.—My presence shall go with thee, and I will give thee rest.

Whither shall I go from thy Spirit? or whither shall I flee from thy presence? If I ascend up into heaven, thou art there: if I make my bed in hell, behold, thou art there.—Am I a God at hand, saith the LORD, and not a God afar off? Can any hide himself in secret places that I shall not see him? saith the LORD. Do not I fill heaven and earth? saith the LORD.

Behold, the heaven and heaven of heavens cannot contain thee; how much less this house that I have builded?—Thus saith the high and lofty One that inhabiteth eternity, whose name is Holy: I dwell in the high and holy place, with him also that is of a contrite and humble spirit, to revive the spirit of the humble, and to revive the heart of the contrite ones.

GENESIS 28: 16. Matthew 18: 20.—Matthew 28: 20.— Exodus 33: 14. Psalms 139: 7, 8.—Jeremiah 23: 23, 24. I Kings 8: 27.—Isaiah 57: 15.

MAY 3

Be ye perfect, even as your Father which is in heaven is perfect.

I AM the Almighty God; walk before me, and be thou perfect.—Ye shall be holy unto me: for I the LORD am holy, and have severed you from other people, that ye should be mine.

Ye are bought with a price: therefore glorify God in your body, and in your spirit, which are God's.

Ye are complete in him, which is the head of all principality and power.—Who gave himself for us, that he might redeem us from all iniquity.—Be diligent that ye may be found of him in peace, without spot, and blameless.

Blessed are the undefiled in the way, who walk in the law of the LORD.—Whoso looketh into the perfect law of liberty, and continueth therein, he being not a forgetful hearer, but a doer of the work, this man shall be blessed in his deed.—Search me, O God, and know my heart: try me, and know my thoughts: and see if there be any wicked way in me, and lead me in the way everlasting.

MATTHEW 5: 48. Genesis 17: 1.—Leviticus 20: 26. I Corinthians 6: 20. Colossians 2: 10.—Titus 2: 14.—II Peter 3: 14. Psalms 119: 1.—James 1: 25.—Psalms 139: 23, 24.

Behold, the Lord's hand is not shortened, that it cannot save; neither his ear heavy, that it cannot hear.

In the day when I cried thou answeredst me, and strengthenedst me with strength in my soul.—While I was speaking in prayer, even the man Gabriel, whom I had seen in the vision at the beginning, being caused to fly swiftly, touched me about the time of the evening oblation.

Hide not thy face far from me; put not thy servant away in anger: thou hast been my help; leave me not, neither forsake me, O God of my salvation.—Be not thou far from me, O Lord: O my strength, haste thee to help me.

Ah Lord God! behold, thou hast made the heaven and the earth by thy great power and stretched-out arm, and there is nothing too hard for thee.—Who delivered us from so great a death and doth deliver: in whom we trust that he will yet deliver us.—Shall not God avenge his own elect, which cry day and night unto him, though he bear long with them? I tell you that he will avenge them speedily.

ISAIAH 59: 1. Psalms 138: 3.—Daniel 9: 21. Psalms 27: 9.—Psalms 22: 19. Jeremiah 32: 17.—II Corinthians 1: 10. —Luke 18: 7, 8.

MAY 5

Take no thought, saying, What shall we eat? or, What shall we drink? or, Wherewithal shall we be clothed? for your heavenly Father knoweth that ye have need of all these things.

O FEAR the Lord, ye his saints: for there is no want to them that fear him. The young lions do lack, and suffer hunger: but they that seek the LORD shall not want any good thing.—No good thing will he withhold from them that walk uprightly. O LORD of hosts, blessed is the man that trusteth in thee.

I would have you without carefulness.—Be careful for nothing; but in everything by prayer and supplication with thanksgiving let your requests be made known unto God.

Are not two sparrows sold for a farthing? and one of them shall not fall on the ground without your Father. The very hairs of your head are all numbered. Fear ye not, therefore, ye are of more value than many sparrows.—Why are ye so fearful? how is it that ye have no faith? Have faith in God.

MATTHEW 6: 31, 32. Psalms 34: 9, 10.—Psalms 84: 11, 12.
I Corinthians 7: 32.—Philippians 4: 6. Matthew 10: 29-31.—
Mark 4: 40.—Mark 11: 22.

Mercy and truth are met together; righteousness and peace have kissed each other.

A JUST God and a Saviour.

The LORD is well pleased for his righteousness' sake; he will magnify the law, and make it honorable.

God was in Christ, reconciling the world unto himself, not imputing their trespasses unto them.—Whom God hath set forth to be a propitiation through faith in his blood, to declare his righteousness for the remission of sins that are past, through the forbearance of God: to declare, I say, at this time his righteousness: that he might be just, and the justifier of him which believeth in Jesus.—He was wounded for our transgressions, he was bruised for our iniquities, the chastisement of our peace was upon him, and with his stripes we are healed. Who shall lay anything to the charge of God's elect? It is God that justifieth. —To him that worketh not, but believeth on him that justifieth the ungodly, his faith is counted for righteousness.

PSALMS 85: 10. Isaiah 45: 21. Isaiah 42: 21. II Corinthians 5: 19.—Romans 3: 25, 26.—Isaiah 53: 5.—Romans 8: 33.—Romans 4: 5.

MAY 7

Ye shall hear of wars and rumors of wars: see that ye be not troubled.

GOD is our refuge and strength, a very present help in trouble. Therefore will not we fear, though the earth be removed, and though the mountains be carried into the midst of the sea; though the waters thereof roar and be troubled, though the mountains shake with the swelling thereof.—Come, my people, enter thou into thy chambers, and shut thy doors about thee: hide thyself as it were for a little moment, until the indignation be overpast. For, behold, the Lord cometh out of his place to punish the inhabitants of the earth for their iniquity.—In the shadow of thy wings will I make my refuge, until these calamities be overpast.—Your life is hid with Christ in God.

He shall not be afraid of evil tidings: his heart is fixed, trusting in the LORD.

These things I have spoken unto you, that in me ye might have peace. In the world ye shall have tribulation: but be of good cheer; I have overcome the world.

MATTHEW 24: 6. Psalms 46: 1-3.—Isaiah 26: 20, 21. Psalms 57: 1.—Colossians 3: 3. Psalms 112: 7. John 16: 33.

It pleased the Lord to bruise him; he hath put him to grief.

Now is my soul troubled; and what shall I say? Father, save me from this hour: but for this cause came I unto this hour. Father, glorify thy name. Then came there a voice from heaven, saying, I have both glorified it, and will glorify it again.—Father, if thou be willing, remove this cup from me: nevertheless not my will, but thine, be done. And there appeared an angel unto him from heaven, strengthening him.

Being found in fashion as a man, he humbled himself, and became obedient unto death, even the death of the cross.—Therefore doth my Father love me, because I lay down my life, that I might take it again. —For I came down from heaven, not to do mine own will, but the will of him that sent me.—The cup which my Father hath given me, shall I not drink it?

The Father hath not left me alone; for I do always those things that please him.—My beloved Son, in whom I am well pleased.

ISAIAH 53: 10. John 12: 27, 28.—Luke 22: 42, 43. Philippians 2: 8.—John 10: 17.—John 6: 38.—John 18: 11. John 8: 29.—Matthew 3: 17.—Isaiah 42: 1.

MAY 9

Faith is the substance of things hoped for, the evidence of things not seen.

If in this life only we have hope in Christ, we are of all men most miserable.

Eye hath not seen, nor ear heard, neither have entered into the heart of man, the things which God hath prepared for them that love him. But God hath revealed them unto us by his Spirit.—After that ye believed, ye were sealed with that holy Spirit of promise, which is the earnest of our inheritance until the redemption of the purchased possession.

Jesus saith unto him, Thomas, because thou hast seen me, thou hast believed: blessed are they that have not seen, and yet have believed.—Whom having not seen, ye love; in whom, though now ye see him not, yet believing, ye rejoice with joy unspeakable and full of glory: receiving the end of your faith, even the salvation of your souls.

We walk by faith, not by sight.—Cast not away therefore your confidence, which hath great recompense of reward.

HEBREWS 11: 1. I Corinthians 15: 19. I Corinthians 2: 9, 10.—Ephesians 1: 13, 14. John 20: 29.—I Peter 1: 8, 9. II Corinthians 5: 7.—Hebrews 10: 35.

For this purpose the Son of God was manifested, that he might destroy the works of the devil.

WE wrestle not against flesh and blood, but against principalities, against powers, against the rulers of the darkness of this world, against spiritual wickedness in high places.—Forasmuch . . . as the children are partakers of flesh and blood, he also himself likewise took part of the same; that through death he might destroy him that had the power of death, that is, the devil.—And having spoiled principalities and powers, he made a show of them openly, triumphing over them.—I heard a loud voice saying in heaven, Now is come salvation, and strength, and the kingdom of our God, and the power of his Christ: for the accuser of our brethren is cast down, which accused them before our God day and night. And they overcame him by the blood of the Lamb, and by the word of their testimony; and they loved not their lives unto the death.

Thanks be to God, which giveth us the victory through our Lord Jesus Christ.

I JOHN 3: 8. Ephesians 6: 12.—Hebrews 2: 14.—Colossians 2: 15.—Revelation 12: 10, 11. I Corinthians 15: 57.

MAY 11

Awake to righteousness, and sin not.

Y E are all the children of light, and the children of the day. Therefore let us not sleep, as do others; but let us watch and be sober.

It is high time to awake out of sleep: for now is our salvation nearer than when we believed. The night is far spent, the day is at hand: let us therefore cast off the works of darkness, and let us put on the armor of light.—Wherefore take unto you the whole armor of God, that ye may be able to withstand in the evil day, and having done all, to stand. Cast away from you all your transgressions, whereby ye have transgressed; and make you a new heart and a new spirit.—Lay apart all filthiness and superfluity of naughtiness, and receive with meekness the engrafted word, which is able to save your souls.

Little children, abide in him; that, when he shall appear, we may have confidence, and not be ashamed before him at his coming. If ye know that he is righteous, ye know that every one that doeth righteousness is born of him.

I CORINTHIANS 15: 34. I Thessalonians 5: 5, 6. Romans 13: 11, 12.—Ephesians 6: 13.—Ezekiel 18: 31.—James 1: 21. I John 2: 28: 29.

Beloved, let us love one another: for love is of
God; and every one that loveth is born of God,
and knoweth God.

T HE love of God is shed abroad in our hearts by
the Holy Ghost, which is given unto us.—Ye have
not received the spirit of bondage again to fear; but
ye have received the Spirit of adoption, whereby we
cry Abba, Father. The Spirit itself beareth witness
with our spirit, that we are the children of God.—He
that believeth on the Son of God hath the witness in
himself.

In this was manifested the love of God toward us,
because that God sent his only begotten Son into the
world, that we might live through him.—In whom we
have redemption through his blood, the forgiveness
of sins, according to the riches of his grace.—That in
the ages to come he might show the exceeding riches
of his grace in his kindness toward us through Christ
Jesus.

Beloved, if God so loved us, we ought also to love
one another.

I JOHN 4: 7. Romans 5: 5.—Romans 8: 15, 16.—I John
5: 10. I John 4: 9.—Ephesians 1: 7.—Ephesians 2: 7. I John
4: 11.

Pray everywhere, lifting up holy hands, without wrath and doubting.

THE true worshippers shall worship the Father in spirit and in truth: for the Father seeketh such to worship him. God is a spirit: and they that worship him must worship him in spirit and in truth.—Then shalt thou call, and the Lord shall answer; thou shalt cry, and he shall say, Here I am.—When ye stand praying, forgive, if ye have aught against any.

Without faith it is impossible to please him: for he that cometh to God must believe that he is, and that he is a rewarder of them that diligently seek him.— Let him ask in faith, nothing wavering. For he that wavereth is like a wave of the sea, driven with the wind and tossed. For let not that man think that he shall receive anything of the Lord.

If I regard iniquity in my heart, the Lord will not hear me.—My little children, these things write I unto you, that ye sin not. And if any man sin, we have an advocate with the Father, Jesus Christ the righteous.

I TIMOTHY 2: 8. John 4: 23, 24.—Isaiah 58: 9.—Mark 11: 25. Hebrews 11: 6.—James 1: 6, 7. Psalms 66: 18.— I John 2: 1.

The fellowship of His sufferings.

It is enough for the disciple that he be as his master, and the servant as his lord.

He is despised and rejected of men; a man of sorrows, and acquainted with grief: and we hid as it were our faces from him: he was despised, and we esteemed him not.—Because ye are not of the world, but I have chosen you out of the world, therefore the world hateth you.

I looked for some to take pity, but there was none. —At my first answer no man stood with me, but all men forsook me.

The foxes have holes, and the birds of the air have nests; but the Son of man hath not where to lay his head.—Here have we no continuing city, but we seek one to come.

Let us run with patience the race that is set before us, looking unto Jesus the author and finisher of our faith; who for the joy that was set before him endured the cross, despising the shame, and is set down at the right hand of the throne of God.

PHILIPPIANS 3: 10. Matthew 10: 25. Isaiah 53: 3.—John 15: 19. Psalms 69: 20.—II Timothy 4: 16. Matthew 8: 20.— Hebrews 13: 14. Hebrews 12: 1, 2.

God shall wipe away all tears: . . . there shall
be no more death, neither sorrow, . . . for the
former things are passed away.

He will swallow up death in victory; and the Lord
God will wipe away tears from off all faces; and the
rebuke of his people shall he take away from off all
the earth: for the LORD hath spoken it.—Thy sun
shall no more go down; neither shall thy moon withdraw itself: for the LORD shall be thine everlasting
light, and the days of thy mourning shall be ended.—
The inhabitant shall not say, I am sick: the people
that dwell therein shall be forgiven their iniquity.—
The voice of weeping shall be no more heard in her,
nor the voice of crying.—Sorrow and sighing shall flee
away.

I will ransom them from the power of the grave;
I will redeem them from death: O death, I will be
thy plagues; O grave, I will be thy destruction.—The
last enemy that shall be destroyed is death. Then
shall be brought to pass the saying that is written,
Death is swallowed up in victory.

REVELATION 21: 4. Isaiah 25: 8.—Isaiah 60: 20.—Isaiah
33: 24.—Isaiah 65: 19.—Isaiah 35: 10. Hosea 13: 14.—I Corinthians 15: 26, 54.

A servant of Jesus Christ.

Y E call me Master and Lord, and ye say well; for so
I am.—If any man serve me, let him follow me; and
where I am, there shall also my servant be: if any
man serve me, him will my Father honor.—Take my
yoke upon you, and learn of me; for I am meek and
lowly in heart: and ye shall find rest unto your souls.
For my yoke is easy, and my burden is light.

What things were gain to me, those I counted loss
for Christ.—Being made free from sin, and become
servants to God, ye have your fruit unto holiness, and
the end everlasting life.

Henceforth I call you not servants; for the servant
knoweth not what his lord doeth: but I have called
you friends; for all things that I have heard of my
Father, I have made known unto you.

Stand fast therefore in the liberty wherewith Christ
hath made us free, and be not entangled again with
the yoke of bondage. For, brethren, ye have been
called unto liberty; only use not liberty for an occasion to the flesh.

ROMANS 1: 1. John 13: 13.—John 12: 26.—Matthew 11:
29, 30. Philippians 3: 7.—Romans 6: 22. John 15: 15. Galatians 5: 1, 13.

MAY 17

I am the Lord your God; walk in my statutes, and keep my judgments, and do them.

As he which hath called you is holy, so be ye holy in all manner of conversation.—He that saith he abideth in him ought himself also so to walk, even as he walked. If ye know that he is righteous, ye know that every one that doeth righteousness is born of him.—Circumcision is nothing, and uncircumcision is nothing, but the keeping of the commandments of God.—Whosoever shall keep the whole law, and yet offend in one point, he is guilty of all.

Not that we are sufficient . . . to think anything, as of ourselves; but our sufficiency is of God.—Teach me, O Lord, the way of thy statutes.

Work out your own salvation with fear and trembling. For it is God which worketh in you both to will and to do of his good pleasure.—The God of peace . . . make you perfect in every work to do his will, working in you that which is well pleasing in his sight, through Jesus Christ.

EZEKIEL 20: 19. I Peter 1: 15.—I John 2: 6, 29.—I Corinthians 7: 19.—James 2: 10. II Corinthians 3: 5.— Psalms 119: 33. Philippians 2: 12, 13.—Hebrews 13: 20, 21.

As the Father hath life in himself; so hath he
given to the Son to have life in himself.

Our Saviour Jesus Christ hath abolished death,
and hath brought life and immortality to light
through the gospel.—I am the resurrection and the
life.—Because I live, ye shall live also.—We are made
partakers of Christ.—Partakers of the Holy Ghost.—
Partakers of the divine nature.—The first man Adam
was made a living soul; the last Adam was made a
quickening spirit. Behold, I show you a mystery; We
shall not all sleep, but we shall all be changed, in a
moment, in the twinkling of an eye, at the last trump:
for the trumpet shall sound, and the dead shall be
raised incorruptible, and we shall be changed.

Holy, holy, holy, Lord God Almighty, which was,
and is, and is to come. . . . Who liveth for ever and
ever.—The blessed and only Potentate, the King of
kings, and Lord of lords; who only hath immortality.
—Unto the King eternal . . . be honor and glory for
ever and ever. Amen.

JOHN 5: 26. II Timothy 1: 10.—John 11: 25.—John 14:
19.—Hebrews 3: 14.—Hebrews 6: 4.—II Peter 1: 4.—I Corinthians 15: 45, 51, 52. Revelation 4: 8, 9.—I Timothy 6:
15, 16.—I Timothy 1: 17.

Wash me thoroughly from mine iniquity.

I WILL cleanse them from all their iniquity, whereby they have sinned against me; and I will pardon all their iniquities, whereby they have sinned, and whereby they have transgressed against me.—Then will I sprinkle clean water upon you, and ye shall be clean: from all your filthiness and from all your idols will I cleanse you.

Except a man be born of water and of the Spirit, he cannot enter into the kingdom of God.—If the blood of bulls, and of goats, and the ashes of a heifer sprinkling the unclean, sanctifieth to the purifying of the flesh: how much more shall the blood of Christ, who through the eternal Spirit offered himself without spot to God, purge your conscience from dead works to serve the living God!

He saved them for his name's sake, that he might make his mighty power to be known.—Not unto us, O LORD, not unto us, but unto thy name give glory, for thy mercy, and for thy truth's sake. We will bless the LORD from this time forth and for evermore. Praise the Lord.

PSALMS 51: 2. Jeremiah 33: 8.—Ezekiel 36: 25. John 3: 5.—Hebrews 9: 13, 14. Psalms 106: 8.—Psalms 115: 1, 18.

Take heed unto thyself.

E VERY man that striveth for the mastery is temperate in all things. Now they do it to obtain a corruptible crown; but we an incorruptible. I therefore so run, not as uncertainly; so fight I, not as one that beateth the air: but I keep under my body, and bring it into subjection: lest that by any means, when I have preached to others, I myself should be a castaway.

Put on the whole armor of God, that ye may be able to stand against the wiles of the devil. For we wrestle not against flesh and blood, but against principalities, against powers, against the rulers of the darkness of this world, against spiritual wickedness in high places.

They that are Christ's have crucified the flesh with the affections and lusts. If we live in the Spirit, let us also walk in the Spirit.—For as many as are led by the Spirit of God, they are the sons of God.—Meditate upon these things; give thyself wholly to them; that thy profiting may appear to all.

I TIMOTHY 4: 16. I Corinthians 9: 25-27. Ephesians 6: 11, 12. Galatians 5: 24, 25.—Romans 8: 14.—I Timothy 4: 15.

MAY 21

My brethren, be strong in the Lord, and in the power of his might.

My grace is sufficient for thee: for my strength is made perfect in weakness. Most gladly therefore will I rather glory in my infirmities, that the power of Christ may rest upon me. Therefore I take pleasure in infirmities, in reproaches, in necessities, in persecutions, in distresses for Christ's sake: for when I am weak, then am I strong.—I will go in the strength of the Lord God: I will make mention of thy righteousness, even of thine only.—The gospel of Christ . . . is the power of God unto salvation.

I can do all things through Christ which strengtheneth me.—I also labor, striving according to his working which worketh in me mightily.—We have this treasure in earthen vessels, that the excellency of the power may be of God, and not of us.

The joy of the Lord is your strength.—Strengthened with all might, according to his glorious power, unto all patience and long-suffering with joyfulness.

EPHESIANS 6: 10. II Corinthians 12: 9, 10.—Psalms 71: 16.—Romans 1: 16. Philippians 4: 13.—Colossians 1: 29.—II Corinthians 4: 7. Nehemiah 8: 10.—Colossians 1: 11.

Peace I leave with you, my peace I give unto you: not as the world giveth, give I unto you.

THE world passeth away, and the lust thereof.—Surely every man walketh in a vain show: surely they are disquieted in vain: he heapeth up riches, and knoweth not who shall gather them.—What fruit had ye then in those things whereof ye are now ashamed? for the end of those things is death.

Martha, Martha, thou art careful and troubled about many things: but one thing is needful: and Mary hath chosen that good part, which shall not be taken away from her.

These things I have spoken unto you, that in me ye might have peace. In the world ye shall have tribulation: but be of good cheer; I have overcome the world.—The Lord of peace himself give you peace always by all means.—The LORD bless thee, and keep thee; the LORD make his face shine upon thee, and be gracious unto thee: the Lord lift up his countenance upon thee, and give thee peace.

JOHN 14: 27. I John 2: 17.—Psalms 39: 6.—Romans 6: 21. Luke 10: 41, 42. John 16: 33.—II Thessalonians 3: 16.—Numbers 6: 24-26.

Thou shalt put the two stones upon the shoulders of the ephod for stones of memorial unto the children of Israel; and Aaron shall bear their names before the Lord.

Jesus . . . because he continueth ever, hath an unchangeable priesthood. Wherefore he is able also to save them to the uttermost that come unto God by him, seeing he ever liveth to make intercession for them.—Him that is able to keep you from falling, and to present you faultless before the presence of his glory.

Seeing . . . that we have a great high priest, that is passed into the heavens, Jesus the Son of God, let us hold fast our profession. For we have not a high priest which cannot be touched with the feeling of our infirmities: but was in all points tempted like as we are, yet without sin. Let us therefore come boldly unto the throne of grace.

The beloved of the Lord shall dwell in safety by Him; and the Lord shall cover him all the day long, and he shall dwell between his shoulders.

EXODUS 28: 12. Hebrews 7: 24, 25.—Jude 24. Hebrews 4: 14-16. Deuteronomy 33: 12.

Grieve not the Holy Spirit of God, whereby ye are sealed unto the day of redemption.

THE love of the Spirit.—The Comforter, which is the Holy Ghost.—In all their affliction he was afflicted, and the Angel of his presence saved them: in his love and in his pity he redeemed them; and he bare them, and carried them all the days of old. But they rebelled, and vexed his Holy Spirit: therefore he was turned to be their enemy, and he fought against them.

Hereby know we that we dwell in him, and he in us, because he hath given us of his Spirit.—After that ye believed, ye were sealed with that Holy Spirit of promise, which is the earnest of our inheritance until the redemption of the purchased possession.—This I say then, Walk in the Spirit, and ye shall not fulfil the lust of the flesh. For the flesh lusteth against the spirit, and the spirit against the flesh: and these are contrary the one to the other: so that ye cannot do the things that ye would.

The Spirit helpeth our infirmities.

EPHESIANS 4: 30. Romans 15: 30.—John 14: 26.—Isaiah 63: 9, 10. I John 4: 13.—Ephesians 1: 13, 14.—Galatians 5: 16, 17. Romans 8: 26.

MAY 25

How great is thy goodness, which thou hast laid up for them that fear thee!

SINCE the beginning of the world men have not heard, nor perceived by the ear, neither hath the eye seen, O God, beside thee, what he hath prepared for him that waiteth for him.—Eye hath not seen, nor ear heard, neither have entered into the heart of man, the things which God hath prepared for them that love him. But God hath revealed them unto us by his Spirit.—Thou wilt show me the path of life: in thy presence is fullness of joy: at thy right hand there are pleasures for evermore.

How excellent is thy living kindness, O God! therefore the children of men put their trust under the shadow of thy wings. They shall be abundantly satisfied with the fatness of thy house; and thou shalt make them drink of the river of thy pleasures.

Godliness is profitable unto all things, having promise of the life that now is, and of that which is to come.

PSALMS 31: 19. Isaiah 64: 4.—I Corinthians 2: 9, 10.— Psalms 16: 11. Psalms 36: 7, 8. I Timothy 4: 8.

Our Lord Jesus, that great shepherd of the sheep.

I AM the good shepherd, and know my sheep, and am known of mine. My sheep hear my voice, and I know them, and they follow me: and I give unto them eternal life; and they shall never perish, neither shall any man pluck them out of my hand.

The LORD is my shepherd; I shall not want. He maketh me to lie down in green pastures: he leadeth me beside the still waters. He restoreth my soul: he leadeth me in the paths of righteousness for his name's sake.

All we like sheep have gone astray; we have turned every one to his own way; and the LORD hath laid on him the iniquity of us all.—I am the good shepherd: the good shepherd giveth his life for the sheep.—I will seek that which was lost, and bring again that which was driven away, and will bind up that which was broken, and will strengthen that which was sick. —Ye were as sheep going astray; but are now returned unto the Shepherd and Bishop of your souls.

HEBREWS 13: 20. John 10: 14, 27, 28. Psalms 23: 1-3. Isaiah 53: 6.—John 10: 11.—Ezekiel 34: 16.—I Peter 2: 25.

MAY 27

The Lord is good, a stronghold in the day of trouble; and he knoweth them that trust in him.

PRAISE the Lord of hosts; for the Lord is good; for his mercy endureth for ever.—God is our refuge and strength, a very present help in trouble.—I will say of the LORD, He is my refuge and my fortress: my God; in him will I trust.—Who is like unto thee, O people saved by the LORD, the shield of thy help, and who is the sword of thy excellency!—As for God, his way is perfect; the word of the Lord is tried: he is a buckler to all them that trust in him. For who is God, save the LORD? and who is a rock, save our God?

If any man love God, the same is known of Him.— The foundation of God standeth sure, having this seal, The Lord knoweth them that are his. And, Let every one that nameth the name of Christ depart from iniquity.—The LORD knoweth the way of the right-eous: but the way of the ungodly shall perish.—Thou hast found grace in my sight, and I know thee by name.

NAHUM 1: 7. Jeremiah 33: 11.—Psalms 46: 1.—Psalms 91: 2.—Deuteronomy 33: 29.—II Samuel 22: 31, 32. I Corin-thians 8: 3.—II Timothy 2: 19.—Psalms 1: 6.—Exodus 33: 17.

We look for the Saviour.

THE grace of God that bringeth salvation hath appeared to all men, teaching us that, denying ungodliness and worldly lusts, we should live soberly, righteously, and godly, in this present world; looking for that blessed hope, and the glorious appearing of the great God and our Saviour Jesus Christ; who gave himself for us, that he might redeem us from all iniquity, and purify unto himself a peculiar people, zealous of good works.—We, according to his promise, look for new heavens and a new earth, wherein dwelleth righteousness. Wherefore, beloved, seeing that ye look for such things, be diligent that ye may be found of him in peace, without spot, and blameless.

Christ was once offered to bear the sins of many; and unto them that look for him shall he appear the second time without sin unto salvation.—And it shall be said in that day, Lo, this is our God; we have waited for him and he will save us: this is the LORD; we have waited for him, we will be glad and rejoice in his salvation.

PHILIPPIANS 3: 20. Titus 2: 11-14.—II Peter 3: 13, 14. Hebrews 9: 28.—Isaiah 25: 9.

The life of the flesh is in the blood: and I have given it to you upon the altar to make an atonement for your souls: for it is the blood that maketh an atonement for the soul.

Behold the Lamb of God, which taketh away the sin of the world.—The blood of the Lamb.—The precious blood of Christ, as of a lamb without blemish and without spot.

Without shedding of blood is no remission.—The blood of Jesus Christ his Son cleanseth us from all sin.

By his own blood he entered in once into the holy place, having obtained eternal redemption for us.—Having therefore, brethren, boldness to enter into the holiest by the blood of Jesus, by a new and living way, which he hath consecrated for us, through the veil, that is to say, his flesh; let us draw near with a true heart in full assurance of faith.

Ye are bought with a price: therefore glorify God in your body, and in your spirit which are God's.

LEVITICUS 17: 11. John 1: 29.—Revelation 7: 14.—I Peter 1: 19. Hebrews 9: 22.—I John 1: 7. Hebrews 9: 12.—Hebrews 10: 19, 20, 22.—I Corinthians 6: 20.

Let us labor to enter into that rest.

Enter ye in at the strait gate: for wide is the gate, and broad is the way, that leadeth to destruction: . . . strait is the gate, and narrow is the way, which leadeth unto life, and few there be that find it.—The kingdom of heaven suffereth violence, and the violent take it by force.—Labor not for the meat which perisheth, but for that meat which endureth unto everlasting life, which the Son of man shall give unto you.

Give diligence to make your calling and election sure; . . . for so an entrance shall be ministered unto you abundantly into the everlasting kingdom of our Lord and Saviour Jesus Christ.—So run, that ye may obtain. And every man that striveth for the mastery is temperate in all things. Now they do it to obtain a corruptible crown; but we an incorruptible.

For he that is entered into his rest, he also hath ceased from his own works as God did from his.—The Lord shall be unto thee an everlasting light, and thy God thy glory.

HEBREWS 4: 11. Matthew 7: 13, 14.—Matthew 11: 12.—John 6: 27. II Peter 1: 10, 11.—I Corinthians 9: 24, 25. Hebrews 4: 10.—Isaiah 60: 19.

MAY 31

Thy name shall be called Israel: for as a prince hast thou power with God and with men, and hast prevailed.

B<small>Y</small> his strength he had power with God: yea, he had power over the angel, and prevailed: he wept, and made supplication unto him.—[Abraham] staggered not at the promise of God through unbelief; but was strong in faith, giving glory to God.

Have faith in God. For verily I say unto you, That whosoever shall say unto this mountain, Be thou removed, and be thou cast into the sea; and shall not doubt in his heart, but shall believe that those things which he saith shall come to pass; he shall have whatsoever he saith. Therefore I say unto you, What things soever ye desire, when ye pray, believe that ye receive them, and ye shall have them.—If thou canst believe all things are possible to him that believeth. —Blessed is she that believed: for there shall be a performance of those things which were told her from the Lord.

Lord, increase our faith.

GENESIS 32: 28. Hosea 12: 3, 4.—Romans 4: 20. Mark 11: 22-24.—Mark 9: 23.—Luke 1: 45. Luke 17: 5.

The fruit of the Spirit is long-suffering, gentleness.

THE LORD, the LORD God, merciful and gracious, long-suffering, and abundant in goodness and truth.

Walk worthy of the vocation wherewith ye are called, with all lowliness and meekness, with long-suffering, forbearing one another in love.—Be ye kind one to another, tender-hearted, forgiving one another, even as God for Christ's sake hath forgiven you.—The wisdom that is from above is first pure, then peaceable, gentle, and easy to be entreated.—Charity suffereth long, and is kind.

In due season, we shall reap, if we faint not.—Be patient therefore, brethren, unto the coming of the Lord. Behold, the husbandman waiteth for the precious fruit of the earth, and hath long patience for it, until he receive the early and latter rain. Be ye also patient; stablish your hearts: for the coming of the Lord draweth nigh.

GALATIANS 5: 22. Exodus 34: 6. Ephesians 4: 1, 2.—Ephesians 4: 32.—James 3: 17.—I Corinthians 13: 4. Galatians 6: 9.—James 5: 7, 8.

JUNE 2

Thus shall ye eat it: with your loins girded, and ye shall eat it in haste: it is the Lord's passover.

Arise ye, and depart; for this is not your rest.—Here have we no continuing city, but we seek one to come. —There remaineth therefore a rest to the people of God.

Let your loins be girded about, and your lights burning; and ye yourselves like unto men that wait for their lord, when he will return from the wedding; that when he cometh and knocketh, they may open unto him immediately. Blessed are those servants, whom the lord when he cometh shall find watching. —Gird up the loins of your mind, be sober, and hope to the end for the grace that is to be brought unto you at the revelation of Jesus Christ.

This one thing I do, forgetting those things which are behind, . . . I press toward the mark for the prize of the high calling of God in Christ Jesus. Let us therefore, as many as be perfect, be thus minded.

EXODUS 12: 11. Micah 2: 10.—Hebrews 13: 14.—Hebrews 4: 9. Luke 12: 35-37.—I Peter 1: 13. Philippians 3: 13-15.

Watch, for ye know neither the day nor the hour
wherein the Son of man cometh.

TAKE heed to yourselves, lest at any time your hearts
be overcharged with surfeiting, and drunkenness, and
cares of this life, and so that day come upon you
unawares. For as a snare shall it come on all them
that dwell on the face of the earth. Watch ye, therefore, and pray always, that ye may be counted worthy
to escape all these things that shall come to pass, and
to stand before the Son of man.

The day of the Lord so cometh as a thief in the
night. For when they shall say, Peace and safety;
then sudden destruction cometh upon them, as travail
upon a woman with child; and they shall not escape.
But ye, brethren, are not in darkness, that that day
should overtake you as a thief. Ye are all the children
of light, and the children of the day; we are not of
the night, nor of darkness. Therefore let us not sleep,
as do others; but let us watch and be sober.

MATTHEW 25: 13. Luke 21: 34-36. I Thessalonians 5: 2-6.

JUNE 4

The glory of this latter house shall be greater
than the former, and in this place will I give
peace.

THE house that is to be builded for the LORD must
be exceeding magnifical, of fame and of glory
throughout all countries.—The glory of the LORD . . .
filled the LORD's house.

Destroy this temple, and in three days I will raise
it up. He spake of the temple of his body.—That
which was made glorious had no glory in this respect,
by reason of the glory that excelleth.—The Word was
made flesh, and dwelt among us, (and we beheld his
glory, the glory as of the only begotten of the Father,)
full of grace and truth.—God . . . hath in these last
days spoken unto us by his Son, whom he hath appointed heir of all things, by whom also he made
the worlds.

Glory to God in the highest, and on earth peace,
good will toward men.—The Prince of Peace.—He is
our peace.—The peace of God, which passeth all
understanding, shall keep your hearts and minds
through Christ Jesus.

HAGGAI 2: 9. I Chronicles 22: 5.—II Chronicles 7: 2. John
2: 19, 21.—II Corinthians 3: 10. John 1: 14.—Hebrews 1: 1,
2. Luke 2: 14.—Isaiah 9: 6.—Ephesians 2: 14.—Philippians
4: 7.

156

When ye shall have done all those things which are commanded you, say, We are unprofitable servants.

WHERE is boasting then? It is excluded. By what law? of work? Nay: but by the law of faith.—What hast thou that thou didst not receive? Now if thou didst receive it, why dost thou glory, as if thou hadst not received it?—By grace are ye saved through faith; and that not of yourselves: it is the gift of God: not of works, lest any man should boast. For we are his workmanship, created in Christ Jesus unto good works, which God hath before ordained that we should walk in them.

By the grace of God I am what I am: and his grace which was bestowed upon me was not in vain; but I labored more abundantly than they all; yet not I, but the grace of God which was with me.—For of him, and through him, and to him, are all things.— Of thine own have we given thee.

Enter not into judgment with thy servant: for in thy sight shall no man living be justified.

LUKE 17: 10. Romans 3: 27.—I Corinthians 4: 7.— Ephesians 2: 8-10. I Corinthians 15: 10.—Romans 11: 36.— I Chronicles 29: 14. Psalms 143: 2.

JUNE 6

He will rest in his love.

THE LORD did not set his love upon you, nor choose you, because ye were more in number than any people; for ye were the fewest of all people: but because the Lord loved you.—We love him, because he first loved us.—You . . . hath he reconciled in the body of his flesh through death, to present you holy and unblamable and unreprovable in his sight.

Herein is love, not that we loved God, but that he loved us, and sent his Son to be the propitiation for our sins.—God commendeth his love toward us, in that while we were yet sinners, Christ died for us.

Lo, a voice from heaven, saying, This is my beloved Son, in whom I am well pleased.—Therefore doth my Father love me, because I lay down my life, that I might take it again.—His Son, . . . who being the brightness of his glory, and the express image of his person, and upholding all things by the word of his power, when he had by himself purged our sins, sat down on the right hand of the Majesty on high.

ZEPHANIAH 3: 17. Deuteronomy 7: 7, 8.—I John 4: 19.
—Colossians 1: 21, 22. I John 4: 10.—Romans 5: 8. Matthew
₹· 17.—John 10: 17.—Hebrews 1: 2, 3.

Men ought always to pray, and not to faint.

Which of you shall have a friend, and shall go unto him at midnight, and say unto him, Friend, lend me three loaves; for a friend of mine in his journey is come to me, and I have nothing to set before him? And he from within shall answer and say, Trouble me not: the door is now shut, and my children are with me in bed; I cannot rise and give thee. I say unto you, Though he will not rise and give him because he is his friend, yet because of his importunity he will rise and give him as many as he needeth. —Praying always with all prayer and supplication in the Spirit, and watching thereunto with all perseverance and supplication for all saints.

I will not let thee go, except thou bless me. As a prince hast thou power with God and with men.— Continue in prayer, and watch in the same with thanksgiving.

[Jesus] went out into a mountain to pray, and continued all night in prayer to God.

LUKE 18: 1. Luke 11: 5-8.—Ephesians 6: 18. Genesis 32: 26, 28.—Colossians 4: 2. Luke 6: 12.

JUNE 8

The Lord made all that he did to prosper in his hand.

Blessed is every one that feareth the Lord; that walketh in his ways. For thou shalt eat the labor of thy hands: happy shalt thou be, and it shall be well with thee.—Trust in the Lord, and do good, so shalt thou dwell in the land, and verily thou shalt be fed. Delight thyself also in the Lord; and he shall give thee the desires of thy heart.—Be not afraid, neither be thou dismayed: for the Lord thy God is with thee whithersoever thou goest.

Seek ye first the kingdom of God, and his righteousness; and all these things shall be added unto you.

As long as he sought the Lord, God made him to prosper.—Beware that thou forget not the Lord thy God, in not keeping his commandments, and his judgments, and his statutes, which I command thee this day: and thou say in thy heart, My power and the might of my hand hath gotten me this wealth.

Is not the Lord your God with you? and hath he not given you rest on every side?

GENESIS 39: 3. Psalms 128: 1, 2.—Psalms 37: 3, 4.—Joshua 1: 9. Matthew 6: 33. II Chronicles 26: 5.—Deuteronomy 8: 11, 17. I Chronicles 22: 18.

Never man spake like this man.

THOU art fairer than the children of men: grace is poured into thy lips: therefore God hath blessed thee for ever.—The Lord God hath given me the tongue of the learned, that I should know how to speak a word in season to him that is weary.—His mouth is most sweet: yea, he is altogether lovely. This is my beloved, and this is my friend.

All bare him witness, and wondered at the gracious words which proceeded out of his mouth.—He taught them as one having authority, and not as the scribes.

Let the word of Christ dwell in you richly in all wisdom.—The sword of the Spirit . . . is the word of God.—The word of God is quick, and powerful, and sharper than any two-edged sword.—The weapons of our warfare are not carnal, but mighty through God to the pulling down of strongholds; casting down imaginations, and every high thing that exalteth itself against the knowledge of God, and bringing into captivity every thought to the obedience of Christ.

JOHN 7: 46. Psalms 45: 2.—Isaiah 50: 4.—Canticles 5: 16. Luke 4: 22.—Matthew 7: 29. Colossians 3: 16.—Ephesians 6: 17.—Hebrews 4: 12.—II Corinthians 10: 4, 5.

JUNE 10

The younger son took his journey into a far country, and there wasted his substance with riotous living.

SUCH were some of you: but ye are washed, but ye are sanctified, but ye are justified in the name of the Lord Jesus, and by the Spirit of our God.

We . . . were by nature the children of wrath, even as others. But God, who is rich in mercy, for his great love wherewith he loved us, even when we were dead in sins, hath quickened us together with Christ, (by grace ye are saved) and hath raised us up together, and made us sit together in heavenly places in Christ Jesus.

Herein is love, not that we loved God, but that he loved us, and sent his Son to be the propitiation for our sins.

God commendeth his love toward us, in that, while we were yet sinners, Christ died for us. If, when we were enemies, we were reconciled to God by the death of his Son, much more, being reconciled, we shall be saved by his life.

LUKE 15: 13. I Corinthians 6: 11. Ephesians 2: 3-6. I John 4: 10. Romans 5: 8, 10.

He arose and came to his father. But when he
was yet a great way off, his father saw him, and
ran, and fell on his neck, and kissed him.

THE LORD is merciful and gracious, slow to anger,
and plenteous in mercy. He will not always chide:
neither will he keep his anger for ever. He hath not
dealt with us after our sins; nor rewarded us
according to our iniquities. For as the heaven is
high above the earth, so great is his mercy toward
them that fear him. As far as the east is from the
west, so far hath he removed our transgressions from
us. Like as a father pitieth his children, so the LORD
pitieth them that fear him.

Ye have received the Spirit of adoption, whereby
we cry, Abba, Father. The Spirit itself beareth
witness with our spirit, that we are the children of
God.—Ye who sometime were far off are made nigh
by the blood of Christ. Now therefore ye are no more
strangers and foreigners, but fellow-citizens with the
saints, and of the household of God.

LUKE 15: 20. Psalms 103: 8-13. Romans 8: 15, 16.—
Ephesians 2: 13, 19.

JUNE 12

Everything that may abide the fire, ye shall make it go through the fire, and it shall be clean.

THE LORD your God proveth you, to know whether ye love the LORD your God with all your heart and with all your soul.—He shall sit as a refiner and purifier of silver; and he shall purify the sons of Levi, and purge them as gold and silver, that they may offer unto the LORD an offering in righteousness. —Every man's work shall be made manifest: for the day shall declare it, because it shall be revealed by fire; and the fire shall try every man's work of what sort it is.

I will turn my hand upon thee, and purely purge away thy dross, and take away all thy tin.—I will melt them, and try them.

Thou, O God, hast proved us; thou hast tried us, as silver is tried. We went through fire and through water: but thou broughtest us out into a wealthy place.

When thou walkest through the fire, thou shalt not be burned; neither shall the flame kindle upon thee.

NUMBERS 31: 23. Deuteronomy 13: 3.—Malachi 3: 3.— I Corinthians 3: 13. Isaiah 1: 25.—Jeremiah 9: 7. Psalms 66: 10, 12. Isaiah 43: 2.

Abide in me, and I in you.

I AM crucified with Christ: nevertheless I live; yet not I, but Christ liveth in me: and the life which I now live in the flesh I live by the faith of the Son of God, who loved me, and gave himself for me.

I know that in me (that is, in my flesh) dwelleth no good thing: for to will is present with me; but how to perform that which is good I find not. O wretched man that I am! who shall deliver me from the body of this death? I thank God through Jesus Christ our Lord.

If Christ be in you, the body is dead because of sin; but the Spirit is life because of righteousness.— If ye continue in the faith grounded and settled, and be not moved away from the hope of the gospel, which ye have heard.

Little children, abide in Him; that, when He shall appear, we may have confidence, and not be ashamed before Him at his coming.—He that saith he abideth in Him ought himself also so to walk, even as He walked.

JOHN 15: 4. Galatians 2: 20. Romans 7: 18, 24, 25. Romans 8: 10.—Colossians 1: 23. I John 2: 28.—II John 2: 6.

JUNE 14

As the sufferings of Christ abound in us, so our consolation also aboundeth by Christ.

THE fellowship of his sufferings.—Rejoice, inasmuch as ye are partakers of Christ's sufferings; that, when his glory shall be revealed, ye may be glad also with exceeding joy.—For if we be dead with him, we shall also live with him.—If children, then heirs; heirs of God, and joint heirs with Christ; if so be that we suffer with him, that we may be also glorified together.

God willing more abundantly to show unto the heirs of promise the immutability of his counsel, confirmed it by an oath: that by two immutable things, in which it was impossible for God to lie, we might have a strong consolation, who have fled for refuge to lay hold upon the hope set before us.—Our Lord Jesus Christ himself, and God, even our Father, which hath loved us, and hath given us everlasting consolation and good hope through grace, comfort your hearts, and stablish you in every good word and work.

II CORINTHIANS 1: 5. Philippians 3: 10.—I Peter 4: 13.
—II Timothy 2: 11.—Romans 8: 17. Hebrews 6: 17, 18.—II
Thessalonians 2: 16, 17.

The secret things belong unto the Lord our God:
but those which are revealed belong unto us.

Lord, my heart is not haughty, nor mine eyes lofty;
neither do I exercise myself in great matters, or in
things too high for me. Surely I have behaved and
quieted myself, as a child that is weaned of his
mother: my soul is even as a weaned child.

The secret of the Lord is with them that fear him:
and he will show them his covenant.—There is a God
in heaven that revealeth secrets.

Lo, these are parts of his ways: but how little a
portion is heard of him?

Henceforth I call you not servants; for the servant
knoweth not what his lord doeth: but I have called
you friends; for all things that I have heard of my
Father I have made known unto you.—If ye love me,
keep my commandments. And I will pray the Father,
and he shall give you another Comforter, that he may
abide with you for ever; even the Spirit of truth.

DEUTERONOMY 29: 29. Psalms 131: 1, 2. Psalms 25:
14.—Daniel 2: 28. Job 26: 14. John 15: 15.—John 14: 15-17.

JUNE 16

See that ye walk circumspectly, not as fools, but as wise, redeeming the time, because the days are evil.

TAKE diligent heed to do the commandment and the law, . . . to love the LORD your God, and to walk in all his ways, and to keep his commandments, and to cleave unto him, and to serve him with all your heart and with all your soul.—Walk in wisdom toward them that are without, redeeming the time. Let your speech be always with grace, seasoned with salt, that ye may know how ye ought to answer every man.— Abstain from all appearance of evil.

While the bridegroom tarried, they all slumbered and slept. And at midnight there was a cry made, Behold, the bridegroom cometh; go ye out to meet him. Watch therefore, for ye know neither the day nor the hour when the Son of man cometh.

Brethren, give diligence to make your calling and election sure; for if ye do these things, ye shall never fall. Blessed are those servants, whom the Lord when he cometh shall find watching.

EPHESIANS 5: 15, 16. Joshua 22: 5.—Colossians 4: 5, 6.—I Thessalonians 5: 22. Matthew 25: 5, 6, 18. II Peter 1: 10.—Luke 12: 37.

In everything by prayer and supplication with thanksgiving let your requests be made known unto God.

I Love the LORD because he hath heard my voice and my supplications. Because he hath inclined his ear unto me, therefore will I call upon him, as long as I live.

When ye pray, use not vain repetitions, as the heathen do: for they think that they shall be heard for their much speaking.—The spirit . . . helpeth our infirmities: for we know not what we should pray for as we ought; but the Spirit itself maketh intercession for us with groanings which cannot be uttered.

I will therefore that men pray everywhere, lifting up holy hands, without wrath and doubting.—Praying always with all prayer and supplication in the Spirit, and watching thereunto with all perseverance and supplication for all saints.

If two of you shall agree on earth as touching anything that they shall ask, it shall be done for them of my Father which is in heaven.

PHILIPPIANS 4: 6. Psalms 116: 1, 2. Matthew 6:7.— Romans 8: 26. I Timothy 2: 8.—Ephesians 6: 17.—Matthew 18: 19.

JUNE 18

Thou shalt put the mercy-seat above upon the ark, and there I will meet with thee.

THE way into the holiest of all was not yet made manifest.—Jesus, when he had cried again with a loud voice, yielded up the ghost. And, behold, the veil of the temple was rent in twain from the top to the bottom.

Having, . . . brethren, boldness to enter into the holiest by the blood of Jesus, by a new and living way, which he hath consecrated for us, through the veil, that is to say, his flesh; . . . let us draw near with a true heart in full assurance of faith.—Let us therefore come boldly unto the throne of grace, that we may obtain mercy and find grace to help in time of need.

Christ Jesus: whom God hath set forth to be a propitiation [mercy seat] through faith in his blood, to declare his righteousness for the remission of sins that are past, through the forbearance of God.—Through Him we . . . have access by one Spirit unto the Father.

EXODUS 25: 21, 22. Hebrews 9: 8.—Matthew 27: 50, 51. Hebrews 10: 19, 20, 22.—Hebrews 4: 16. Romans 3: 24, 25.—Ephesians 2: 18.

Holiness, without which no man shall see the
Lord.

Except a man be born again, he cannot see the
kingdom of God.—There shall in no wise enter into
it anything that defileth.—There is no spot in thee.

Ye shall be holy: for I the Lord your God am
holy.—As obedient children, not fashioning yourselves
according to the former lusts in your ignorance: but
as he which hath called you is holy, so be ye holy in
all manner of conversation; because it is written, Be
ye holy; for I am holy. And if ye call on the Father,
who without respect of persons judgeth according to
every man's work, pass the time of your sojourning
here in fear.

Put off concerning the former conversation the old
man, which is corrupt according to the deceitful
lusts; and be renewed in the spirit of your mind;
and . . . put on the new man, which after God is
created in righteousness and true holiness.—He hath
chosen us in him before the foundation of the world,
that we should be holy and without blame before him
in love.

HEBREWS 12: 14. John 3: 3. Revelation 21: 27.—
Canticles 4: 7. Leviticus 19: 2.—I Peter 1: 14-17. Ephesians
4: 22-24.—Ephesians 1: 4.

JUNE 20

Take this child away, and nurse it for me, and
I will give thee thy wages.

Go ye . . . into the vineyard, and whatsoever is
right I will give you.—Whosoever shall give you a cup
of water to drink in my name, because ye belong to
Christ, verily I say unto you, he shall not lose his
reward.

The liberal soul shall be made fat: and he that
watereth shall be watered also himself.—God is not
unrighteous to forget your work and labor of love,
. . . in that ye have ministered to the saints.

Every man shall receive his own reward according
to his own labor.

Lord, when saw we thee a hungered, and fed thee?
or thirsty, and gave thee drink? When saw we thee
a stranger, and took thee in? or naked, and clothed
thee? And the King shall answer and say unto them,
. . . Inasmuch as ye have done it unto one of the
least of these my brethren, ye have done it unto me.
Come, ye blessed of my Father, inherit the kingdom
prepared for you from the foundation of the world.

EXODUS 2: 9. Matthew 20: 4.—Mark 9: 41. Proverbs
11: 25.—Hebrews 6: 10. I Corinthians 3: 8. Matthew 25: 37,
38, 40, 34.

Christ suffered for us, leaving us an example that ye should follow his steps.

Even the Son of man came not to be ministered unto, but to minister.—Whosoever of you will be the chiefest, shall be servant of all.

Jesus of Nazareth . . . went about doing good.—Bear ye one another's burdens, and so fulfil the law of Christ.

The meekness and gentleness of Christ.—In lowliness of mind let each esteem other better than themselves.

Father, forgive them: for they know not what they do.—Be ye kind one to another, tender-hearted, forgiving one another, even as God for Christ's sake hath forgiven you.

He that saith he abideth in Him, ought himself also so to walk, even as He walked.—Looking unto Jesus the author and finisher of our faith; who for the joy that was set before him endured the cross, despising the shame, and is set down at the right hand of the throne of God.

I PETER 2: 21. Mark 10: 45.—Mark 10: 44. Acts 10: 38.—Galatians 6: 2. II Corinthians 10: 1.—Philippians 2: 3. Luke 23: 34.—Ephesians 4: 32. I John 2: 6.—Hebrews 12: 2.

Ye are dead, and your life is hid with Christ in God.

How shall we, that are dead to sin, live any longer therein?—I am crucified with Christ, nevertheless I live; yet not I, but Christ liveth in me: and the life which I now live in the flesh, I live by the faith of the Son of God, who loved me, and gave himself for me.— He died for all, that they which live should not henceforth live unto themselves, but unto him which died for them, and rose again.—If any man be in Christ, he is a new creature: old things are passed away; behold, all things are become new.

We are in Him that is true, even in his Son Jesus Christ.—As thou, Father, art in me, and I in thee, that they also may be one in us.—Ye are the body of Christ, and members in particular.—Because I live, ye shall live also.

To him that overcometh will I give to eat of the hidden manna, and will give him a white stone, and in the stone a new name written, which no man knoweth saving he that receiveth it.

COLOSSIANS 3: 3. Romans 6: 2.—Galatians 2: 20.—II Corinthians 5: 15.—II Corinthians 5: 17. I John 5: 20.— John 17: 21.—I Corinthians 12: 27.—John 14: 19. Revelation 2: 17.

I will pray the Father, and he shall give you another Comforter, even the Spirit of truth.

I T is expedient for you that I go away: for if I go not away, the Comforter will not come unto you; but if I depart, I will send him unto you.

The Spirit itself beareth witness with our spirit, that we are the children of God.—Ye have not received the spirit of bondage again to fear, but ye have recived the Spirit of adoption, whereby we cry, Abba, Father.—The Spirit . . . helpeth our infirmities: for we know not what we should pray for as we ought: but the Spirit itself maketh intercession for us with groanings which cannot be uttered.

The God of hope fill you with all joy and peace in believing, that ye may abound in hope, through the power of the Holy Ghost.—Hope maketh not ashamed; because the love of God is shed abroad in our hearts by the Holy Ghost which is given unto us.

Hereby know we that we dwell in him, and he in us, because he hath given us of his Spirit.

JOHN 14: 16, 17. John 16: 7. Romans 8: 16.—Romans 8: 15.—Romans 8: 26. Romans 15: 13.—Romans 5: 5. I John 4: 13.

JUNE 24

The ark of the covenant of the Lord went before them to search out a resting place for them.

M Y times are in thy hand.—He shall choose our inheritance for us.

Lead me, O Lord, in thy righteousness; . . . make thy way straight before my face.

Commit thy way unto the LORD; trust also in him; and he shall bring it to pass.—In all thy ways acknowledge him, and he shall direct thy paths.—Thine ears shall hear a word behind thee, saying, This is the way, walk ye in it, when ye turn to the right hand, and when ye turn to the left.

The Lord is my shepherd; I shall not want. He maketh me to lie down in green pastures: he leadeth me beside the still waters.—Like as a father pitieth his children, so the Lord pitieth them that fear him. For he knoweth our frame; he remembereth that we are dust.—Your heavenly Father knoweth that ye have need of all these things.—Casting all your care upon him; for he careth for you.

NUMBERS 10: 33. Psalms 31: 15.—Psalms 47: 4. Psalms 5: 8. Psalms 37: 5.—Proverbs 3: 6.—Isaiah 30: 21. Psalms 23: 1, 2.—Psalms 103: 13, 14.—Matthew 6: 32.—I Peter 5: 7.

When he shall appear, we shall be like him: for
we shall see him as he is.

A s many as received him, to them gave he power to
become the sons of God, even to them that believe
on his name.—Whereby are given unto us exceeding
great and precious promises: that by these ye might
be partakers of the divine nature, having escaped the
corruption that is in the world through lust.

Since the beginning of the world men have not
heard, nor perceived by the ear, neither hath the eye
seen, O God, beside thee, what he hath prepared for
him that waiteth for him.

Now we see through a glass, darkly; but then face
to face: now I know in part; but then shall I know
even as also I am known.—Christ . . . shall change
our vile body, that it may be fashioned like unto his
glorious body, according to the working whereby he
is able even to subdue all things unto himself.—As
for me, I will behold thy face in righteousness: I shall
be satisfied, when I awake, with thy likeness.

I JOHN 3: 2. John 1: 12.—II Peter 1: 4. Isaiah 64: 4.
—I Corinthians 13: 12.—Philippians 3: 20, 21.—Psalms 17:
15.

Oh, that thou wouldest bless me indeed, and that thou wouldest keep me from evil! And God granted him that which he requested.

THE blessing of the LORD, it maketh rich, and he addeth no sorrow with it.—When he giveth quietness, who then can make trouble? and when he hideth his face, who then can behold him?

Salvation belongeth unto the LORD: thy blessing is upon thy people.—How great is thy goodness, which thou hast laid up for them that fear thee; which thou hast wrought for them that trust in thee before the sons of men——I pray not that thou shouldest take him out of the world, but that thou shouldest keep them from the evil.

Ask, and it shall be given you: seek, and ye shall find; knock, and it shall be opened unto you: for every one that asketh receiveth; and he that seeketh findeth; and to him that knocketh it shall be opened.—The LORD redeemeth the soul of his servants: and none of them that trust in him shall be desolate.

I CHRONICLES 4: 10. Proverbs 10: 22.—Job 34: 29. Psalms 3: 8.—Psalms 31: 19.—John 17: 15. Matthew 7: 7, 8.—Psalms 34: 22.

Who shall be able to stand?

Who may abide the day of his coming? and who shall stand when he appeareth? for he is like a refiner's fire, and like fuller's soap.

I beheld, and lo, a great multitude, which no man could number, of all nations, and kindreds, and people, and tongues, stood before the throne, and before the Lamb, clothed with white robes, and palms in their hands. These are they which came out of great tribulation, and have washed their robes, and made them white in the blood of the Lamb. They shall hunger no more, neither thirst any more; neither shall the sun light on them, nor any heat. For the Lamb, which is in the midst of the throne, shall feed them, and shall lead them unto living fountains of waters: and God shall wipe away all tears from their eyes.

There is no condemnation to them which are in Christ Jesus, who walk not after the flesh, but after the Spirit.—Stand fast therefore in the liberty wherewith Christ hath made us free.

REVELATION 6: 17. Malachi 3: 2. Revelation 7: 9, 14-17. Romans 8: 1.—Galatians 5: 1.

JUNE 28

I know that my Redeemer liveth.

IF when we were enemies, we were reconciled to God by the death of his Son, much more, being reconciled, we shall be saved by his life.—This man, because he continueth ever, hath an unchangeable priesthood. Wherefore he is able also to save them to the uttermost that come unto God by him, seeing he ever liveth to make intercession for them.

Because I live, ye shall live also.—If in this life only we have hope in Christ, we are of all men most miserable. But now is Christ risen from the dead, and become the first-fruits of them that slept.

The Redeemer shall come to Zion, and unto them that turn from transgression in Jacob, saith the Lord.—We have redemption through his blood, the forgiveness of sins, according to the riches of his grace.—Ye were not redeemed with corruptible things, as silver and gold, from your vain conversation received by tradition from your fathers; but with the precious blood of Christ, as of a lamb without blemish and without spot.

JOB 19: 25. Romans 5: 10.—Hebrews 7: 24, 25. John 14: 19.—I Corinthians 15: 19, 20. Isaiah 59: 20.—Ephesians 1: 7.—I Peter 1: 18, 19.

His commandments are not grievous.

THIS is the will of Him that sent me, that every one which seeth the Son, and believeth on him, may have everlasting life.—Whatsoever we ask, we receive of him, because we keep his commandments, and do those things that are pleasing in his sight.

My yoke is easy, and my burden is light.—If ye love me, keep my commandments. He that hath my commandments, and keepeth them, he it is that loveth me: and he that loveth me shall be loved of my Father, and I will love him, and will manifest myself to him.

Happy is the man that findeth wisdom, and the man that getteth understanding. Her ways are ways of pleasantness, and all her paths are peace.—Great peace have they which love thy law: and nothing shall offend them.

This is his commandment, That we should believe on the name of his Son Jesus Christ, and love one another.—Love worketh no ill to his neighbor: therefore love is the fulfilling of the law.

I JOHN 5: 3. John 6: 40.—I John 3: 22. Matthew 11: 30.—John 14: 15, 21. Proverbs 3: 13, 17.—Psalms 119: 165.—Romans 7: 22. I John 3: 23.—Romans 13: 10.

JUNE 30

As many as I love, I rebuke and chasten.

MY son, despise not thou the chastening of the LORD, nor faint when thou art rebuked of him: for whom the LORD loveth he chasteneth, and scourgeth every son whom he receiveth.—Even as a father the son in whom he delighteth.

He maketh sore, and bindeth up: he woundeth, and his hands make whole.—Humble yourselves therefore under the mighty hand of God, that he may exalt you in due time.—I have chosen thee in the furnace of affliction.

He doth not afflict willingly, nor grieve the children of men.—He hath not dealt with us after our sins; nor rewarded us according to our iniquities. For as the heaven is high above the earth, so great is his mercy toward them that fear him. As far as the east is from the west, so far hath he removed our transgressions from us. Like as a father pitieth his children, so the LORD pitieth them that fear him. For he knoweth our frame; he remembereth that we are dust.

REVELATION 3: 19. Hebrews 12: 5, 6.—Proverbs 3: 12. Job 5: 18.—I Peter 5: 6.—Isaiah 48: 10. Lamentations 3: 33.—Psalms 103: 10-14.

The fruit of the Spirit is goodness.

LOVE your enemies, bless them that curse you, do good to them that hate you, and pray for them which despitefully use you and persecute you: that ye may be the children of your Father which is in heaven: for he maketh his sun to rise on the evil and on the good, and send the rain on the just and on the unjust.—Be ye therefore merciful, as your Father also is merciful.

The fruit of the Spirit is in all goodness and righteousness and truth.

After that the kindness and love of God our Saviour toward man appeared, not by works of righteousness which we have done, but according to his mercy he saved us, by the washing of regeneration, and renewing of the Holy Ghost.—The LORD is good to all: and his tender mercies are over all his works.—He that spared not his own Son, but delivered him up for us all, how shall he not with him also freely give us all things?

GALATIANS 5: 22. Ephesians 5: 1.—Matthew 5: 44, 45.— Luke 6: 3.—Ephesians 5: 9. Titus 3: 4-6.—Psalms 145: 9.— Romans 8: 32.

JULY 2

This is the ordinance of the passover. There shall no stranger eat thereof.

WE have an altar, whereof they have no right to eat which serve the tabernacle.—Except a man be born again, he cannot see the kingdom of God.—At that time ye were without Christ, being aliens from the commonwealth of Israel, and strangers from the covenants of promise. But now, in Christ Jesus, ye who sometime were afar off, are made nigh by the blood of Christ.

For he is our peace, who hath made both one, . . . having abolished in his flesh the enmity, even the law of commandments contained in ordinances; for to make in himself of twain one new man, so making peace.

Now, therefore, ye are no more strangers and foreigners, but fellow-citizens with the saints, and of the household of God.

Behold, I stand at the door and knock: if any man hear my voice, and open the door, I will come in to him, and will sup with him, and he with me.

EXODUS 12: 43. Hebrews 13: 10.—John 3: 3.—Ephesians 2: 12, 13. Ephesians 2: 14, 15. Ephesians 2: 19. Revelation 3: 20.

If children, then heirs; heirs of God, and joint-heirs with Christ.

IF ye be Christ's, then are ye Abraham's seed, and heirs according to the promise.

Behold, what manner of love the Father hath bestowed upon us, that we should be called the sons of God.—Thou art no more a servant, but a son; and if a son, then an heir of God through Christ.—Having predestinated us unto the adoption of children by Jesus Christ to himself, according to the good pleasure of his will.

Father, I will that they also, whom thou hast given me, be with me where I am; that they may behold my glory, which thou hast given me.

He that overcometh, and keepeth my works unto the end, to him will I give power over the nations.— To him that overcometh will I grant to sit with me in my throne, even as I also overcame, and am set down with my Father in his throne.

ROMANS 8: 17. Galatians 3: 29. I John 3: 1.—Galatians 4: 7.—Ephesians 1: 5. John 17: 24. Revelation 2: 26.— Revelation 3: 21.

JULY 4

Leaning on Jesus' bosom.

As one whom his mother comforteth, so will I comfort you.—They brought young children to him, that he should touch them. And he took them up in his arms, put his hands upon them, and blessed them.

Jesus called his disciples unto him, and said, I have compassion on the multitude, because they continue with me now three days, and have nothing to eat; and I will not send them away fasting, lest they faint by the way.—A High Priest . . . touched with the feeling of our infirmities.—In his love and in his pity he redeemed them.

I will not leave you comfortless [marg. orphans]: I will come to you.—Can a woman forget her sucking child, that she should not have compassion on the son of her womb? yea, they may forget, yet will I not forget thee.

The Lamb which is in the midst of the throne shall feed them, and shall lead them unto living fountains of waters: and God shall wipe away all tears from their eyes.

JOHN 13: 23. Isaiah 66: 13.—Mark 10: 13, 16. Matthew 15: 32.—Hebrews 4: 15.—Isaiah 63: 9. John 14: 18.—Isaiah 49: 15. Revelation 7: 17.

We have known and believed the love that God
hath to us.

GOD who is rich in mercy, for his great love wherewith he loved us, even when we were dead in sins,
hath quickened us together with Christ (by grace ye
are saved) and hath raised us up together, and made
us sit together in heavenly places in Christ Jesus:
that in the ages to come he might show the exceeding
riches of his grace in his kindness toward us through
Christ Jesus.

God so loved the world, that he gave his only begotten Son, that whosoever believeth in him should
not perish, but have everlasting life.—He that spared
not his own Son, but delivered him up for us all,
how shall he not with him also freely give us all
things?—The LORD is good to all: and his tender
mercies are over all his works.

We love him, because he first loved us.

Blessed is she that believed: for there shall be a
performance of those things which were told her from
the Lord.

I JOHN 4: 16. Ephesians 2: 4-7. John 3: 16.—Romans 8:
32.—Psalms 145: 9. I John 4: 19. Luke 1: 45.

JULY 6

Let your speech be always with grace.

A WORD fitly spoken, is like apples of gold in pictures of silver. As an ear-ring of gold, and an ornament of fine gold, so is a wise reprover upon an obedient ear.—Let no corrupt communication proceed out of your mouth, but that which is good to the use of edifying, that it may minister grace unto the hearers.—A good man out of the treasure of the heart bringeth forth good things: and an evil man out of the evil treasure bringeth forth evil things. By thy words thou shalt be justified.—The tongue of the wise is health.

They that feared the LORD spake often one to another: and the LORD hearkened and heard it, and a book of remembrance was written before him for them that feared the LORD and that thought upon his name.

If thou take forth the precious from the vile, thou shalt be as my mouth.—Therefore, as ye abound in everything, in faith, and utterance, and knowledge, and in all diligence, . . . see that ye abound in this grace also.

COLOSSIANS 4: 6. Proverbs 25: 11, 12.—Ephesians 4: 29. —Matthew 12: 35, 37.—Proverbs 12: 18. Malachi 3: 16. Jeremiah 15: 19.—I Corinthians 8: 7.

Then was Jesus led up of the spirit into the wilderness to be tempted of the devil.

In the days of his flesh, when he had offered up prayers and supplications with strong crying and tears unto him that was able to save him from death, and was heard in that he feared; though he were a Son, yet learned he obedience by the things which he suffered; and being made perfect, he became the author of eternal salvation unto all them that obey him.

We have not a high-priest which cannot be touched with the feeling of our infirmities; but was in all points tempted like as we are, yet without sin.

There hath no temptation taken you but such as is common to man: but God is faithful, who will not suffer you to be tempted above that ye are able; but will with the temptation also make a way to escape, that ye may be able to bear it.—My grace is sufficient for thee: for my strength is made perfect in weakness.

MATTHEW 4: 1. Hebrews 5: 7-9. Hebrews 4: 15. I Corinthians 10: 13.—I Corinthians 12: 9.

JULY 8

If we confess our sins, he is faithful and just to forgive us our sins, and to cleanse us from all unrighteousness.

I ACKNOWLEDGE my transgressions: and my sin is ever before me. Against thee, thee only, have I sinned, and done this evil in thy sight.

And he arose, and came to his father. But when he was yet a great way off, his father saw him, and had compassion, and ran, and fell on his neck, and kissed him.—I have blotted out as a thick cloud, thy transgressions, and, as a cloud, thy sins return unto me; for I have redeemed thee.—Your sins are forgiven you for his name's sake.—God for Christ's sake hath forgiven you.—That he might be just, and the justifier of him which believeth in Jesus.

Then will I sprinkle clean water upon you, and ye shall be clean.—They shall walk with me in white: for they are worthy.

This is he that came by water and blood, even Jesus Christ: not by water only, but by water and blood.

I JOHN 1: 9. Psalms 51: 3, 4. Luke 15: 20.—Isaiah 44: 22.—I John 2: 12.—Ephesians 4: 32.—Romans 3: 26. Ezekiel 36: 25.—Revelation 1: 4. I John 5: 6.

I have caused thine iniquity to pass from thee, and I will clothe thee with change of raiment.

Blessed is he whose transgression is forgiven, whose sin is covered.—We are all as an unclean thing.—I know that in me (that is, in my flesh) dwelleth no good thing: for to will is present with me; but how to perform that which is good I find not.

As many of you as have been baptized into Christ have put on Christ. Ye have put off the old man with his deeds; and have put on the new man, which is renewed in knowledge after the image of Him that created him.—Not having mine own righteousness which is of the law, but . . . the righteousness which is of God by faith.

Bring forth the best robe, and put it on him.—The fine linen is the righteousness of saints.—I will greatly rejoice in the Lord, my soul shall be joyful in my God; for he hath clothed me with the garments of salvation, he hath covered me with the robe of righteousness.

ZECHARIAH 3: 4. Psalms 32: 1.—Isaiah 64: 6.—Romans 7: 18. Galatians 3: 27.—Colossians 3: 9, 10.—Philippians 3: 9. Luke 15: 22.—Revelation 19: 8.—Isaiah 61: 10.

JULY 10

The disciple is not above his Master.

Y<small>E</small> call me Master and Lords and ye say well; for so I am.

It is enough for the disciple that he be as his master, and the servant as his lord.—If they have persecuted me, they will also persecute you; if they have kept my saying, they will keep yours also.—I have given them thy word; and the world hath hated them, because they are not of the world, even as I am not of the world.

Consider him that endured such contradiction of sinners against himself, lest ye be wearied and faint in your minds. Ye have not yet resisted unto blood, striving against sin.

Let us run with patience the race that is set before us, looking unto Jesus the author and finisher of our faith; who for the joy that was set before him endured the cross, despising the shame, and is set down at the right hand of the throne of God.—Forasmuch . . . as Christ hath suffered for us in the flesh, arm yourselves likewise with the same mind.

MATTHEW 10: 24. John 13: 13. Matthew 10: 25.—John 15: 20.—John 17: 14. Hebrews 12: 3, 4. Hebrews 12: 1, 2. —I Peter 4: 1.

I am with thee to save thee.

SHALL the prey be taken from the mighty, or the lawful captive delivered? But thus saith the Lord, Even the captives of the mighty shall be taken away, and the prey of the terrible shall be delivered; for I will contend with him that contendeth with thee. And all flesh shall know that I the Lord am thy Saviour and thy Redeemer, the mighty One of Jacob. —Fear thou not; for I am with thee: be not dismayed; for I am thy God: I will strengthen thee: yea, I will help thee; yea, I will uphold thee with the right hand of my righteousness.

We have not a high-priest which cannot be touched with the feeling of our infirmities; but was in all points tempted like as we are, yet without sin.—In that he himself hath suffered being tempted, he is able to succor them that are tempted.

The steps of a good man are ordered by the Lord: and He delighteth in his way. Though he fall, he shall not be utterly cast down: for the Lord upholdeth him with his hand.

JEREMIAH 15: 20. Isaiah 49: 24-26.—Isaiah 41: 10. Hebrews 4: 15.—Hebrews 2: 18. Psalms 37: 23, 24.

JULY 12

My presence shall go with thee, and I will give thee rest.

Be strong and of good courage, fear not, nor be afraid of them: for the Lord thy God, he it is that doth go with thee; he will not fail thee, nor forsake thee. The LORD, he it is that doth go before thee; he will be with thee, he will not fail thee, neither forsake thee: fear not, neither be dismayed.—Have not I commanded thee? Be strong and of a good courage; be not afraid, neither be thou dismayed: for the Lord thy God is with thee whithersoever thou goest.—In all thy ways acknowledge him, and he shall direct thy paths.

He hath said, I will never leave thee, nor forsake thee. So that we may boldly say, The Lord is my helper, and I will not fear what man shall do unto me.—Our sufficiency is of God.

Lead us not into temptation.—O Lord, I know that the way of man is not in himself: it is not in man that walketh to direct his steps.

My times are in thy hand.

EXODUS 33: 14. Deuteronomy 31: 6, 8.—Joshua 1: 9.— Proverbs 3: 6. Hebrews 13: 5, 6.—II Corinthians 3: 5. Matthew 6: 13.—Jeremiah 10: 23. Psalms 31: 15.

I am my Beloved's and His desire is toward me.

I KNOW whom I have believed, and am persuaded that he is able to keep that which I have committed unto him against that day.—I am persuaded, that neither death, nor life, nor angels, nor principalities, nor powers, nor things present, nor things to come, nor height, nor depth, nor any other creature, shall be able to separate us from the love of God, which is in Christ Jesus our Lord.—Those that thou gavest me I have kept, and none of them is lost.

THE LORD taketh pleasure in his people.—My delights were with the sons of men.—His great love wherewith he loved us.—Greater love hath no man than this, that a man lay down his life for his friends.

Ye are bought with a price: therefore glorify God in your body, and in your spirit, which are God's.—Whether we live, we live unto the Lord: and whether we die, we die unto the LORD: whether we live therefore, or die, we are the LORD's.

CANTICLES 7: 10. II Titus 1: 12.—Romans 8: 38, 39.—John 17: 12. Psalms 149: 4.—Proverbs 8: 31.—Ephesians 2: 4.—John 15: 13. I Corinthians 6: 19.—Romans 14: 8.

JULY 14

Out of the abundance of the heart the mouth speaketh.

Let the word of Christ dwell in you richly in all wisdom.

Keep thy heart with all diligence; for out of it are the issues of life.—Death and life are in the power of the tongue.—The mouth of the righteous speaketh wisdom, and his tongue talketh of judgment. The law of his God is in his heart: none of his steps shall slide.

Let not corrupt communication proceed out of your mouth, but that which is good to the use of edifying, that it may minister grace unto the hearers.

We cannot but speak the things which we have seen and heard.—I believed, therefore have I spoken.

Whosoever . . . shall confess me before men, him will I confess also before my Father which is in heaven.—With the heart man believeth unto righteousness; and with the mouth confession is made unto salvation.

MATTHEW 12: 34. Colossians 3: 16. Proverbs 4: 23.—
Proverbs 18: 21.—Psalms 37: 30, 31. Ephesians 4: 29. Acts
4: 20.—Psalms 116: 10. Matthew 10: 32.—Romans 10: 10.

Thy will be done in earth, as it is in heaven.

Bless the Lord, ye his angels, that excel in strength, that do his commandments, hearkening unto the voice of his word. Bless ye the Lord, all ye his hosts; ye ministers of his that do his pleasure.

I came down from heaven, not to do mine own will, but the will of him that sent me.—I delight to do thy will, O my God: yea, thy law is within my heart.—O my Father, if this cup may not pass away from me, except I drink it, thy will be done.

Not every one that saith unto me, Lord, Lord, shall enter into the kingdom of heaven: but he that doeth the will of my Father which is in heaven.—Not the hearers of the law are just before God, but the doers of the law shall be justified.—If ye know these things, happy are ye if ye do them.—To him that knoweth to do good, and doeth it not, to him it is sin.

Be not conformed to this world: but be ye transformed by the renewing of your mind.

MATTHEW 6: 10. Psalms 103: 20, 21. John 6: 38.— Psalms 40: 8.—Matthew 26: 42. Matthew 7: 21.—Romans 2: 13.—John 13: 17.—James 4: 17. Romans 12: 2.

JULY 16

Ye shall be unto me a kingdom of priests, and a holy nation.

Thou wast slain, and hast redeemed us to God by thy blood out of every kindred, and tongue, and people, and nation; and hast made us unto our God kings and priests.—Ye are a chosen generation, a royal priesthood, a holy nation, a peculiar people, that ye should show forth the praises of him who hath called you out of darkness into his marvellous light.

Ye shall be named the Priests of the Lord: men shall call you the Ministers of our God.—Priests of God and of Christ.

Wherefore, holy brethren, partakers of the heavenly calling, consider the Apostle and High Priest of our profession, Christ Jesus.—By him therefore let us offer the sacrifice of praise to God continually, that is, the fruit of our lips giving thanks to his name.

For we are his workmanship, created in Christ Jesus unto good works, which God hath before ordained that we should walk in them.—The temple of God is holy, which temple ye are.

EXODUS 19: 6. Revelation 5: 9, 10.—I Peter 2: 9. Isaiah 61: 6.—Revelation 20: 6. Hebrews 3: 1.—Hebrews 13: 15. Ephesians 2: 10.—I Corinthians 3: 17.

Thou art a gracious God, and merciful, slow to
anger, and of great kindness, and repentest thee
of the evil.

I BESEECH thee, let the power of my LORD be great,
according as thou hast spoken, saying, The LORD is
long-suffering, and of great mercy, forgiving iniquity
and transgresion, and by no means clearing the
guilty; visiting the iniquity of the fathers upon the
children unto the third and fourth generation.

O remember not against us former iniquities: let
thy tender mercies speedily prevent us. Help us, O
God of our salvation, for the glory of thy name: and
deliver us, and purge away our sins, for thy name's
sake.—O LORD, though our iniquities testify against
us, do thou it for thy name's sake: for our back-
slidings are many; we have sinned against thee. We
acknowledge, O LORD, our wickedness, and the iniquity of our fathers: for we have sinned against thee.

If thou, LORD, shouldest mark iniquities, O LORD,
who shall stand? But there is forgiveness with thee,
that thou mayest be feared.

JONAH 4: 2. Numbers 14: 17, 18. Psalms 79: 8, 9.—
Jeremiah 14: 7, 20. Psalms 130: 3, 4.

> He calleth his own sheep by name, and leadeth
> them out.

THE foundation of God standeth sure, having this
seal, The Lord knoweth them that are his; and, Let
every one that nameth the name of Christ, depart
from iniquity.—Many will say to me in that day, Lord,
Lord, have we not prophesied in thy name? and in
thy name have cast out devils? and in thy name done
many wonderful works? And then will I profess unto
them, I never knew you: depart from me, ye that
work iniquity.—The LORD knoweth the way of the
righteous: but the way of the ungodly shall perish.

Behold, I have graven thee upon the palms of my
hands; thy walls are continually before me.—Set me
as a seal upon thy heart, as a seal upon thine arm.—
The Lord is good, a stronghold in the day of trouble;
and he knoweth them that trust in him.

I go to prepare a place for you. And if I go and
prepare a place for you, I will come again, and receive you unto myself; that where I am, there ye may
be also.

JOHN 10: 3. II Timothy 2: 19.—Matthew 7: 22, 23.—Psalms
1: 6. Isaiah 49: 16.—Canticles 8: 6.—Nahum 1: 7. John 14:
2, 3.

He that is mighty hath done to me great things;
and holy is his name.

Who is like unto thee, O Lord, among the gods?
who is like thee, glorious in holiness, fearful in
praises, doing wonders?—Among the gods there is
none like unto thee, O Lord: neither are there any
works like unto thy works.—Who shall not fear thee,
O Lord, and glorify thy name? for thou only art
holy.—Hallowed be thy name.

Blessed be the Lord God of Israel; for he hath
visited and redeemed his people.

Who is this that cometh from Edom, with dyed garments from Bozrah? this that is glorious in his
apparel, travelling in the greatness of his strength?
I that speak in righteousness, mighty to save.—I
have laid help upon one that is mighty; I have
exalted one chosen out of the people.

Now unto him that is able to do exceeding abundantly above all that we ask or think, according to
the power that worketh in us, . . . be glory.

LUKE 1: 49. Exodus 15: 11.—Psalms 86: 8.—Revelation
15: 4.—Matthew 6: 9. Luke 1: 68. Isaiah 63: 1.—Psalms 89:
19. Ephesians 3: 20.

JULY 20

They are not of the world, even as I am not of the world.

HE is despised and rejected of men; a man of sorrows, and acquainted with grief.—Ye are partakers of Christ's sufferings; that when his glory shall be revealed, ye may be glad also with exceeding joy.

Such a high priest became us, who is holy, harmless, undefiled, separate from sinners.—That ye may be blameless and harmless, the sons of God, without rebuke, in the midst of a crooked and perverse nation.

Jesus of Nazareth . . . went about doing good, and healing all that were oppressed of the devil; for God was with him.—As we have therefore opportunity, let us do good unto all men, especially unto them who are of the household of faith.

That was the true Light, which lighteth every man that cometh into the world.—Ye are the light of the world. A city that is set on a hill cannot be hid. Let your light so shine before men, that they may see your good works, and glorify your Father which is in heaven.

JOHN 17: 16. Isaiah 53: 3.—I Peter 4: 13. Hebrews 7: 26.—Philippians 2: 15. Acts 10: 38.—Galatians 6: 10. John 1: 9.—Matthew 5: 14, 16.

What profit is there of circumcision?

Much every way.—Circumcise yourselves to the Lord, and take away the foreskins of your heart.—If . . . their uncircumcised hearts be humbled, and they then accept of the punishment of their iniquity: then will I remember my covenant with Jacob, and also my covenant with Isaac, and also my covenant with Abraham will I remember.

Jesus Christ was a minister of the circumcision for the truth of God, to confirm the promises made unto the fathers.—In whom also ye are circumcised with the circumcision made without hands, in putting off the body of the sins of the flesh by the circumcision of Christ.—You, being dead in your sins and the uncircumcision of your flesh, hath he quickened together with him, having forgiven you all trespasses.

Put off concerning the former conversation the old man, which is corrupt according to the deceitful lusts; and be renewed in the spirit of your mind; and . . . put on the new man, which after God is created in righteousness and true holiness.

ROMANS 3: 1. Romans 3: 2.—Jeremiah 4: 4.—Leviticus 26: 41, 42. Romans 15: 8.—Colossians 2: 11.—Colossians 2: 13. Ephesians 4: 22-24.

In that he died, he died unto sin once; but in
that he liveth, he liveth unto God.

H<small>E</small> was numbered with the transgressors.—Christ
was once offered to bear the sins of many.—Who his
own self bare our sins in his own body on the tree,
that we, being dead to sins, should live unto righteousness.—By one offering he hath perfected for ever
them that are sanctified.

This man, because he continueth ever, hath an unchangeable priesthood. Wherefore he is able also to
save them to the uttermost that come unto God by
him, seeing he ever liveth to make intercession for
them.—While we were yet sinners, Christ died for us.
Much more then, being now justified by his blood,
we shall be saved from wrath through him.

Forasmuch . . . as Christ hath suffered for us in
the flesh, arm yourselves likewise with the same mind:
for he that hath suffered in the flesh hath ceased from
sin; that he no longer should live the rest of his time
in the flesh to the lusts of men, but to the will of God.

ROMANS 6: 10. Isaiah 53: 12.—Hebrews 9: 28.—I Peter
2: 24.—Hebrews 10: 14. Hebrews 7: 24, 25.—Romans 5: 8,
9. I Peter 4: 1, 2.

Then cometh the end.

O F that day and that hour knoweth no man, no, not the angels which are in heaven, neither the Son, but the Father. Take ye heed, watch and pray: for ye know not when the time is. And what I say unto you I say unto all, Watch.—The Lord is not slack concerning his promise, as some men count slackness; but is long-suffering to us-ward, not willing that any should perish, but that all should come to repentance.—The coming of the Lord draweth nigh. The judge standeth before the door.—Surely I come quickly.

Seeing . . . that all these things shall be dissolved, what manner of persons ought ye to be in all holy conversation and godliness?

The end of all things is at hand: be ye therefore sober, and watch unto prayer.—Let your loins be girded about, and your lights burning; and ye yourselves like unto men that wait for their lord, when he will return from the wedding; that when he cometh and knocketh, they may open unto him immediately.

I CORINTHIANS 15: 24. Mark 13: 32, 33, 37.—II Peter 3: 9.—James 5: 8, 9.—Revelation 22: 20. II Peter 3: 11. I Peter 4: 7.—Luke 12: 35, 36.

Patient in tribulation.

IT is the LORD: let him do what seemeth him good.—
Whom, though I were righteous, yet would I not
answer, but I would make supplication to my judge.—
The LORD gave, and the LORD hath taken away;
blessed be the name of the LORD.—What? shall we
receive good at the hand of God, and shall we not
receive evil?

Jesus wept.—A man of sorrows, and acquainted
with grief. . . . Surely he hath borne our griefs, and
carried our sorrows.

Whom the Lord loveth he chasteneth, and
scourgeth every son whom he receiveth. Now no
chastening for the present seemeth to be joyous, but
grievous: nevertheless afterward it yieldeth the peaceable fruit of righteousness unto them which are
exercised thereby.—Strengthened with all might, according to his glorious power, unto all patience and
long-suffering with joyfulness.—In the world ye shall
have tribulation: but be of good cheer; I have overcome the world.

ROMANS 12: 12. I Samuel 3: 18.—Job 9: 15.—Job 1: 21.
—Job 2: 10. John 11: 35.—Isaiah 53: 3, 4. Hebrews 12: 6,
11.—Colossians 1: 11.—John 16: 33.

We know that we have passed from death unto life.

H E that heareth my word, and believeth on Him that sent me, hath everlasting life, and shall not come into condemnation; but is passed from death unto life.—He that hath the Son hath life; and he that hath not the Son of God hath not life.

He which stablisheth us with you in Christ, and hath anointed us, is God; who hath also sealed us, and given the earnest of the Spirit in our hearts.

Hereby we know that we are of the truth, and shall assure our hearts before him. Beloved, if our heart condemn us not, then have we confidence toward God.—We know that we are of God, and the whole world lieth in wickedness.

You hath he quickened, who were dead in trespasses and sins. Quickened . . . together with Christ.—Who hath delivered us from the power of darkness, and hath translated us into the kingdom of his dear Son.

I JOHN 3: 14. John 5: 24.—I John 5: 12. II Corinthians 1: 21, 22. I John 3: 19, 21.—I John 5: 19. Ephesians 2: 1, 5.—Colossians 1: 13.

> By faith Abraham, . . called to go out into a place which he should after receive for an inheritance, obeyed.

He shall choose our inheritance for us.—He led him about, he instructed him, he kept him as the apple of his eye. As an eagle stirreth up her nest, fluttereth over her young, spreadeth abroad her wings, taketh them, beareth them on her wings, so the LORD alone did lead him, and there was no strange god with him.

I am the LORD thy God, which teacheth thee to profit, which leadeth thee by the way that thou shouldest go.—Who teacheth like Him?

We walk by faith, not by sight.—Here have we no continuing city, but we seek one to come.

Dearly beloved, I beseech you as strangers and pilgrims, abstain from fleshly lusts, which war against the soul.—Arise ye and depart; for this is not your rest: because it is polluted, it shall destroy you, even with a sore destruction.

HEBREWS 11: 8. Psalms 47: 4.—Deuteronomy 32: 10-12. Isaiah 48: 17.—Job 36: 22. II Corinthians 5: 7.—Hebrews 13: 14. I Peter 2: 11.—Micah 2: 10.

Christ, who is the image of God.

THE glory of the LORD shall be revealed, and all flesh shall see it together.—No man hath seen God at any time; the only begotten Son, which is in the bosom of the Father, he hath declared him. And the Word was made flesh, and dwelt among us, and we beheld his glory, the glory as of the only-begotten of the Father, full of grace and truth.

He that hath seen me hath seen the Father.—The brightness of his glory, and the express image of his person.—God was manifest in the flesh.

In whom we have redemption through his blood, even the forgiveness of sins: who is the image of the invisible God, the first-born of every creature.— Whom he did foreknow, he also did predestinate to be conformed to the image of his Son, that he might be the first-born among many brethren.

As we have borne the image of the earthy, we shall also bear the image of the heavenly.

II CORINTHIANS 4: 4. Isaiah 40: 5.—John 1: 18, 14. John 14: 9.—Hebrews 1: 3.—I Timothy 3: 16. Colossians 1: 14, 15.—Romans 8: 29. I Corinthians 15: 49.

JULY 28

Walk in love.

A NEW commandment I give unto you, That ye love one another; as I have loved you, that ye also love one another.—Above all things have fervent charity among yourselves: for charity shall cover the multitude of sins.—Love covereth all sins.

When ye stand praying, forgive, if ye have aught against any: that your Father also which is in heaven may forgive you your trespasses.—Love ye your enemies, and do good, and lend, hoping for nothing again. —Rejoice not when thine enemy falleth, and let not thy heart be glad when he stumbleth.—Not rendering evil for evil, or railing for railing: but contrariwise blessing; knowing that ye are thereunto called, that ye should inherit a blessing.—If it be possible, as much as lieth in you, live peaceably with all men.—Be ye kind one to another, tender-hearted, forgiving one another, even as God for Christ's sake hath forgiven you.

My little children, let us not love in word, neither in tongue; but in deed and in truth.

EPHESIANS 5: 2. John 13: 34.—I Peter 4: 8.—Proverbs 10: 12. Mark 11: 25.—Luke 6: 35.—Proverbs 24: 17.—I Peter 3: 9.—Romans 12: 18.—Ephesians 4: 32. I John 3: 18

Oh that thou wouldest rend the heavens, that thou wouldest come down.

MAKE haste, my beloved, and be thou like to a roe or to a young hart upon the mountains of spices.—We ourselves groan within ourselves, waiting for the adoption, to wit, the redemption of our body.—Bow thy heavens, O LORD, and come down: touch the mountains, and they shall smoke.

This same Jesus, which is taken up from you into heaven, shall so come in like manner as ye have seen him go into heaven.—Unto them that look for him shall he appear the second time without sin unto salvation.—It shall be said in that day, Lo, this is our God; we have waited for him, and he will save us: this is the LORD; we have waited for him, we will be glad and rejoice in his salvation.

He which testifieth these things saith, Surely I come quickly. Amen. Even so, come, Lord Jesus.—That blessed hope, . . . the glorious appearing of the great God and our Saviour Jesus Christ.—Our conversation is in heaven.

ISAIAH 64: 1. Canticles 8: 14.—Romans 8: 23.—Psalms 144: 5. Acts 1: 11.—Hebrews 9: 28.—Isaiah 25: 9. Revelation 22: 20.—Titus 2: 13.—Philippians 3: 20.

JULY 30

Seek those things which are above, where Christ sitteth on the right hand of God.

GET wisdom, get understanding.—The wisdom that is from above.—The depth saith, It is not in me: and the sea saith, It is not with me.—We are buried with him by baptism into death: that like as Christ was raised up from the dead by the glory of the Father, even so we also should walk in newness of life. For if we have been planted together in the likeness of his death, we shall be also in the likeness of his resurrection.

Let us lay aside every weight, and the sin which doth so easily beset us, and let us run with patience the race that is set before us.—God . . . hath quickened us together with Christ, . . . and hath raised us up together, and made us sit together in heavenly places in Christ Jesus.

They that say such things declare plainly that they seek a country.—Seek ye the LORD, all ye meek of the earth, which have wrought his judgment; seek righteousness, seek meekness.

COLOSSIANS 3: 1. Proverbs 4: 5.—James 3: 17.—Job 28: 14.—Romans 6: 4, 5. Hebrews 12: 1.—Ephesians 2: 4-6. Hebrews 11: 14.—Zephaniah 2: 3.

Endure hardness, as a good soldier of Jesus Christ.

I HAVE given him for a witness to the people, a leader and commander to the people.

It became him, for whom are all things, and by whom are all things, in bringing many sons unto glory, to make the captain of their salvation perfect through sufferings.—We must through much tribulation enter into the kingdom of God.

We wrestle not against flesh and blood, but against principalities, against powers, against the rulers of the darkness of this world, against spiritual wickedness in high places. Wherefore take unto you the whole armor of God.—We do not war after the flesh: for the weapons of our warfare are not carnal, but mighty through God to the pulling down of strongholds.

The God of all grace, who hath called us unto his eternal glory by Christ Jesus, after that ye have suffered a while, make you perfect, stablish, strengthen, settle you.

II TIMOTHY 2: 3. Isaiah 55: 4. Hebrews 2: 10.—Acts 14: 22. Ephesians 6: 12, 13.—II Corinthians 10: 3, 4. I Peter 5: 10.

AUGUST 1

The fruit of the Spirit is faith.

By grace are ye saved through faith; and that not of yourselves: it is the gift of God.—Without faith it is impossible to please him.—He that believeth on him is not condemned: but he that believeth not is condemned already, because he hath not believed.

Whoso keepeth his word, in him verily is the love of God perfected: hereby know we that we are in him.—Faith worketh by love.—Faith without works is dead.

We walk by faith, not by sight.—I am crucified with Christ: nevertheless I live; yet not I, but Christ liveth in me: and the life which I now live in the flesh I live by the faith of the Son of God, who loved me, and gave himself for me.—Whom having not seen, ye love; in whom, though now ye see him not, yet believing, ye rejoice with joy unspeakable and full of glory, receiving the end of your faith, even the salvation of your souls.

GALATIANS 5: 22. Ephesians 2: 8.—Hebrews 11: 6.—John 3: 18.—Mark 9: 24. I John 2: 5.—Galatians 5: 6.—James 2: 20. II Corinthians 5: 7.—Galatians 2: 20.—I Peter 1: 8, 9.

The Lamb slain from the foundation of the
world.

Y<small>OUR</small> lamb shall be without blemish, . . . and the
whole assembly of the congregation of Israel shall kill
it in the evening. And they shall take of the blood,
and strike it on the two side-posts and on the upper
door-post of the houses, wherein they shall eat it.
. . . and when I see the blood, I will pass over you.
—The blood of sprinkling.—Christ our passover is
sacrificed for us.—Being delivered by the determinate
counsel and fore-knowledge of God.—According to
his own purpose and grace, which was given us in
Christ Jesus before the world began.

We have redemption through his blood, the forgiveness of sins.

Forasmuch then as Christ hath suffered for us in the
flesh, arm yourselves likewise with the same mind:
for he that hath suffered in the flesh hath ceased from
sin; that he no longer should live the rest of his time
in the flesh to the lusts of men, but to the will of
God.

REVELATION 13: 8. Exodus 12: 5-7, 13.—Hebrews 12:
24.—I Corinthians 5: 7.—Acts 2: 23.—II Timothy 1: 9.
Ephesians 1: 7. I Peter 4: 1, 2.

AUGUST 3

His mercy is on them that fear Him.

O<small>H</small> how great is thy goodness, which thou hast laid up for them that fear thee; which thou hast wrought for them that trust in thee before the sons of men! Thou shalt hide them in the secret of thy presence from the pride of man: thou shalt keep them secretly in a pavilion from the strife of tongues.

If ye call on the Father, who without respect of persons judgeth according to every man's work, pass the time of your sojourning here in fear.—The LORD is nigh unto all them that call upon him . . . in truth. He will fulfil the desire of them that fear him: he also will hear their cry, and will save them.

Because thy heart was tender, and thou hast humbled thyself before the LORD, . . . and hast rent thy clothes, and wept before me; I also have heard thee, saith the LORD.—To this man will I look, even to him that is poor and of a contrite spirit, and trembleth at my word.—The LORD is nigh unto them that are of a broken heart; and saveth such as be of a contrite spirit.

LUKE 1: 50. Psalms 31: 19, 20. I Peter 1: 17.—Psalms 145: 18, 19. II Kings 22: 19.—Isaiah 66: 2.—Psalms 34: 18.

It is finished: and he bowed his head, and gave up the ghost.

Jesus the author and finisher of our faith.—I have glorified thee on the earth: I have finished the work which thou gavest me to do.—We are sanctified through the offering of the body of Jesus Christ once for all. And every priest standeth daily ministering and offering often-times the same sacrifices, which can never take away sins: but this man, after he had offered one sacrifice for sins for ever, sat down on the right hand of God; from henceforth expecting till his enemies be made his footstool. For by one offering he hath perfected for ever them that are sanctified. —Blotting out the handwriting of ordinances that was against us, which was contrary to us, and took it out of the way, nailing it to his cross.

I lay down my life, that I might take it again. No man taketh it from me, but I lay it down of myself. I have power to lay it down, and I have power to take it again.—Greater love hath no man than this, that a man lay down his life for his friends.

JOHN 19: 30. Hebrews 12: 2.—John 17: 4.—Hebrews 10: 10-14.—Colossians 2: 14. John 10: 17, 18.—John 15: 13.

AUGUST 5

Walk in newness of life.

As ye have yielded your members servants to uncleanness and to iniquity unto iniquity; even so now
yield your members servants to righteousness unto
holiness.—I beseech you, . . . brethren, by the mercies of God, that ye present your bodies a living
sacrifice, holy, acceptable unto God, which is your
reasonable service. And be not conformed to this
world: but be ye transformed by the renewing of your
mind.

If any man be in Christ, he is a new creature; old
things are passed away; behold, all things are become
new.—In Christ Jesus neither circumcision availeth
anything, nor uncircumcision, but a new creature.
And as many as walk according to this rule, peace be
on them, and mercy.—This I say therefore and testify
in the Lord, that ye henceforth walk not as other
Gentiles walk, in the vanity of their mind. Ye have
not so learned Christ; if so be that ye have heard him,
and have been taught by him, as the truth is in
Jesus. Put on the new man, which after God is created
in righteousness and true holiness.

ROMANS 6: 4. Romans 6: 19.—Romans 12: 1, 2. II
Corinthians 5: 17.—Galatians 6: 15, 16.—Ephesians 4: 17,
20, 21, 24.

Whom the Lord loveth he correcteth.

SEE now that I, even I, am he, and there is no god with me; I kill and I make alive; I wound, and I heal; neither is there any that can deliver out of my hand.

I know the thoughts that I think toward you, saith the LORD, thoughts of peace, and not of evil, to give you an expected end.—My thoughts are not your thoughts, neither are your ways my ways, saith the LORD.

I will allure her, and bring her into the wilderness, and speak comfortably unto her.—As a man chasteneth his son, so the LORD thy God chasteneth thee.—Now no chastening for the present seemeth to be joyous, but grievous: nevertheless afterward it yieldeth the peaceable fruit of righteousness unto them which are exercised thereby.—Humble yourselves therefore under the mighty hand of God, that he may exalt you in due time.

I know, O LORD, that thy judgments are right, and that thou in faithfulness hast afflicted me.

PROVERBS 3: 12. Deuteronomy 32: 39. Jeremiah 29: 11.— Isaiah 55: 8. Hosea 2: 14.—Deuteronomy 8: 5.—Hebrews 12: 11.—I Peter 5: 6. Psalms 119: 75.

AUGUST 7

The Comforter, which is the Holy Ghost, whom
the Father will send in my name.

If thou knewest the gift of God, and who it is that
saith to thee, Give me to drink; thou wouldest have
asked of him, and he would have given thee living
water.—If ye . . . being evil, know how to give good
gifts unto your children: how much more shall your
heavenly Father give the Holy Spirit to them that
ask him?—Verily, verily, I say unto you, Whatsoever
ye shall ask the Father in my name, he will give it
you. Hitherto have ye asked nothing in my name:
ask, and ye shall receive, that your joy may be full.

When . . . the Spirit of truth is come, he will
guide you into all truth: for he shall not speak of
himself; but whatsoever he shall hear, that shall he
speak: and he will show you things to come. He shall
glorify me: for he shall receive of mine, and shall
show it unto you.

They rebelled, and vexed his Holy Spirit: therefore he was turned to be their enemy, and he fought
against them.

JOHN 14: 26. John 4: 10.—Luke 11: 13.—John 16: 23,
24. John 16: 13, 14. Isaiah 63: 10.

The path of the just is as the shining light, that shineth more and more unto the perfect day.

Nᴏᴛ as though I had already attained, either were perfect: but I follow after, if that I may apprehend that for which also I am apprehended of Christ Jesus.

Then shall the righteous shine forth as the sun in the kingdom of their Father.—We all, with open face beholding as in a glass the glory of the Lord, are changed into the same image from glory to glory, even as by the Spirit of the Lord.—When that which is perfect is come, then that which is in part shall be done away. For now we see through a glass, darkly, but then face to face: now I know in part; but then shall I know even as also I am known.

Beloved, now are we the sons of God; and it doth not yet appear what we shall be: but we know that, when he shall appear, we shall be like him; for we shall see him as he is. And every man that hath this hope in him purifieth himself, even as he is pure.

PROVERBS 4: 18. Philippians 3: 12.—Hosea 6: 3. Matthew 13: 43.—II Corinthians 3: 18.—I Corinthians 13: 10, 12. I John 3: 2, 3.

Thou art all fair, my love; there is no spot in
thee.

THE whole head is sick, and the whole heart faint.
From the sole of the foot even unto the head there
is no soundness in it; but wounds, and bruises, and
putrefying sores: they have not been closed, neither
mollified with ointment.—We are all as an unclean
thing, and all our righteousnesses are as filthy rags.—
I know that in me (that is, in my flesh) dwelleth no
good thing.

Ye are washed, . . . ye are sanctified, . . . ye are
justified in the name of the Lord Jesus, and by the
Spirit of our God.—The King's daughter is all glorious
within.—Perfect through my comeliness, which I had
put upon thee, saith the Lord.

Let the beauty of the LORD our God be upon us.

These are they which . . . have washed their
robes, and made them white in the blood of the
Lamb.—A glorious church, not having spot, or
wrinkle, or any such thing; but . . . holy and without blemish.—Ye are complete in him.

CANTICLES 4: 7. Isaiah 1: 5, 6.—Isaiah 64: 6.—Romans
7: 18. I Corinthians 6: 11.—Psalms 45: 13.—Ezekiel 16: 14.
Psalms 90: 17. Revelation 7: 14.—Ephesians 5: 27.—Colossians 2: 10.

I pray not that thou shouldest take them out of the world, but that thou shouldest keep them from the evil.

BLAMELESS and harmless, the sons of God, without rebuke, in the midst of a crooked and perverse nation, among whom ye shine as lights in the world.—Ye are the salt of the earth, . . . the light of the world. Let your light so shine before men, that they may see your good works, and glorify your Father which is in heaven.

I also withheld thee from sinning against me.

The Lord is faithful, who shall stablish you, and keep you from evil.—So did not I, because of the fear of God.—Who gave himself for our sins, that he might deliver us from this present evil world, according to the will of God and our Father.—Now unto him that is able to keep you from falling, and to present you faultless before the presence of his glory with exceeding joy, to the only wise God our Saviour, be glory and majesty, dominion and power both now and ever. Amen.

JOHN 17: 15. Philippians 2: 15.—Matthew 5: 13, 14, 16. Genesis 20: 6. II Thessalonians 3: 3.—Nehemiah 5: 15.— Galatians 1: 4.—Jude 24, 25.

AUGUST 11

**That through death He might destroy him that
had the power of death.**

Our Saviour Jesus Christ . . . hath abolished
death, and hath brought life and immortality to light
through the gospel.—He will swallow up death in
victory; and the Lord God will wipe away tears from
off all faces; and the rebuke of his people shall he
take away from off all the earth: for the LORD hath
spoken it.—When this corruptible shall have put on
incorruption, and this mortal shall have put on immortality, then shall be brought to pass the saying
that is written, Death is swallowed up in victory. O
death, where is thy sting? O grave, where is thy victory? The sting of death is sin; and the strength of
sin is the law. But thanks be to God, which giveth us
the victory through our Lord Jesus Christ.

God hath not given us the spirit of fear; but of
power, and of love, and of a sound mind.—Yea, though
I walk through the valley of the shadow of death, I will
fear no evil: for thou art with me; thy rod and thy
staff they comfort me.

HEBREWS 2: 14. II Timothy 1: 10.—Isaiah 25: 8.—I
Corinthians 15: 54-57. II Timothy 1: 7.—Psalms 23: 4.

The Lord will not cast off for ever: but though he cause grief, yet will he have compassion.

Fear thou not, . . . saith the Lord: for I am with thee; I will not make a full end of thee, but correct thee in measure.—For a small moment have I forsaken thee; but with great mercies will I gather thee. In a little wrath I hid my face from thee for a moment; but with everlasting kindness will I have mercy on thee, saith the Lord thy Redeemer. For the mountains shall depart, and the hills be removed; but my kindness shall not depart from thee, neither shall the covenant of my peace be removed, saith the Lord that hath mercy on thee. O thou afflicted, tossed with tempest, and not comforted, behold, I will lay thy stones with fair colors, and lay thy foundations with sapphires.

I will bear the indignation of the Lord, because I have sinned against him, until he plead my cause, and execute judgment for me: he will bring me forth to the light, and I shall behold his righteousness.

LAMENTATIONS 3: 31, 32. Jeremiah 46: 28.—Isaiah 54: 7, 8, 10, 11. Micah 7: 9.

AUGUST 13

He hath prepared for them a city.

IF I go and prepare a place for you, I will come again, and receive you unto myself; that where I am, there ye may be also.—An inheritance incorruptible, and undefiled, and that fadeth not away, reserved in heaven for you.—Here have we no continuing city, but we seek one to come.

This same Jesus, which is taken up from you into heaven, shall so come in like manner as ye have seen him go into heaven.—Be patient therefore, brethren, unto the coming of the Lord. Behold, the husband-man waiteth for the precious fruit of the earth, and hath long patience for it, until he receive the early and latter rain. Be ye also patient; stablish your hearts: for the coming of the Lord draweth nigh.— Yet a little while, and he that shall come will come, and will not tarry.

We which are alive and remain shall be caught up together with them in the clouds, to meet the Lord in the air: and so shall we ever be with the Lord. Wherefore comfort one another with these words.

HEBREWS 11: 16. John 14: 3.—I Peter 1: 4.—Hebrews 13: 14. Acts 1: 11.—James 5: 7, 8.—Hebrews 10: 37. I Thessalonians 4: 17, 18.

The joy of the Lord is your strength.

Sing, O heavens; and be joyful, O earth; and break forth into singing, O mountains: for the LORD hath comforted his people, and will have mercy upon his afflicted.—Behold, God is my salvation; I will trust, and not be afraid: for the LORD JEHOVAH is my strength and my song; he also is become my salvation.

The LORD is my strength and my shield; my heart trusted in him, and I am helped: therefore my heart greatly rejoiceth; and with my song will I praise him. —My soul shall be joyful in my God; for he hath clothed me with the garments of salvation, he hath covered me with the robe of righteousness, as a bridegroom decketh himself with ornaments, and as a bride adorneth herself with her jewels.

I have therefore whereof I may glory through Jesus Christ in those things which pertain to God.—We . . . joy in God through our Lord Jesus Christ, by whom we have now received the atonement.—I will joy in the God of my salvation.

NEHEMIAH 8: 10. Isaiah 49: 13.—Isaiah 12: 2. Psalms 28: 7.—Isaiah 61: 10. Romans 15: 17.—Romans 5: 11.— Habakkuk 3: 18.

AUGUST 15

The God of peace make you perfect in every good work to do his will.

B<small>E</small> perfect, be of good comfort, be of one mind, live in peace; and the God of love and peace shall be with you.

By grace are ye saved through faith; and that not of yourselves: it is the gift of God: not of works, lest any man should boast.—Every good gift and every perfect gift is from above, and cometh down from the Father of lights, with whom is no variableness, neither shadow of turning.

Work out your own salvation with fear and trembling. For it is God which worketh in you both to will and to do of his good pleasure.—Be ye transformed by the renewing of your mind, that ye may prove what is that good, and acceptable, and perfect will of God.—Being filled with the fruits of righteousness, which are by Jesus Christ, unto the glory and praise of God.

Not that we are sufficient of ourselves to think anything as of ourselves; but our sufficiency is of God.

HEBREWS 13: 20, 21. II Corinthians 13: 11. Ephesians 2: 8, 9.—James 1: 17. Philippians 2: 12, 13.—Romans 12: 2.—Philippians 1: 11. II Corinthians 3: 5.

**The house that is to be builded for the Lord
must be exceeding magnifical**

Ye . . . as lively stones, are built up a spiritual
house.—Know ye not that ye are the temple of God,
and that the Spirit of God dwelleth in you? If any
man defile the temple of God, him shall God destroy;
for the temple of God is holy, which temple ye are.—
Your body is the temple of the Holy Ghost which is
in you, which ye have of God, and ye are not your
own. For ye are bought with a price: therefore glorify
God in your body, and in your spirit, which are
God's.—What agreement hath the temple of God with
idols? for ye are the temple of the living God; as
God hath said, I will dwell in them, and walk in
them; and I will be their God, and they shall be my
people.

Ye . . . are built upon the foundation of the
apostles and prophets, Jesus Christ himself being the
chief corner-stone; in whom all the building fitly
framed together groweth unto a holy temple in the
Lord: in whom ye also are builded together for a
habitation of God through the Spirit.

II CHRONICLES 22: 5. I Peter 2: 5.—I Corinthians 3:
16, 17.—I Corinthians 6: 19, 20.—II Corinthians 6: 16. Ephesians 2: 19-22.

Pray one for another, that ye may be healed.

ABRAHAM answered and said, Behold now, I have taken upon me to speak unto the Lord, which am but dust and ashes: peradventure there shall lack five of the fifty righteous: wilt thou destroy all the city for lack of five? And he saith, If I find there forty and five, I will not destroy it.

Father, forgive them; for they know not what they do.—Pray for them which despitefully use you, and persecute you.

I pray for them: I pray not for the world, but for them which thou hast given me; for they are thine. Neither pray I for these alone, but for them also which shall believe on me through their word.—Bear ye one another's burdens, and so fulfil the law of Christ.

The effectual fervent prayer of a righteous man availeth much. Elias was a man subject to like passions as we are, and he prayed earnestly that it might not rain: and it rained not on the earth by the space of three years and six months.

JAMES 5: 16. Genesis 18: 27, 28. Luke 23: 34.—Matthew 5: 44. John 17: 9, 20.—Galatians 6: 2. James 5: 16, 17.

What god is there in heaven or in earth, that
can do according to thy works, and according
to thy might?

WHO in the heaven can be compared unto the
LORD? who among the sons of the mighty can be
likened unto the LORD? O LORD God of hosts, who is
a strong LORD like thee? or to thy faithfulness round
about thee?—Among the gods there is none like unto
thee, O Lord; neither are there any works like unto
thy works.—For thy word's sake, and according to
thine own heart, hast thou done all these great things,
to make thy servant know them. Wherefore thou art
great, O LORD God: for there is none like thee, neither
is there any God beside thee, according to all that
we have heard with our ears.

Eye hath not seen, nor ear heard, neither have
entered into the heart of man, the things which God
hath prepared for them that love him. But God hath
revealed them unto us by his Spirit.—The secret
things belong unto the LORD our God: but those things
which are revealed belong unto us and to our children.

DEUTERONOMY 3: 24. Psalms 89: 6, 8.—Psalms 86: 8.—
II Samuel 7: 21, 22. I Corinthians 2: 9, 10.—Deuteronomy
29: 29.

AUGUST 19

As he which hath called you is holy, so be ye holy in all manner of conversation.

Ye know how we exhorted . . . and charged every one of you, . . . that ye would walk worthy of God, who hath called you unto his kingdom and glory.— That ye should show forth the praises of Him who hath called you out of darkness into his marvellous light.

Ye were sometime darkness, but now are ye light in the Lord: walk as children of light (for the fruit of the Spirit is in all goodness and righteousness and truth); proving what is acceptable unto the Lord. And have no fellowship with the unfruitful works of darkness, but rather reprove them.—Being filled with the fruits of righteousness, which are by Jesus Christ, unto the glory and praise of God.

Let your light so shine before men, that they may see your good works, and glorify your Father which is in heaven.—Whether therefore ye eat, or drink, or whatsoever ye do, do all to the glory of God.

I PETER 1: 15. I Thessalonians 2: 11, 12.—I Peter 2: 9. Ephesians 5: 8-11.—Philippians 1: 11. Matthew 5: 16.—I Corinthians 10: 31.

God is not a man, that he should lie; neither the son of man, that he should repent.

THE Father of lights, with whom is no variableness, neither shadow of turning.—Jesus Christ, the same yesterday, and today, and for ever.

His truth shall be thy shield and buckler.

God, willing more abundantly to show unto the heirs of promise the immutability of his counsel, confirmed it by an oath; that by two immutable things, in which it was impossible for God to lie, we might have a strong consolation, who have fled for refuge to lay hold upon the hope set before us.

The faithful God, which keepeth covenant and mercy with them that love him and keep his commandments to a thousand generations.—All the paths of the LORD are mercy and truth unto such as keep his covenant and his testimonies.—Happy is he that hath the God of Jacob for his help, whose hope is in the Lord his God . . . which keepeth truth for ever.

NUMBERS 23: 19. James 1: 17.—Hebrews 13: 8. Psalms 91: 4. Hebrews 6: 17, 18. Deuteronomy 7: 9.—Psalms 25: 10.—Psalms 146: 5, 6.

AUGUST 21

Thou art my portion, O Lord.

ALL things are yours; . . . and ye are Christ's; and Christ is God's.—Our Saviour Jesus Christ . . . gave himself for us.—God gave him to be the head over all things to the church.—Christ loved the church, and gave himself for it; that he might present it to himself a glorious church, not having spot, or wrinkle, or any such thing; but that it should be holy and without blemish.

My soul shall make her boast in the Lord.—I will greatly rejoice in the LORD, my soul shall be joyful in my God; for he hath clothed me with the garments of salvation, he hath covered me with the robe of righteousness.

Whom have I in heaven but thee? and there is none upon earth that I desire beside thee. My flesh and my heart faileth: but God is the strength of my heart, and my portion for ever.—O my soul, thou hast said unto the LORD, Thou art my Lord. The LORD is the portion of mine inheritance and of my cup: thou maintainest my lot.

PSALMS 119: 57. I Corinthians 3: 21, 23.—Titus 2: 13, 14.—Ephesians 1: 22.—Ephesians 5: 25, 27. Psalms 34: 2.—Isaiah 61: 10. Psalms 73: 25, 26.—Psalms 16: 2, 5, 6.

None of us liveth to himself, and no man dieth to himself.

Whether we live, we live unto the Lord; and whether we die, we die unto the Lord: whether we live therefore, or die, we are the Lord's.—Let no man seek his own: but every man another's wealth.—Ye are bought with a price: therefore glorify God in your body, and in your spirit, which are God's.

Christ shall be magnified in my body, whether it be by life, or by death. For to me to live is Christ, and to die is gain. But if I live in the flesh, this is the fruit of my labor: yet what I shall choose I wot not. For I am in a strait betwixt two, having a desire to depart, and to be with Christ; which is far better.

I through the law am dead to the law, that I might live unto God. I am crucified with Christ: nevertheless I live; yet not I, but Christ liveth in me: and the life which I now live in the flesh I live by the faith of the Son of God, who loved me, and gave himself for me.

ROMANS 14: 7. Romans 14: 8.—I Corinthians 10: 24. I Corinthians 6: 20. Philippians 1: 20-23. Galatians 2: 19, 20.

AUGUST 23

I have loved thee with an everlasting love: therefore with loving-kindness have I drawn thee.

WE are bound to give thanks always to God for you, brethren beloved of the Lord, because God hath from the beginning chosen you to salvation through sanctification of the Spirit and belief of the truth: whereunto he called you by our gospel, to the obtaining of the glory of our Lord Jesus Christ.—God . . . hath saved us, and called us with a holy calling, not according to our works, but according to his own purpose and grace, which was given us in Christ Jesus before the world began.—Thine eyes did see my substance, yet being imperfect: and in thy book all my members were written, which in continuance were fashioned, when as yet there was none of them.

God so loved the world, that he gave his only begotten Son, that whosoever believeth in him should not perish, but have everlasting life.

Herein is love, not that we loved God, but that he loved us, and sent his Son to be the propitiation for our sins.

JEREMIAH 31: 3. II Thessalonians 2: 13, 14.—II Timothy 1: 9.—Psalms 139: 16. John 3: 16. I John 4: 10.

I know their sorrows.

A MAN of sorrows, and acquainted with grief.—
Touched with the feeling of our infirmities.

Himself took our infirmities, and bare our sicknesses.—Jesus . . . being wearied with his journey,
sat thus on the well.

When Jesus . . . saw her weeping, and the Jews
also weeping which came with her, he groaned in
the spirit, and was troubled. Jesus wept.—For in that
he himself hath suffered, being tempted, he is able to
succor them that are tempted.

He hath looked down from the height of his sanctuary: from heaven did the LORD behold the earth;
to hear the groaning of the prisoner; to loose those
that are appointed to death.—He knoweth the way
that I take: when he hath tried me, I shall come forth
as gold.—When my spirit was overwhelmed within
me, then thou knewest my path.

He that toucheth you toucheth the apple of his
eye.—In all their affliction he was afflicted: and the
Angel of his presence saved them.

EXODUS 3: 7. Isaiah 53: 3.—Hebrews 4: 15. Matthew 8:
17.—John 4: 6. John 11: 33, 35.—Hebrews 2: 18. Psalms
102: 19, 20.—Job 23: 10.—Psalms 142: 3. Zechariah 2: 8.—
Isaiah 63: 9.

AUGUST 25

Look unto the rock whence ye are hewn, and to the hole of the pit whence ye are digged.

Behold, I was shapen in iniquity.—None eye pitied thee, . . . but thou wast cast out in the open field, to the loathing of thy person, in the day that thou was born. And when I passed by thee, and saw thee polluted in thine own blood, I said unto thee, . . . Live.

He brought me up . . . out of a horrible pit, out of the miry clay, and set my feet upon a rock, and established my goings. And he hath put a new song in my mouth, even praise unto our God.

When we were yet without strength, in due time Christ died for the ungodly. For scarcely for a righteous man will one die: yet peradventure for a good man some would even dare to die. But God commendeth his love toward us, in that, while we were yet sinners, Christ died for us.—God, who is rich in mercy for his great love wherewith he loved us, even when we were dead in sins, hath quickened us together with Christ.

ISAIAH 51: 1. Psalms 51: 5.—Ezekiel 16: 5, 6. Psalms 40: 2, 3. Romans 5: 6-8.—Ephesians 2: 4, 5.

Thou shalt make a plate of pure gold, and grave
upon it, like the engravings of a signet,

HOLINESS TO THE LORD.

Holiness, without which no man shall see the Lord.
—God is a Spirit: and they that worship him must
worship him in spirit and in truth.—I will be sanctified in them that come nigh me, and before all the
people I will be glorified.—But we are all as an unclean thing, and all our righteousnesses are as filthy
rags.

This is the law of the house: Upon the top of the
mountain the whole limit thereof round about shall
be most holy.—Holiness becometh thy house, O Lord,
for ever.

For their sakes I sanctify myself, that they also
might be sanctified through the truth.—Seeing . . .
that we have a great High Priest, that is passed into
the heavens, Jesus the Son of God, let us . . . come
boldly unto the throne of grace, that we may obtain
mercy, and find grace to help in time of need.

EXODUS 28: 36. Hebrews 12: 14.—John 4: 24.—Leviticus
10: 3.—Isaiah 64: 6. Ezekiel 43: 12.—Psalms 93: 5. John 17:
19.—Hebrews 4: 14, 16.

AUGUST 27

Thy word is a lamp unto my feet, and a light unto my path.

By the word of thy lips I have kept me from the paths of the destroyer. Hold up my goings in thy paths, that my footsteps slip not.

When thou goest, it shall lead thee; when thou sleepest, it shall keep thee; and when thou awakest, it shall talk with thee. For the commandment is a lamp; and the law is light.—Thine ears shall hear a word behind thee, saying, This is the way, walk ye in it, when ye turn to the right hand, and when ye turn to the left.

I am the light of the world: he that followeth me shall not walk in darkness, but shall have the light of life.—We have also a . . . sure word of prophecy; whereunto ye do well that ye take heed, as unto a light that shineth in a dark place.—Now we see through a glass, darkly; but then face to face: now I know in part, but then shall I know even as also I am known.—They need no candle, neither light of the sun; for the Lord God giveth them light: and they shall reign for ever and ever.

PSALMS 119: 105. Psalms 17: 4, 5. Proverbs 6: 22, 23.—
Isaiah 30: 21. John 8: 2.—II Peter 1: 19.—I Corinthians 13:
12.—Revelation 22: 5.

The accuser of our brethren is cast down, which accused them before our God day and night.

THEY overcame him by the blood of the Lamb, and by the word of their testimony.

Who shall lay anything to the charge of God's elect? It is God that justifieth. Who is he that condemneth? It is Christ that died, yea, rather, that is risen again, who is even at the right hand of God, who also maketh intercession for us.

Having spoiled principalities and powers, he made a show of them openly.—That through death he might destroy him that had the power of death, that is, the devil; and deliver them who through fear of death were all their lifetime subject to bondage.—In all these things we are more than conquerors, through him that loved us.—Put on the whole armor of God, that ye may be able to stand against the wiles of the devil. And take the sword of the Spirit, which is the word of God.—Thanks be to God, which giveth us the victory through our Lord Jesus Christ.

REVELATION 12: 10. Revelation 12: 11. Romans 8: 33, 34. Colossians 2: 15.—Hebrews 2: 14, 15.—Romans 8: 37.—Ephesians 6: 11, 17.—I Corinthians 15: 57.

AUGUST 29

Whoso trusteth in the Lord, happy is he.

[ABRAHAM] staggered not at the promise of God through unbelief; but was strong in faith, giving glory to God; and being fully persuaded that, what he had promised, he was able also to perform.—The children of Judah prevailed, because they relied upon the LORD God of their fathers.

God is our refuge and strength, a very present help in trouble. Therefore will not we fear, though the earth be removed, and though the mountains be carried into the midst of the sea.—It is better to trust in the LORD than to put confidence in man. It is better to trust in the LORD than to put confidence in princes. —The steps of a good man are ordered by the LORD: and he delighteth in his way. Though he fall, he shall not be utterly cast down: for the LORD upholdeth him with his hand.

O taste and see that the Lord is good: blessed is the man that trusteth in him. O fear the Lord, ye his saints: for there is no want to them that fear him.

PROVERBS 16: 20. Romans 4: 20, 21.—II Chronicles 13: 18. Psalms 46: 1, 2.—Psalms 118: 8, 9.—Psalms 37: 23, 24. Psalms 34: 8, 9.

The king held out the golden sceptre. So Esther
drew near, and touched the top of the sceptre.

It shall come to pass, when he crieth unto me, that
I will hear; for I am gracious.

We have known and believed the love that God
hath to us. God is love; and he that dwelleth in love
dwelleth in God, and God in him. Herein is our
love made perfect, that we may have boldness in the
day of judgment. . . . There is no fear in love; but
perfect love casteth out fear: because fear hath tor-
ment. He that feareth is not made perfect in love. We
love him, because he first loved us.

Let us draw near with a true heart, in full assurance of faith, having our hearts sprinkled from an
evil conscience, and our bodies washed with pure
water.

Through him we . . . have access by one Spirit
unto the Father.—We have boldness and access with
confidence by the faith of him.—Let us therefore come
boldly unto the throne of grace, that we may obtain
mercy, and find grace to help in time of need.

ESTHER 5: 2. Exodus 22: 27. I John 4: 16-19. Hebrews
10: 22. Ephesians 2: 18.—Ephesians 3: 12.—Hebrews 4: 16.

The free gift is of many offences unto justification.

THOUGH your sins be as scarlet, they shall be as white as snow; though they be red like crimson, they shall be as wool.

I, even I, am he that blotteth out thy transgressions for mine own sake, and will not remember thy sins. Put me in remembrance: let us plead together: declare thou, that thou mayest be justified.—I have blotted out, as a thick cloud, thy transgressions, and, as a cloud, thy sins: return unto me; for I have redeemed thee.

God so loved the world, that he gave his only begotten Son, that whosoever believeth in him should not perish, but have everlasting life.—Not as the offence, so also is the free gift. For if through the offence of one many be dead, much more the grace of God, and the gift by grace, which is by one man, Jesus Christ, hath abounded unto many.—And such were some of you: but ye are washed, but ye are sanctified, but ye are justified in the name of the Lord Jesus, and by the Spirit of our God.

ROMANS 5: 16. Isaiah 1: 18. Isaiah 43: 25, 26.—Isaiah 44: 22. John 3: 16.—Romans 5: 15.—I Corinthians 6: 11.

The fruit of the spirit is meekness.

THE meek . . . shall increase their joy in the LORD, and the poor among men shall rejoice in the Holy One of Israel.

Except ye be converted, and become as little children, ye shall not enter into the kingdom of heaven. Whosoever therefore shall humble himself as this little child, the same is greatest in the kingdom of heaven.—The ornament of a meek and quiet spirit . . . is in the sight of God of great price.—Charity vaunteth not itself, is not puffed up.

Follow after meekness.—Take my yoke upon you and learn of me, for I am meek and lowly in heart. —He was oppressed, and he was afflicted, yet he opened not his mouth: he is brought as a lamb to the slaughter, and as a sheep before her shearers is dumb, so he openeth not his mouth.—Leaving us an example, that ye should follow his steps: who . . . , when he was reviled, reviled not again.

GALATIANS 5: 22. Isaiah 29: 19. Matthew 18: 3, 4.— I Peter 3: 4.—I Corinthians 13: 4. I Timothy 6: 11.—Matthew 11: 29.—Isaiah 53: 7.—I Peter 2: 21-23.

SEPTEMBER 2

Wait on the Lord: be of good courage, and he shall strengthen thy heart.

Hast thou not known? hast thou not heard, that the everlasting God, the Lord, the Creator of the ends of the earth, fainteth not, neither is weary? He giveth power to the faint; and to them that have no might he increaseth strength.—Fear thou not; for I am with thee: be not dismayed; for I am thy God: I will strengthen thee; yea, I will help thee; yea, I will uphold thee with the right hand of my righteousness.—Thou hast been a strength to the poor, a strength to the needy in his distress, a refuge from the storm, a shadow from the heat, when the blast of the terrible ones is as a storm against the wall.

The trying of your faith worketh patience. But let patience have her perfect work, that ye may be perfect and entire, wanting nothing.—Cast not away therefore your confidence, which hath great recompense of reward. For ye have need of patience, that, after ye have done the will of God, ye might receive the promise.

PSALMS 27: 14. Isaiah 40: 28, 29.—Isaiah 41: 10.—Isaiah 25: 4. James 1: 3, 4.—Hebrews 10: 35, 36.

Neither shall there be leaven seen with thee in
all thy quarters.

THE fear of the LORD is to hate evil.—Abhor that
which is evil.—Abstain from all appearance of evil.—
Looking diligently lest any man fail of the grace of
God; lest any root of bitterness springing up trouble
you, and thereby many be defiled.

If I regard iniquity in my heart, the Lord will not
hear me.

Know ye not that a little leaven leaveneth the
whole lump? Purge out therefore the old leaven, that
ye may be a new lump, as ye are unleavened. For
even Christ our passover is sacrificed for us: therefore let us keep the feast, not with old leaven, neither
with the leaven of malice and wickedness: but with
the unleavend bread of sincerity and truth.—Let a
man examine himself, and so let him eat of that
bread, and drink of that cup.

Let every one that nameth the name of Christ depart from iniquity.—Such a high priest became us, who
is holy, harmless, undefiled, separate from sinners.—
In Him is no sin.

EXODUS 13: 7. Proverbs 8: 13.—Romans 12: 9.—I Thessalonians 5: 22.—Hebrews 12: 15. Psalms 66: 18. I Corinthians 5: 6-8.—I Corinthians 11: 28. II Timothy 2: 19.—
Hebrews 7: 26.—I John 3: 5.

SEPTEMBER 4

Sit still, my daughter.

Take heed, and be quiet; fear not, neither be faint-hearted.—Be still, and know that I am God.—Said I not unto thee, that, if thou wouldest believe, thou shouldest see the glory of God?—The loftiness of man shall be bowed down, and the haughtiness of men shall be made low: and the Lord alone shall be exalted in that day.

Mary . . . sat at Jesus' feet, and heard his word. Mary hath chosen that good part, which shall not be taken away from her.—In returning and rest shall ye be saved; in quietness and in confidence shall be your strength.—Commune with your own heart upon your bed, and be still.

Rest in the Lord, and wait patiently for him: fret not thyself because of him who prospereth in his way, because of the man who bringeth wicked devices to pass.

He shall not be afraid of evil tidings: his heart is fixed, trusting in the Lord. His heart is established.

He that believeth shall not make haste.

RUTH 3: 18. Isaiah 7: 4.—Psalms 46: 10.—John 11: 40.
—Isaiah 2: 17. Luke 10: 39, 42.—Isaiah 30: 15.—Psalms 4:
4. Psalms 17: 7. Psalms 112: 7, 8. Isaiah 28: 16.

As the body is one and hath many members, so also is Christ.

HE is the head of the body, the church.—The head over all things to the church, which is his body, the fulness of him that filleth all in all.

We are members of his body, of his flesh, and of his bones.

A body hast thou prepared me.—Thine eyes did see my substance, yet being unperfect; and in thy book all my members were written, which in continuance were fashioned, when as yet there was none of them.

Thine they were, and thou gavest them me.—He hath chosen us in him before the foundation of the world. —Whom he did foreknow, he also did predestinate to be conformed to the image of his Son.

Grow up into him in all things, which is the head, even Christ: from whom the whole body fitly joined together, and compacted by that which every joint supplieth, . . . maketh increase of the body unto the edifying of itself in love.

I CORINTHIANS 12: 12. Colossians 1: 18.—Ephesians 1: 22, 23. Ephesians 5: 30. Hebrews 10: 5.—Psalms 139: 16. John 17: 6.—Ephesians 1: 4.—Romans 8: 29. Ephesians 4: 15, 16.

SEPTEMBER 6

Let us lift up our heart with our hands unto God in the heavens.

WHO is like unto the LORD our God, who dwelleth on high, who humbleth himself to behold the things that are in heaven and in the earth.—Unto thee, O LORD, do I lift up my soul!—I stretch forth my hands unto thee: my soul thirsteth after thee, as a thirsty land. Hide not thy face from me, lest I be like unto them that go down into the pit. Cause me to hear thy loving-kindness in the morning; for in thee do I trust: cause me to know the way wherein I should walk; for I lift up my soul unto thee.

Because thy living-kindness is better than life, my lips shall praise thee. Thus will I bless thee while I live: I will lift up my hands in thy name.—Rejoice the soul of thy servant: for unto thee, O Lord, do I lift up my soul. For thou, Lord, art good, and ready to forgive; and plenteous in mercy unto all them that call upon thee.

Whatsoever ye shall ask in my name, that will I do.

LAMENTATIONS 3: 41. Psalms 113: 5, 6.—Psalms 25: 1.—Psalms 143: 6-8. Psalms 63: 3, 4.—Psalms 86: 4, 5. John 14: 13.

Rejoicing in hope.

THE hope which is laid up for you in heaven.—If in this life only we have hope in Christ, we are of all men most miserable—We must through much tribulation enter into the kingdom of God.—Whosoever doth not bear his cross, and come after me, cannot be my disciple.—No man should be moved by these afflictions: for yoursleves know that we are appointed thereunto.

Rejoice in the Lord alway: and again I say, Rejoice.—The God of hope fill you with all joy and peace in believing, that ye may abound in hope through the power of the Holy Ghost.—Blessed be the God and Father of our Lord Jesus Christ, which according to his abundant mercy hath begotten us again unto a lively hope by the resurrection of Jesus Christ from the dead.—Whom having not seen, ye love; in whom, though now ye see him not, yet believing, ye rejoice with joy unspeakable and full of glory.—By whom also we have access by faith into this grace wherein we stand, and rejoice in hope of the glory of God.

ROMANS 12: 12. Colossians 1: 5.—I Corinthians 15: 19.—Acts 14: 22.—Luke 14: 27.—I Thessalonians 3: 3. Philippians 4: 4.—Romans 15: 13.—I Peter 1: 3.—I Peter 1: 8.—Romans 5: 2.

SEPTEMBER 8

Thou art weighed in the balances and art found wanting.

THE LORD is a God of knowledge, and by him actions are weighed.

That which is highly estimated among men is abomination in the sight of God.—The LORD seeth not as man seeth, for man looketh on the outward appearance, but the Lord looketh on the heart.—Be not deceived; God is not mocked: for whatsoever a man soweth, that shall he also reap. For he that soweth to his flesh shall of the flesh reap corruption; but he that soweth to the Spirit shall of the Spirit reap life everlasting.

What is a man profited, if he shall gain the whole world, and lose his own soul? or what shall a man give in exchange for his soul?—What things were gain to me, those I counted loss for Christ.

Behold, thou desirest truth in the inward parts.— Thou hast proved my heart; thou hast visited me in the night; thou hast tried me, and shalt find nothing.

DANIEL 5: 27. I Samuel 2: 3.—Luke 16: 15.—I Samuel 16: 17.—Galatians 6: 7, 8. Matthew 16: 26.—Philippians 3: 7. Psalms 51: 6.—Psalms 17: 3.

He hath filled the hungry with good things; and the rich he hath sent empty away.

THOU sayest, I am rich, and increased with goods, and have need of nothing; and knowest not that thou art wretched, and miserable, and poor, and blind, and naked: I counsel thee to buy of me the gold tried in the fire, that thou mayest be rich. As many as I love, I rebuke and chasten: be zealous therefore and repent.

Blessed are they which do hunger and thirst after righteousness: for they shall be filled.—When the poor and needy seek water, and there is none, and their tongue faileth for thirst, I the LORD will hear them, I the God of Israel will not forsake them.—I am the Lord thy God, . . . open thy mouth wide, and I will fill it.

Wherefore do ye spend money for that which is not bread? and your labor for that which satisfieth not? hearken diligently unto me, and eat ye that which is good, and let your soul delight itself in fatness.—I am the bread of life.

LUKE 1: 53. Revelation 3: 17-19. Matthew 5: 6.—Isaiah 41: 17.—Psalms 81: 10. Isaiah 55: 2.—John 5: 35.

SEPTEMBER 10

I will give them one heart, and one way, that
they may fear me for ever, for the good of them,
and of their children after them.

A NEW heart . . . will I give you, and a new spirit
will I put within you.—Good and upright is the Lord:
therefore will he teach sinners in the way. The meek
will he guide in judgment: and the meek will he
teach his way. All the paths of the LORD are mercy
and truth unto such as keep his covenant and his
testimonies.

That they all may be one; as thou, Father, art in
me, and I in thee, that they also may be one in us:
that the world may believe that thou hast sent me.

I . . . beseech you that ye walk worthy of the vocation wherewith ye are called, with all lowliness and
meekness . . . endeavoring to keep the unity of the
Spirit in the bond of peace. There is one body, and
one Spirit, even as ye are called in one hope of your
calling: one Lord, one faith, one baptism, one God
and Father of all, who is above all, and through all,
and in you all.

JEREMIAH 32: 39. Ezekiel 36: 26.—Psalms 25: 8-10. John
17: 21. Ephesians 4: 1-6.

Be not conformed to this world: but be ye transformed by the renewing of your mind.

Know ye not that the friendship of the world is enmity with God? whosoever therefore will be a friend of the world is the enemy of God.

What fellowship hath righteousness with unrighteousness? and what communion hath light with darkness? And what concord hath Christ with Belial? or what part hath he that believeth with an infidel? And what agreement hath the temple of God with idols?—Love not the world, neither the things that are in the world. If any man love the world, the love of the Father is not in him. The world passeth away, and the lust thereof: but he that doeth the will of God abideth for ever.

In time past ye walked according to the course of this world, according to the prince of the power of the air, the spirit that now worketh in the children of disobedience.—Ye have not so learned Christ; if so be that ye that have heard him, . . . as the truth is in Jesus.

ROMANS 12: 2. James 4: 4. II Corinthians 6: 14-16.—
I John 2: 15-17. Ephesians 2: 2.—Ephesians 4: 20, 21.

SEPTEMBER 12

I have seen his ways, and will heal him.

I AM the LORD that healeth thee.

O LORD, thou hast searched me, and known me.
Thou knowest my downsitting and mine uprising,
thou understandest my thoughts afar off. Thou com-
passeth my path and my lying down, and art acquainted with all my ways.—Thou hast set our
iniquities before thee, our secret sins in the light of
thy countenance.—All things are naked and opened
unto the eyes of him with whom we have to do.

Come now, and let us reason together, saith the
LORD: though your sins be as scarlet, they shall be
as white as snow; though they be red like crimson,
they shall be as wool.—He is gracious unto him, and
saith, Deliver him from going down to the pit: I have
found a ransom.—He was wounded for our transgressions, he was bruised for our iniquities: the chastisement of our peace was upon him; and with his stripes
we are healed.—Thy faith hath made thee whole.

ISAIAH 57: 18. Exodus 15: 26. Psalms 139: 1-3.—Psalms
90: 8.—Hebrews 4: 13. Isaiah 1: 18.—Job 33: 24.—Isaiah 53:
5.—Mark 3: 34.

If any man thirst, let him come unto me, and drink.

My soul longeth, yea, even fainteth for the courts of the Lord: my heart and my flesh crieth out for the living God.—O God, thou art my God; early will I seek thee: my soul thirsteth for thee, my flesh longeth for thee in a dry and thirsty land where no water is; to see thy power and thy glory, so as I have seen thee in the sanctuary.

Ho, every one that thirsteth, come ye to the waters, and he that hath no money; come ye, buy, and eat; yea, come, buy wine and milk without money and without price.—The Spirit and the bride say, Come. And let him that heareth say, Come. And let him that is athirst come. And whosoever will, let him take the water of life freely.—Whosoever drinketh of the water that I shall give him shall never thirst; but the water that I shall give him shall be in him a well of water springing up into everlasting life.—My blood is drink indeed.

Eat, O friends; drink, yea, drink abundantly, O beloved.

JOHN 7: 37. Psalms 84: 2.—Psalms 63: 1, 2. Isaiah 55: 1.—Revelation 22: 17.—John 4: 14.—John 6: 55. Canticles 5: 1.

SEPTEMBER 14

I, even I, am he that comforteth you.

Blessed be God, even the Father of our Lord Jesus Christ, the Father of mercies, and the God of all comfort; who comforteth us in all our tribulation, that we may be able to comfort them which are in any trouble, by the comfort wherewith we ourselves are comforted of God.—Like as a father pitieth his children, so the Lord pitieth them that fear him. For he knoweth our frame; he remembereth that we are dust. —As one whom his mother comforteth, so will I comfort you.—Casting all your care upon him, for he careth for you.

Thou, O Lord, art a God full of compassion, and gracious, long-suffering, and plenteous in mercy and truth.

Another Comforter . . . even the Spirit of truth. —The Spirit . . . helpeth our infirmities.

God shall wipe away all tears from their eyes; and there shall be no more death, neither sorrow, nor crying, neither shall there be any more pain, for the former things are passed away.

ISAIAH 51: 12. II Corinthians 1: 3, 4.—Psalms 103: 13, 14.—Isaiah 66: 13.—I Peter 5: 7. Psalms 86: 15. John 14: 16, 17.—Romans 8: 26. Revelation 21: 4.

SEPTEMBER 15

> Sin shall not have dominion over you: for ye
> are not under the law, but under grace.

WHAT then? shall we sin, because we are not under the law, but under grace? God forbid.—My brethren, ye . . . are become dead to the law by the body of Christ; that ye should be married to another, even to him who is raised from the dead, that we should bring forth fruit unto God.—Being not without law to God, but under the law to Christ.

The sting of death is sin; and the strength of sin is the law. But thanks be to God, which giveth us the victory through our Lord Jesus Christ.

The law of the Spirit of life in Christ Jesus hath made me free from the law of sin and death.—Whosoever committeth sin is the servant of sin.—If the Son . . . shall make you free, you shall be free indeed.

Stand fast therefore in the liberty wherewith Christ hath made us free, and be not entangled again with the yoke of bondage.

ROMANS 6: 14. Romans 6: 15.—Romans 7: 4.—I Corinthians 9: 21. I Corinthians 15: 56, 57. Romans 8: 2.—John 8: 34, 36. Galatians 5: 1.

259

SEPTEMBER 16

The Lord pondereth the hearts.

THE LORD knoweth the way of the righteous; but the way of the ungodly shall perish.—The LORD will show who are his, and who is holy.—Thy Father which seeth in secret himself shall reward thee openly.

Search me, O God, and know my heart: try me, and know my thoughts: and see if there be any wicked way in me, and lead me in the way everlasting. —There is no fear in love; but perfect love casteth out fear.

Lord, all my desire is before thee; and my groaning is not hid from thee.—When my spirit was overwhelmed within me, then thou knewest my path.—He that searcheth the hearts knoweth what is the mind of the Spirit, because he maketh intercession for the saints according to the will of God.

The foundation of God standeth sure, having this seal, The Lord knoweth them that are his. And let every one that nameth the name of Christ depart from iniquity.

PROVERBS 21: 2. Psalms 1: 6.—Numbers 16: 5.—Matthew 6: 6. Psalms 139: 23, 24.—I John 4: 18. Psalms 38: 9.— Psalms 142: 3.—Romans 8: 27. II Timothy 2: 19.

A bruised reed shall he not break.

THE sacrifices of God are a broken spirit: a broken and a contrite heart, O God, thou wilt not despise. —He healeth the broken in heart, and bindeth up their wounds.—Thus saith the high and lofty One that inhabiteth eternity, whose name is Holy; I dwell in the high and holy place, with him also that is of a contrite and humble spirit, to revive the spirit of the humble, and to revive the heart of the contrite ones. For I will not contend for ever, neither will I be always wroth: for the spirit should fail before me, and the souls which I have made.

I will seek that which was lost, and bring again that which was driven away, and will bind up that which was broken, and will strengthen that which was sick.—Wherefore lift up the hands which hang down, and the feeble knees; and make straight paths for your feet, lest that which is lame be turned out of the way; but let it rather be healed.

Behold, your God . . . will come and save you.

MATTHEW 12: 20. Psalms 51: 17.—Psalms 147: 3.—Isaiah 57: 15, 16. Ezekiel 34: 16.—Hebrews 12: 12, 13. Isaiah 35: 4.

SEPTEMBER 18

Open thou mine eyes, that I may behold wondrous things out of thy law.

THEN opened he their understanding, that they might understand the Scriptures.—It is given unto you to know the mysteries of the kingdom of heaven, but to them it is not given.—I thank thee, O Father, Lord of heaven and earth, because thou hast hid these things from the wise and prudent, and hast revealed them unto babes. Even so, Father: for so it seemed good in thy sight.—We have received, not the spirit of the world, but the Spirit which is of God; that we might know the things that are freely given to us of God.—How precious are thy thoughts unto me, O God! how great is the sum of them! If I should count them, they are more in number than the sand. O the depth of the riches both of the wisdom and knowledge of God! how unsearchable are his judgments, and his ways past finding out! For who hath known the mind of the Lord? or who hath been his counsellor? For of him, and through him, and to him are all things: to whom be glory for ever. Amen.

PSALMS 119: 18. Luke 24: 45.—Matthew 13: 11.—Matthew 11: 25, 26.—I Corinthians 2: 12.—Psalms 139: 17, 18.—Romans 11: 33, 34, 36.

The God of all grace.

I WILL proclaim the name of the LORD before thee: and will be gracious to whom I will be gracious.—He is gracious unto him, and saith, Deliver him from going down to the pit: I have found a ransom.—Being justified freely by his grace, through the redemption that is in Christ Jesus: whom God hath set forth to be a propitiation through faith in his blood, to declare his righteousness for the remission of sins that are past, through the forbearance of God.—Grace and truth came by Jesus Christ.

By grace are ye saved through faith; and that not of yourselves; it is the gift of God.—Grace, mercy, and peace, from God our Father and Jesus Christ our Lord.—Unto every one of us is given grace according to the measure of the gift of Christ.—As every man hath received the gift, even so minister the same one to another, as good stewards of the manifold grace of God.—He giveth more grace.

Grow in grace, and in the knowledge of our Lord and Saviour Jesus Christ. To him be glory both now and for ever.

I PETER 5: 10. Exodus 33: 19.—Job 33: 24.—Romans 3: 24, 25.—John 1: 17. Ephesians 2: 8.—I Timothy 1: 2.—Ephesians 4: 1.—I Peter 4: 10.—James 4: 6. II Peter 3: 18.

SEPTEMBER 20

Happy is the man that findeth wisdom, and the man that getteth understanding.

Whoso findeth me findeth life, and shall obtain favor of the LORD.

Thus saith the LORD, Let not the wise man glory in his wisdom, neither let the mighty man glory in his might: . . . but let him that glorieth glory in this, that he understandeth and knoweth me, that I am the LORD.—The fear of the Lord is the beginning of wisdom.

What things were gain to me, those I counted loss for Christ. Yea, doubtless, and I count all things but loss for the excellency of the knowledge of Christ Jesus my Lord: for whom I have suffered the loss of all things, and do count them but dung that I may win Christ.—In whom are hid all the treasures of wisdom and knowledge.—Counsel is mine, and sound wisdom: I am understanding; I have strength.

Christ Jesus . . . is made unto us wisdom, and righteousness, and sanctification, and redemption.— He that winneth souls is wise.

PROVERBS 3: 13. Proverbs 8: 35. Jeremiah 9: 23, 24.— Proverbs 9: 10. Philippians 3: 7, 8.—Colossians 2: 3.— Proverbs 8: 14. I Corinthians 1: 30.—Proverbs 11: 30.

We know that all things work together for good
to them that love God.

Surely the wrath of man shall praise thee; the remainder of wrath shalt thou restrain.—Ye thought evil against me: but God meant it unto good.

All things are yours; whether . . . the world, or life, or death, or things present, or things to come; all are yours: and ye are Christ's; and Christ is God's.

All things are for your sakes, that the abundant grace might through the thanksgiving of many redound to the glory of God. For which cause we faint not; but though our outward man perish, yet the inward man is renewed day by day. For our light affliction, which is but for a moment, worketh for us a far more exceeding and eternal weight of glory.

My brethren, count it all joy when ye fall into divers temptations; knowing this, that the trying of your faith worketh patience. But let patience have her perfect work, that ye may be perfect and entire, wanting nothing.

ROMANS 8: 28. Psalms 76: 10.—Genesis 50:20. I Corinthians 3: 21-23. I Corinthians 4: 15-17. James 1: 2-4.

SEPTEMBER 22

> My meditation of him shall be sweet: I will be
> glad in the Lord.

As the apple-tree among the trees of the wood, so
is my beloved among the sons. I sat down under his
shadow with great delight, and his fruit was sweet to
my taste.—For who in the heaven can be compared
unto the LORD? who among the sons of the mighty
can be likened unto him?

My beloved is white and ruddy, the chiefest among
ten thousand.—One pearl of great price.—The prince
of the kings of the earth.

His head is as the most fine gold, his locks are
bushy, and black as a raven.—The head over all
things.—He is the head of the body, the church.

His cheeks are as a bed of spices, as sweet flowers.—
He could not be hid.

His lips like lilies, dropping sweetsmelling myrrh.
—Never man spake like this man.

His countenance is as Lebanon, excellent as the
cedars.—Make thy face to shine upon thy servant.—
LORD, lift thou up the light of thy countenance upon
us.

PSALMS 104: 34. Canticles 2: 3.—Psalms 80: 6. Canticles
5: 10.—Matthew 13: 46. Revelation 1: 5. Canticles 5: 11.—
Ephesians 1: 22.—Colossians 1: 18. Canticles 5: 13.—Mark
7: 24. Canticles 5: 13.—John 7: 46. Canticles 5: 15.—
Psalms 31: 16.—Psalms 4: 6.

Our God hath not forsaken us.

Beloved, think it not strange concerning the fiery trial which is to try you, as though some strange thing happened unto you.—If ye endure chastening, God dealeth with you as with sons; for what son is he whom the father chasteneth not? But if ye be without chastisement, whereof all are partakers, then are ye bastards and not sons.

The Lord your God proveth you, to know whether ye love the Lord your God with all your heart and with all your soul.

The Lord will not forsake his people, for his great name's sake; because it hath pleased the Lord to make you his people.—Can a woman forget her sucking child, that she should not have compassion on the son of her womb? yea, they may forget, yet will I not forget thee.—Happy is he that hath the God of Jacob for his help, whose hope is in the Lord his God.

Shall not God avenge his own elect which cry day and night unto him, though he bear long with them? I tell you that he will avenge them speedily.

EZRA 9: 9. I Peter 4: 12.—Hebrews 12: 7, 8. Deuteronomy 13: 3. I Samuel 12: 22.—Isaiah 49: 15.—Psalms 146: 5. Luke 18: 7, 8.

SEPTEMBER 24

It is good for me to draw near to God.

LORD, I have loved the habitation of thy house, and the place where thine honor dwelleth.—A day in thy courts is better than a thousand. I had rather be a doorkeeper in the house of my God, than to dwell in the tents of wickedness.—Blessed is the man whom thou choosest, and causest to approach unto thee, that he may dwell in thy courts: we shall be satisfied with the goodness of thy house, even of thy holy temple.

The LORD is good unto them that wait for him, to the soul that seeketh him.—Therefore will the LORD wait that he may be gracious unto you, and therefore will he be exalted, that he may have mercy upon you: for the LORD is a God of judgment: blessed are all they that wait for him.

Having therefore, brethren, boldness to enter into the holiest by the blood of Jesus, by a new and living way, which he hath consecrated for us; . . . let us draw near with a true heart in full assurance of faith, having our hearts sprinkled from an evil conscience.

PSALMS 73: 28. Psalms 26: 8.—Psalms 84: 10.—Psalms 65: 4. Lamentations 3: 25.—Isaiah 30: 18. Hebrews 10: 19, 20, 22.

> Let patience have her perfect work, that ye may
> be perfect and entire, wanting nothing.

Now for a season, if need be, ye are in heaviness through manifold temptations; that the trial of your faith, being much more precious than of gold that perisheth, though it be tried with fire, might be found unto praise and honor and glory at the appearing of Jesus Christ.—We glory in tribulations: . . . knowing that tribulation worketh patience; and patience, experience; and experience, hope.

It is good that a man should both hope and quietly wait for the salvation of the Lord.—Ye have in heaven a better and an enduring substance. Cast not away therefore your confidence, which hath great recompense of reward. For ye have need of patience, that, after ye have done the will of God, ye might receive the promise.—Our Lord Jesus Christ himself, and God, even our Father, which hath loved us, and hath given us everlasting consolation and good hope through grace, comfort your hearts.

JAMES 1: 4. I Peter 1: 6, 7.—Romans 5: 3, 4. Lamentations 3: 26.—Hebrews 10: 34-36.—II Thessalonians 2: 16, 17.

SEPTEMBER 26

A God of truth and without iniquity, just and right is he.

Hᴜᴍ that judgeth righteously.—We must all appear before the judgment-seat of Christ; that every one may receive the things done in his body, according to that he hath done, whether it be good or bad.—Every one of us shall give account of himself to God.—The soul that sinneth it shall die.

Awake, O sword, against my Shepherd, and against the Man that is my Fellow, saith the Lᴏʀᴅ of hosts: smite the Shepherd.—The Lᴏʀᴅ hath laid on him the iniquity of us all.—Mercy and truth are met together: righteousness and peace have kissed each other.—Mercy rejoiceth against judgment.

The wages of sin is death: but the gift of God is eternal life through Jesus Christ our Lord.

A just God and a Saviour: there is none beside me.—Just, and the justifier of him which believeth in Jesus.—Justified freely by his grace through the redemption that is in Christ Jesus.

DEUTERONOMY 32: 4. I Peter 2: 23.—II Corinthians 5: 10.—Romans 14: 12.—Ezekiel 18: 4. Zechariah 13: 7.—Isaiah 53: 6.—Psalms 85: 10.—James 2: 15. Romans 6: 23. Isaiah 45: 21.—Romans 3: 26.—Romans 3: 24.

Humble yourselves under the mighty hand of God, that he may exalt you in due time.

Every one that is proud in heart is an abomination to the LORD: though hand join in hand he shall not be unpunished.

O LORD, thou art our Father; we are the clay, and thou our potter; and we all are the work of thy hand. Be not wroth very sore, O LORD, neither remember iniquity for ever: behold, see, we beseech thee, we are all thy people.—Thou hast chastised me, and I was chastised, as a bullock unaccustomed to the yoke: turn thou me, and I shall be turned; for thou art the LORD my God. Surely after that I was turned, I repented: and after that I was instructed, I smote upon my thigh: I was ashamed, yea, even confounded, because I did bear the reproach of my youth. —It is good for a man that he bear the yoke in his youth.

Affliction cometh not forth of the dust, neither doth trouble spring out of the ground; yet man is born unto trouble, as the sparks fly upward.

I PETER 5: 6. Proverbs 16: 5. Isaiah 64: 8, 9.—Jeremiah 31: 18, 19. Lamentations 3: 27. Job 5: 6, 7.

SEPTEMBER 28

They shall put my name upon the children of Israel; and I will bless them.

O LORD our God, other lords beside thee have had dominion over us; but by thee only will we make mention of thy name.—We are thine; thou never bearest rule over them; they were not called by thy name.

All people of the earth shall see that thou art called by the name of the LORD: and they shall be afraid of thee.—The LORD will not forsake his people, for his great name's sake: because it hath pleased the LORD to make you his people.

O Lord, hear; O Lord, forgive; O Lord, hearken and do; defer not, for thine own sake, O my God: for thy city and thy people are called by thy name. —Help us, O God of our salvation, for the glory of thy name: and deliver us, and purge away our sins, for thy name's sake. Wherefore should the heathen say, Where is their God?—The name of the Lord is a strong tower: the righteous runneth into it, and is safe.

NUMBERS 6: 27. Isaiah 26: 13.—Isaiah 63: 19. Deuteronomy 28: 10.—I Samuel 12: 22. Daniel 9: 19.—Psalms 79: 9, 10.—Proverbs 18: 10.

Hereby perceive we the love of God, because he
laid down his life for us.

THE love of Christ, which passeth knowledge.—
Greater love hath no man than this, that a man lay
down his life for his friends.—Ye know the grace of
our Lord Jesus Christ, that, though he was rich, yet
for your sakes he became poor, that ye through his
poverty might be rich.—Beloved, if God so loved us,
we ought also to love one another.—Be ye kind one
to another, tender-hearted, forgiving one another,
even as God for Christ's sake hath forgiven you.—
Forbearing one another, and forgiving one another,
if any man have a quarrel against any: even as Christ
forgave you, so also do ye.—For even the Son of man
came not to be ministered unto, but to minister, and
to give his life a ransom for many.—Christ . . . suffered for us, leaving us an example, that ye should
follow his steps.

For I have given you an example, that ye should
do as I have done to you.—We ought to lay down
our lives for the brethren.

I JOHN 3: 16. Ephesians 3: 19.—John 15: 13.—II Corinthians 8: 9.—I John 4: 11.—Ephesians 4: 32.—Colossians
3: 13.—Mark 10: 45.—I Peter 2: 21. John 13: 15.—I John
3: 16.

SEPTEMBER 30

He knoweth the way that I take: when he hath tried me, I shall come forth as gold.

He knoweth our frame.—He doth not afflict willingly nor grieve the children of men.

The foundation of God standeth sure, having this seal, The Lord knoweth them that are his. And, Let every one that nameth the name of Christ depart from iniquity. But in a great house there are not only vessels of gold and of silver, but also of wood and of earth; and some to honor, and some to dishonor. If a man therefore purge himself from these, he shall be a vessel unto honor, sanctified and meet for the master's use, and prepared unto every good work.

He shall sit as a refiner and purifier of silver; and he shall purify the sons of Levi, and purge them as gold and silver, that they may offer unto the Lord an offering in righteousness.—I . . . will refine them as silver is refined, . . . they shall call on my name, and I will hear them: I will say, It is my people: and they shall say, The LORD is my God.

JOB 23: 10. Psalms 103: 14.—Lamentations 3: 33. II Timothy 2: 19-21. Malachi 3: 13.—Zechariah 13: 9.

274

The fruit of the Spirit is temperance.

Every man that striveth for the mastery is temperate in all things. Now they do it to obtain a corruptible crown; but we an incorruptible. I therefore so run, not as uncertainly; so fight I, not as one that beateth the air: but I keep under my body, and bring it into subjection: lest that by any means, when I have preached to others, I myself should be castaway.

Be not drunk with wine, wherein is excess; but be filled with the Spirit.

Let us not sleep, as do others; but let us watch and be sober. For they that sleep, sleep in the night: and they that be drunken are drunken in the night. But let us, who are of the day, be sober.—Denying ungodliness and worldly lusts, we should live soberly, righteously, and godly in this present world.

GALATIANS 5: 22. I Corinthians 9: 25-27. Ephesians 5: 18. Matthew 16: 24. I Thessalonians 5: 6-8.—Titus 2: 12, 13.

OCTOBER 2

The goat shall bear upon him all their iniquities
into a land not inhabited: and he shall let go the
goat in the wilderness.

As far as the east is from the west, so far hath he
removed our transgressions from us.—In those days,
and in that time, saith the LORD, the iniquity of Israel
shall be sought for, and there shall be none: and
the sins of Judah, and they shall not be found: for
I will pardon them whom I reserve.—Thou wilt cast
all their sins into the depths of the sea. Who is a God
like unto thee, that pardoneth iniquity?

All we like sheep have gone astray: we have turned
every one to his own way: and the LORD hath laid on
him the iniquity of us all.—He shall bear their iniquities. Therefore will I divide him a portion with
the great, and he shall divide the spoil with the strong,
because he hath poured out his soul unto death: and
he was numbered with the transgressors; and he bare
the sin of many, and made intercession for the transgressors.—The Lamb of God, which taketh away the
sin of the world.

LEVITICUS 16: 22. Psalms 103: 12.—Jeremiah 50: 20.—
Micah 7: 19, 18. Isaiah 53: 6.—Isaiah 53: 11, 12.—John 1: 29.

Unto him that loved us, and washed us from our sins in his own blood.

MANY waters cannot quench love, neither can the floods drown it. Love is strong as death.—Greater love hath no man than this, that a man lay down his life for his friends.

Who his own self bare our sins in his own body on the tree, that we, being dead to sins, should live unto righteousness: by whose stripes ye were healed. —In whom we have redemption through his blood, the forgiveness of sins, according to the riches of his grace.

Ye are washed, . . . ye are sanctified, . . . ye are justified in the name of the Lord Jesus, and by the Spirit of our God.—Ye are a chosen generation, a royal priesthood, a holy nation, a peculiar people; that ye should show forth the praises of him who hath called you out of darkenss into his marvellous light.

I beseech you . . . brethren, by the mercies of God, that ye present your bodies a living sacrifice, Holy, acceptable unto God, which is your reasonable service.

REVELATION 1: 5. Canticles 8: 7, 6.—John 15: 13. I Peter 2: 24.—Ephesians 1: 7. I Corinthians 6: 11.—I Peter 2: 9. Romans 12: 1.

OCTOBER 4

Moses wist not that the skin of his face shone
while he talked with him.

Not unto us, O Lord, not unto us, but unto thy
name give glory.—Lord, when saw we thee a-hun-
gered, and fed thee? or thirsty, and gave thee drink?
—In lowliness of mind, let each esteem other better
than themselves.—Be clothed with humility.

[Jesus] was transfigured before them: and his face
did shine as the sun, and his raiment was white as
the light.—All that sat in the council, looking steadfastly on [Stephen,] saw his face as it had been the
face of an angel.—The glory which thou gavest me,
I have given them.—We all, with open face beholding
as in a glass the glory of the Lord, are changed into
the same image from glory to glory, even as by the
Spirit of the Lord.

Ye are the light of the world.—A city that is set on
a hill cannot be hid. Neither do men light a candle,
and put it under a bushel, but on a candlestick; and
it giveth light unto all that are in the house.

EXODUS 34: 29. Psalms 115: 1.—Matthew 25: 37.—Philippians 2: 3.—I Peter 5: 5. Matthew 17: 2.—Acts 6: 15.—
John 17: 22.—II Corinthians 3: 18. Matthew 5: 14, 15.

Call upon me in the day of trouble: I will deliver thee, and thou shalt glorify me.

WHY art thou cast down, O my soul? and why art thou disquieted within me? hope thou in God: for I shall yet praise him, who is the health of my countenance, and my God.—LORD, thou hast heard the desire of the humble: thou wilt prepare their heart, thou wilt cause thine ear to hear.—For thou, Lord, art good, and ready to forgive; and plenteous in mercy unto all them that call upon thee.

Jacob said unto his household, . . . Let us arise, and go up to Beth-el, and I will make there an altar unto God, who answered me in the day of my distress, and was with me in the way which I went.

I love the LORD, because he hath heard my voice and my supplications. Because he hath inclined his ear unto me, therefore will I call upon him as long as I live. The sorrows of death compassed me, and the pains of hell gat hold upon me. Then called I on the name of the LORD.

PSALMS 50: 15. Psalms 42: 11.—Psalms 10: 17.—Psalms 86: 5. Genesis 35: 2, 3. Psalms 116: 1-4.

OCTOBER 6

The Lord God omnipotent reigneth.

I KNOW that thou canst do everything.—

The things which are impossible with men are possible with God.—He doeth according to his will in the army of heaven, and among the inhabitants of the earth: and none can stay his hand, or say unto him, What doest thou?—There is none that can deliver out of my hand: I will work, and who shall let it?

Abba, Father, all things are possible unto thee.

Believe ye that I am able to do this! They said unto him, Yea, Lord. Then touched he their eyes, saying, According to your faith be it unto you.—Lord, if thou wilt, thou canst make me clean. And Jesus put forth his hand, and touched him, saying, I will; be thou clean.—The mighty God.—All power is given unto me in heaven and in earth.

Some trust in chariots, and some in horses: but we will remember the name of the LORD our God.— Be strong and courageous, be not afraid nor dismayed, ... there be more with us than with him.

REVELATION 19: 6. Job 42: 2.—Luke 18: 27.—Daniel 4: 35.—Isaiah 43: 13. Mark 14: 36. Matthew 9: 28, 29.—Matthew 8: 2, 3.—Isaiah 9: 6.—Matthew 28: 18. Psalms 20: 7.— II Chronicles 32: 7.

The meek will he teach his way.

Blessed are the meek.

I returned, and saw under the sun, that the race is not to the swift, nor the battle to the strong, neither yet bread to the wise, nor yet riches to men of understanding, nor yet favor to men of skill.—A man's heart deviseth his way: but the Lord directeth his steps.

Unto thee lift I up mine eyes, O thou that dwellest in the heavens. Behold, as the eyes of servants look unto the hand of their masters, and as the eyes of a maiden unto the hand of her mistress: so our eyes wait upon the Lord our God.—Cause me to know the way wherein I should walk; for I lift up my soul unto thee.

O our God, wilt thou not judge them? for we have no might against this great company that cometh against us; neither know we what to do; but our eyes are upon thee.

If any of you lack wisdom, let him ask of God, that giveth to all men liberally, and upbraideth not; and it shall be given him.

PSALMS 25: 9. Matthew 5: 5. Ecclesiastes 9: 11.—Proverbs 16: 9. Psalms 123: 1, 2.—Psalms 143: 8. II Chronicles 20: 12. James 1: 5.

OCTOBER 8

I will not fear what man shall do unto me.

WHO shall separate us from the love of Christ? shall tribulation, or distress, or persecution, or famine, or nakedness, or peril, or sword? Nay, in all these things we are more than conquerors through him that loved us.

Be not afraid of them that kill the body, and after that have no more that they can do. But I will forewarn you whom ye shall fear: Fear him, which after he hath killed hath power to cast into hell; yea, I say unto you, Fear him.

Blessed are they which are persecuted for righteousness' sake: for theirs is the kingdom of heaven. Blessed are ye, when men shall revile you, and persecute you, and shall say all manner of evil against you falsely, for my sake. Rejoice, and be exceeding glad: for great is your reward in heaven.—None of these things move me, neither count I my life dear unto myself, so that I might finish my course with joy.—I will speak of thy testimonies . . . before kings, and will not be ashamed.

HEBREWS 13: 6. Romans 8: 35, 37. Luke 12: 4, 5. Matthew 10-12.—Acts 20: 24.—Psalms 119:46.

Thou art a God ready to pardon, gracious and merciful.

THE LORD is not slack concerning his promise, as some men count slackness; but is long-suffering to us-ward, not willing that any should perish, but that all should come to repentance.—The long-suffering of our Lord is salvation.

For this cause I obtained mercy, that in me first Jesus Christ might show forth all long-suffering, for a pattern to them which should hereafter believe on him to life everlasting.—Whatsoever things were written for our learning, that we through patience and comfort of the Scriptures might have hope.

Despisest thou the riches of his goodness and forbearance and long-suffering; not knowing that the goodness of God leadeth thee to repentance?

Rend your heart, and not your garments, and turn unto the LORD your God: for he is gracious and merciful, slow to anger, and of great kindness, and repenteth him of the evil.

NEHEMIAH 9: 17. II Peter 3: 9.—II Peter 3: 15. I Timothy 1: 16.—Romans 15: 4. Romans 2: 4. Joel 2: 13.

OCTOBER 10

The whole family in heaven and earth.

ONE God and Father of all, who is above all, and through all, and in you all.—Ye are all the children of God by faith in Christ Jesus.—That in the dispensation of the fulness of times, he might gather together in one all things in Christ, both which are in heaven, and which are on earth; even in him.

He is not ashamed to call them brethren.—Behold my mother and my brethren! Whosoever shall do the will of my Father which is in heaven, the same is my brother, and sister, and mother.—Go to my brethren, and say unto them, I ascend unto my Father, and your Father.

I saw under the altar the souls of them that were slain for the word of God, and for the testimony which they held; . . . and white robes were given unto every one of them: and it was said unto them, that they should rest for a little season, until their fellow-servants also and their brethren, that should be killed as they were, should be fulfilled.—That they without us should not be made perfect.

EPHESIANS 3: 15. Ephesians 4: 6.—Galatians 3: 26.—Ephesians 1: 10. Hebrews 2: 11.—Matthew 12: 49, 50.—John 20: 17. Revelation 6: 9-11.—Hebrews 11: 40.

Be not far from me; for trouble is near.

How long wilt thou forget me, O LORD? for ever? how long wilt thou hide thy face from me? How long shall I take counsel in my soul, having sorrow in my heart daily?—Hide not thy face far from me; put not thy servant away in anger: thou hast been my help; leave me not, neither forsake me, O God of my salvation.

He shall call upon me, and I will answer him: I will be with him in trouble; I will deliver him, and honor him.—The LORD is nigh unto all them that call upon him, to all that call upon him in truth. He will fulfil the desire of them that fear him; he also will hear their cry, and will save them.

I will not leave you comfortless: I will come to you.—Lo, I am with you alway, even unto the end of the world.

God is our refuge and strength, a very present help in trouble.—Truly my soul waiteth upon God: from him cometh my salvation. My soul, wait thou only upon God; for my expectation is from him.

PSALMS 22: 11. Psalms 13: 1, 2.—Psalms 27: 9. Psalms 91: 15.—Psalms 145: 18, 19. John 14: 18.—Matthew 28: 20. Psalms 46: 1.—Psalms 62: 1, 5.

OCTOBER 12

> God was in Christ, reconciling the world unto
> himself, not imputing their trespasses unto them.

I T pleased the Father, that in him should all fulness
dwell; and, having made peace through the blood of
his cross, by him to reconcile all things unto himself.
—Mercy and truth are met together; righteousness and
peace have kissed each other.

I know the thoughts that I think toward you, saith
the LORD, thoughts of peace and not of evil.—Come
now, and let us reason together, saith the Lord:
though your sins be as scarlet, they shall be as white
as snow; though they be red like crimson, they shall
be as wool.

Who is a God like unto thee, that pardoneth
iniquity?

Acquaint now thyself with him, and be at peace.
—Work out your own salvation with fear and trembling. For it is God which worketh in you both to
will and to do of his good pleasure.—Lord, thou wilt
ordain peace for us: for thou also hast wrought all
our works in us.

II CORINTHIANS 5: 19. Colossians 1: 19, 20.—Psalms
85: 10. Jeremiah 29: 11.—Isaiah 1: 18. Micah 7: 18. Job
22: 21.—Philippians 2: 12, 13.—Isaiah 26: 12.

From the first day that thou didst set thy heart to chasten thyself before thy God, thy words were heard.

THUS saith the high and lofty One that inhabiteth eternity, whose name is Holy; I dwell in the high and holy place, with him also that is of a contrite and humble spirit, to revive the spirit of the humble, and to revive the heart of the contrite ones.—The sacrifices of God are a broken spirit: a broken and a contrite heart, O God, thou wilt not despise.—Though the LORD be high, yet hath he respect unto the lowly: but the proud he knoweth afar off.—Humble yourselves therefore under the mighty hand of God, that he may exalt you in due time.—God resisteth the proud, but giveth grace unto the humble. Submit yourselves therefore to God.

Thou, Lord, art good, and ready to forgive and plenteous in mercy unto all them that call upon thee. Give ear, O LORD, unto my prayer; and attend to the voice of my supplications. In the day of my trouble I will call upon thee: for thou wilt answer me.

DANIEL 10: 12. Isaiah 57: 15.—Psalms 51: 17.—Psalms 138: 6.—I Peter 5: 6.—James 4: 6, 7. Psalms 86: 5-7.

OCTOBER 14

Christ both died, and rose, and revived, that he might be Lord both of the dead and living.

It pleased the LORD to bruise him: he hath put him to grief: when thou shalt make his soul an offering for sin, he shall see his seed, he shall prolong his days, and the pleasure of the LORD shall prosper in his hand. He shall see of the travail of his soul, and shall be satisfied: by his knowledge shall my righteous servant justify many; for he shall bear their iniquities. —Ought not Christ to have suffered these things, and to enter into his glory?—We thus judge, that if one died for all, then were all dead: and that he died for all, that they which live should not henceforth live unto themselves, but unto him which died for them, and rose again.

Let all the house of Israel know assuredly, that God hath made that same Jesus, whom ye have crucified, both Lord and Christ.—Who verily was foreordained before the foundation of the world, but was manifest in these last times for you, who by him do believe in God.

ROMANS 14: 9. Isaiah 53: 10, 11. Luke 24: 26.—II Corinthians 5: 14, 15. Acts 2: 36.—I Peter 1: 20, 22.

God is my defense.

THE LORD is my rock and my fortress, and my deliverer; the God of my rock; in him will I trust: he is my shield, and the horn of my salvation, my high tower, and my refuge, my Saviour.—The LORD is my strength and my shield; my heart trusted in him, and I am helped: therefore my heart greatly rejoiceth; and with my song will I praise him.

When the enemy shall come in like a flood, the Spirit of the LORD shall lift up a standard against him.—We may boldly say, The LORD is my helper, and I will not fear what man shall do unto me.—The LORD is my light and my salvation; whom shall I fear? the LORD is the strength of my life; of whom shall I be afraid?

As the mountains are round about Jerusalem, so the LORD is round about his people from henceforth even for ever.—Because thou hast been my help, therefore in the shadow of thy wings will I rejoice.

For thy name's sake lead me and guide me.

PSALMS 59: 9. II Samuel 22: 2, 3.—Psalms 28: 7. Isaiah 59: 19.—Hebrews 13: 6.—Psalms 27: 1. Psalms 125: 2.—Psalms 63: 7. Psalms 31: 3.

OCTOBER 16

Not slothful in business; fervent in spirit; serving the Lord.

WHATSOEVER thy hand findeth to do, do it with thy might; for there is no work, nor device, nor knowledge, nor wisdom in the grave, whither thou goest. —Whatsoever ye do, do it heartily, as to the Lord, and not unto men; knowing that of the Lord ye shall receive the reward of the inheritance: for ye serve the Lord Christ.—Whatsoever good thing any man doeth, the same shall he receive of the Lord.

I must work the works of him that sent me, while it is day: the night cometh, when no man can work. —Wist ye not that I must be about my Father's business?—The zeal of thy house hath eaten me up.

Brethren, give diligence to make your calling and election sure: for if ye do these things, ye shall never fall.—We desire that every one of you do show the same diligence to the full assurance of hope unto the end: that ye be not slothful, but followers of them who through faith and patience inherit the promises. So run, that ye may obtain.

ROMANS 12: 11. Ecclesiastes 9: 10.—Colossians 3: 23, 24.—Ephesians 6: 8. John 9: 4.—Luke 2: 49.—John 2: 17. II Peter 1: 10.—Hebrews 6: 11, 12.—I Corinthians 9: 24.

In thy name shall they rejoice all the day; and in thy righteousness shall they be exalted.

IN the LORD have I righteousness and strength, even to him shall men come; and all that are incensed against him shall be ashamed. In the Lord shall all the seed of Israel be justified, and shall glory.—Be glad in the LORD, and rejoice, ye righteous: and shout for joy, all ye that are upright in heart.

The righteousness of God without the law is manifested, being witnessed by the law and the prophets; even the righteousness of God which is by faith of Jesus Christ unto all and upon all them that believe. To declare . . . at this time his righteousness: that he might be just, and the justifier of him which believeth in Jesus.

Whom having not seen, ye love; in whom, though now ye see him not, yet believing, ye rejoice with joy unspeakable and full of glory.

Rejoice in the Lord always: and again I say, Rejoice.

PSALMS 89: 16. Isaiah 45: 24, 25.—Psalms 32: 11. Romans 3: 21, 22, 26. I Peter 1: 8. Philippians 4· 4.

OCTOBER 18

One of the soldiers with a spear pierced his side,
and forthwith there came out blood and water.

BEHOLD the blood of the covenant, which the Lord
hath made with you.—The life of the flesh is in the
blood: and I have given it to you upon the altar to
make an atonement for your souls.—It is not possible
that the blood of bulls and of goats should take away
sins.

Jesus said unto them, This is my blood of the new
testament, which is shed for many.—By his own blood
he entered in once into the holy place, having obtained eternal redemption for us.—Peace through the
blood of his cross.

Ye know that ye were not redeemed with corruptible things, as silver and gold, . . . but with the
precious blood of Christ, as of a lamb without
blemish.

Then will I sprinkle clean water upon you, and
ye shall be clean: . . . from all your idols will I
cleanse you.—Let us draw near with a true heart, in
full assurance of faith, having our hearts sprinkled
from an evil conscience.

JOHN 19: 34. Exodus 24: 8.—Leviticus 17: 11.—Hebrews
10: 4. Mark 14: 24.—Hebrews 9: 12.—Colossians 1: 20.
I Peter 1: 20. I Peter 1: 18, 19. Ezekiel 36: 25.—Hebrews
10: 22.

The Lord shall be thy confidence, and shall keep thy foot from being taken.

SURELY the wrath of man shall praise thee: the remainder of wrath shalt thou restrain.—The king's heart is in the hand of the LORD, as the rivers of water: he turneth it whithersoever he will.—When a man's ways please the LORD, he maketh even his enemies to be at peace with him.

I wait for the LORD, my soul doth wait, and in his word do I hope. My soul waiteth for the Lord more than they that watch for the morning: I say, more than they that watch for the morning.—I sought the LORD, and he heard me, and delivered me from all my fears.

The eternal God is thy refuge, and underneath are the everlasting arms: and he shall thrust out the enemy from before thee; and shall say, Destroy them.—Blessed is the man that trusteth in the Lord, and whose hope the LORD is.

What shall we then say to these things? If God be for us, who can be against us?

PROVERBS 3: 26. Psalms 76: 10.—Proverbs 21: 1.—Proverbs 16: 7. Psalms 130: 5, 6.—Psalms 34: 4. Deuteronomy 33: 27.—Jeremiah 17: 7. Romans 8: 31.

OCTOBER 20

I delight in the law of God after the inward man.

O HOW love I thy law! it is my meditation all the day.—Thy words were found, and I did eat them; and thy word was unto me the joy and rejoicing of my heart.—I sat down under his shadow with great delight, and his fruit was sweet to my taste.—I esteemed the words of his mouth more than my necessary food.

I delight to do thy will, O my God: yea, thy law is within my heart.—My meat is to do the will of him that sent me, and to finish his work.

The statutes of the LORD are right, rejoicing the heart: the comandment of the Lord is pure, enlightening the eyes. More to be desired are they than gold, yea, than much fine gold: sweeter also than honey and the honeycomb.

Be ye doers of the word, and not hearers only, deceiving your own selves. For if any be a hearer of the word, and not a doer, he is like unto a man beholding his natural face in a glass.

ROMANS 7: 22. Psalms 119: 97.—Jeremiah 15: 16.—Canticles 2: 3.—Job 23: 12. Psalms 40: 8.—John 4: 34. Psalms 19: 8, 10. James 1: 22, 23.

Of his fulness have all we received, and grace
for grace.

THIS is my beloved Son, in whom I am well pleased.
—Behold, what manner of love the Father hath be-
stowed upon us, that we should be called the sons of
God.

His Son, whom he hath appointed heir of all
things.—If children, then heirs; heirs of God, and
joint heirs with Christ; if so be that we suffer with
him, that we may be also glorified together.

I and my Father are one. The Father is in me,
and I in him.—My Father, and your Father; and . . .
my God, and your God.—I in them, and thou in me,
that they may be made perfect in one.

The church, which is his body, the fulness of him
that filleth all in all.—He said unto me, My grace is
sufficient for thee; for my strength is made perfect
in weakness.—He giveth more grace.

Having therefore these promises, dearly beloved,
let us cleanse ourselves from all filthiness of the flesh
and spirit, perfecting holiness in the fear of God.

JOHN 1: 16. Matthew 17: 5.—I John 3: 1. Hebrews 1:
2.—Romans 8: 17. John 10: 30, 38.—John 20: 17.—John 17:
23. Ephesians 1: 22, 23.—II Corinthians 12: 9.—James 4:
6.—II Corinthians 7: 1.

OCTOBER 22

O God, my heart is fixed.

THE LORD is my light and my salvation, whom shall I fear? the LORD is the strength of my life; of whom shall I be afraid?

Thou wilt keep him in perfect peace, whose mind is stayed on thee: because he trusteth in thee.—He shall not be afraid of evil tidings: his heart is fixed, trusting in the LORD. His heart is established, he shall not be afraid, until he see his desire upon his enemies.

What time I am afraid, I will trust in thee.—In the time of trouble he shall hide me in his pavilion: in the secret of his tabernacle shall he hide me; he shall set me up upon a rock. And now shall my head be lifted up above mine enemies round about me: therefore will I offer in his tabernacle sacrifices of joy; I will sing, yea, I will sing praises unto the LORD.

The God of all grace, who hath called us unto his eternal glory by Christ Jesus, after that ye have suffered awhile, make you perfect, stablish, strengthen, settle you. To him be glory and dominion for ever and ever.

PSALMS 108: 1. Psalms 27: 1. Isaiah 26: 3.—Psalms 112: 7, 8. Psalms 56: 3.—Psalms 27: 5, 6. I Peter 5: 10, 11.

A man's life consisteth not in the abundance of the things which he possesseth.

A LITTLE that a righteous man hath is better than the riches of many wicked.—Better is little with the fear of the LORD than great treasure and trouble therewith.—Godliness with contentment is great gain. Having food and raiment let us be therewith content.

Give me neither poverty nor riches; feed me with food convenient for me: lest I be full, and deny thee, and say, Who is the LORD? or lest I be poor, and steal, and take the name of my God in vain.—Give us this day our daily bread.

Take no thought for your life, what ye shall eat, or what ye shall drink; nor yet for your body, what ye shall put on.—When I sent you without purse, and scrip, and shoes, lacked ye anything? And they said, Nothing.—Let your conversation be without covetousness: and be content with such things as ye have: for he hath said, I will never leave thee, nor forsake thee.

LUKE 12: 15. Psalms 37: 16.—Proverbs 15: 16.—I Timothy 6: 6, 8. Proverbs 30: 8, 9.—Matthew 6: 11. Matthew 6: 25.—Luke 22: 35.—Hebrews 13: 5.

OCTOBER 24

I am cast out of thy sight; yet I will look again toward thy holy temple.

ZION said, The LORD hath forsaken me, and my Lord hath forgotten me. Can a woman forget her sucking child? yea, they may forget, yet will I not forget thee.

I forgat prosperity. And I said, My strength and my hope is perished from the LORD.—Awake, why sleepest thou, O LORD? arise, cast us not off for ever. —Why sayest thou, O Jacob, and speakest, O Israel, My way is hid from the LORD, and my judgment is passed over from my God?—In a little wrath I hid my face from thee for a moment: but with everlasting kindness will I have mercy on thee, saith the LORD thy Redeemer.

Why art thou cast down, O my soul? and why art thou disquieted within me? hope in God: for I shall yet praise him, who is the health of my countenance. —We are troubled on every side, yet not distressed: we are perplexed, but not in despair; persecuted, but not forsaken; cast down, but not destroyed.

JONAH 2: 4. Isaiah 49: 14, 15. Lamentations 13: 17, 18.— Psalms 44: 23.—Isaiah 40: 27.—Isaiah 54: 8. Psalms 43: 5.— II Corinthians 4: 8, 9.

Lo, I am with you alway, even unto the end of the world.

I<small>F</small> two of you shall agree on earth as touching anything that they shall ask, it shall be done for them of my Father which is in heaven. For where two or three are gathered together in my name, there am I in the midst of them.

He that hath my commandments, and keepeth them, he it is that loveth me: and he that loveth me shall be loved of my Father, and I will love him, and will manifest myself to him.

Lord, how is it that thou wilt manifest thyself unto us, and not unto the world? . . . If a man love me, he will keep my words: and my Father will love him, and we will come unto him, and make our abode with him.

Unto him that is able to keep you from falling, and to present you faultless before the presence of his glory with exceeding joy, to the only wise God our Saviour, be glory and majesty, dominion and power, both now and ever. Amen.

MATTHEW 28: 20. Matthew 18: 19, 20. John 14: 21. John 14: 22, 23. Jude 24, 25.

OCTOBER 26

The Lord reigneth.

FEAR ye not me? saith the LORD: will ye not tremble at my presence, which have placed the sand for the bound of the sea by a perpetual decree, that it cannot pass it: and though the waves thereof toss themselves, yet can they not prevail; though they roar, yet can they not pass over it?—Promotion cometh neither from the east, nor from the west, nor from the south. But God is the judge: he putteth down one, and setteth up another.

He changeth the times and the seasons: he removeth kings, and setteth up kings: he giveth wisdom unto the wise, and knowledge to them that know understanding.—Ye shall hear of wars and rumors of wars: see that ye be not troubled.

If God be for us, who can be against us?—Are not two sparrows sold for a farthing? and one of them shall not fall on the ground without your Father. The very hairs of your head are all numbered. Fear ye not therefore, ye are of more value than many sparrows.

PSALMS 99: 1. Jeremiah 5: 22.—Psalms 75: 6, 7. Daniel 2: 21.—Matthew 24: 6. Romans 8: 31.—Matthew 10: 29-31.

Himself took our infirmities, and bare our sicknesses.

THEN shall the priest command to take for him that is to be cleansed two birds alive and clean, and cedar-wood, and scarlet, and hyssop; and the priest shall command that one of the birds be killed in an earthen vessel over running water: as for the living bird, he shall take it, and the cedar-wood, and the scarlet, and the hyssop, and shall dip them and the living bird in the blood of the bird that was killed over the running water: and he shall sprinkle upon him that is to be cleansed from the leprosy seven times, and shall pronounce him clean, and shall let the living bird loose into the open field.

Behold a man full of leprosy: who seeing Jesus fell on his face, and besought him, saying, LORD, if thou wilt, thou canst make me clean.—And Jesus, moved with compassion, put forth his hand, and touched him, and saith unto him, I will; be thou clean. And as soon as he had spoken, immediately the leprosy departed from him, and he was cleansed.

MATTHEW 8: 17. Leviticus 14: 4-7. Luke 5: 12.—Mark 1: 41, 42.

OCTOBER 28

He saw that there was no man, and wondered that there was no intercessor: therefore his arm brought salvation unto him.

SACRIFICE and offering thou didst not desire: mine ears hast thou opened: burnt offering and sin offering hast thou not required. Then said I, Lo, I come: in the volume of the book it is written of me, I delight to do thy will, O my God: yea, thy law is within my heart.—I lay down my life, that I might take it again. No man taketh it from me, but I lay it down of myself. I have power to lay it down, and I have power to take it again.

There is no God else beside me: a just God and a Saviour; there is none beside me. Look unto me, and be ye saved, all the ends of the earth: for I am God, and there is none else.—There is none other name under heaven given among men, whereby we must be saved.

Ye know the grace of our Lord Jesus Christ, that, though he was rich, yet for your sakes he became poor, that ye through his poverty might be rich.

ISAIAH 59: 16. Psalms 40: 6-8.—John 10: 17, 18. Isaiah 45: 21, 22.—Acts 4: 12. II Corinthians 8: 9.

He is altogether lovely.

M Y meditation of him shall be sweet.—My beloved is . . . the chiefest among ten thousand.—A chief cornerstone, elect, precious: and he that believeth on him shall not be confounded.

Thou art fairer than the children of men: grace is poured into thy lips.—God . . . hath highly exalted him, and given him a name which is above every name.—It pleased the Father that in him should all fulness dwell.

Whom having not seen, ye love; in whom though now ye see him not, yet believing, ye rejoice with joy unspeakable and full of glory.

I count all things but loss, for the excellency of the knowledge of Christ Jesus my Lord: for whom I have suffered the loss of all things, and do count them but dung, that I may win Christ, and be found in him, not having mine own righteousness which is of the law, but that which is through the faith of Christ, the righteousness which is of God by faith.

CANTICLES 5: 16. Psalms 104: 34.—Canticles 5: 10.—
I Peter 2: 6. Psalms 45: 2.—Philippians 2: 9.—Colossians
1: 19. I Peter 1: 8. Philippians 3: 8, 9.

OCTOBER 30

It is good that a man should both hope and quietly wait for the salvation of the Lord.

Hath God forgotten to be gracious? hath he in anger shut up his tender mercies?—I said in my haste, I am cut off from before thine eyes: nevertheless thou heardest the voice of my supplications when I cried unto thee.

Shall not God avenge his own elect, which cry day and night unto him, though he bear long with them? I tell you that he will avenge them speedily.—Wait on the Lord, and he shall save thee.—Rest in the Lord, and wait patiently for him: fret not thyself because of him who prospereth in his way, because of the man who bringeth wicked devices to pass.

Ye shall not need to fight in this battle: set yourselves, stand ye still, and see the salvation of the Lord.

Let us not be weary in well doing: . . . in due season we shall reap, if we faint not.—Behold, the husbandman waiteth for the precious fruit of the earth, and hath long patience for it.

LAMENTATIONS 3: 26. Psalms 77: 9.—Psalms 31: 22. Luke 18: 7, 8.—Proverbs 20: 22.—Psalms 37: 7. II Chronicles 20: 17. Galatians 6: 9.—James 5: 7.

Not by might, nor by power, but by my spirit, saith the Lord of hosts.

Who hath directed the Spirit of the LORD, or being his counsellor, hath taught him?

God hath chosen the foolish things of the world to confound the wise; and God hath chosen the weak things of the world to confound the things which are mighty; and base things of the world, and things which are despised, hath God chosen, yea, and things which are not, to bring to naught things that are: that no flesh should glory in his presence.

The wind bloweth where it listeth, and thou hearest the sound thereof, but canst not tell whence it cometh and whither it goeth: so is every one that is born of the Spirit.—Born not of blood, nor of the will of the flesh, nor of the will of man, but of God.

My Spirit remaineth among you: fear ye not.—The battle is not yours, but God's.

The LORD saveth not with sword and spear; for the battle is the LORD's.

ZECHARIAH 4: 6. Isaiah 40: 13. I Corinthians 1: 27-29. John 3: 8.—John 1: 13. Haggai 2: 5.—II Chronicles 20: 15. I Samuel 17: 47.

NOVEMBER 1

> Blessed is the man that heareth me, watching daily at my gates, waiting at the posts of my doors.

Behold, as the eyes of servants look unto the hand of their masters, and as the eyes of a maiden unto the hand of her mistress, so our eyes wait upon the Lord our God, until that he have mercy upon us.

Where I will meet you, to speak there unto thee.— In all places where I record my name I will come unto thee, and I will bless thee.

Where two or three are gathered together in my name, there am I in the midst of them.

The hour cometh, and now is, when the true worshippers shall worship the Father in spirit and in truth: for the Father seeketh such to worship him. God is a Spirit: and they that worship him must worship him in spirit and in truth.

Praying always with all prayer and supplication in the Spirit.

PROVERBS 8: 34. Psalms 123: 2. Exodus 29: 42.—Exodus 20: 24. Matthew 18: 20. John 4: 23, 24. Ephesians 6: 18.

Ever follow that which is good.

For even hereunto were ye called: because Christ also suffered for us, leaving us an example, that ye should follow his steps: who did no sin, neither was guile found in his mouth: who, when he was reviled, reviled not again; . . . but committed himself to him that judgeth righteously.—Consider him that endured such contradiction of sinners against himself, lest ye be wearied and faint in your minds.

Let us lay aside every weight, and the sin which doth so easily beset us, and let us run with patience the race that is set before us, looking unto Jesus, the author and finisher of our faith; who for the joy that was set before him endured the cross, . . . and is set down at the right hand of the throne of God.

Finally, brethren, whatsoever things are true, whatsoever things are honest, whatsoever things are just, whatsoever things are pure, whatsoever things are lovely, whatsoever things are of good report; if there be any virtue, and if there be any praise, think on these things.

I THESSALONIANS 5: 15. I Peter 2: 21-23.—Hebrews 12: 3. Hebrews 12: 1, 2. Philippians 4: 8.

NOVEMBER 3

The ways of the Lord are right, and the just shall walk in them: but the transgressors shall fall therein.

Unto you . . . which believe he is precious: but unto them which be disobedient, . . . a stone of stumbling and a rock of offence.—The way of the LORD is strength to the upright: but destruction shall be to the workers of iniquity.

He that hath ears to hear, let him hear.—Whoso is wise, and will observe these things, even they shall understand the lovingkindness of the LORD.—The light of the body is the eye: if therefore thine eye be single, thy whole body shall be full of light. But if thine eye be evil, thy whole body shall be full of darkness.—If any man will do his will, he shall know of the doctrine, whether it be of God.—Whosoever hath, to him shall be given.

He that is of God heareth God's words: ye therefore hear them not, because ye are not of God.—Ye will not come unto me, that ye might have life.—My sheep hear my voice, and I know them, and they follow me.

HOSEA 14: 9. I Peter 2: 7, 8.—Proverbs 10: 29. Matthew 11: 15.—Psalms 107: 43.—Matthew 6: 22.—John 7: 17.—Matthew 13: 12. John 8: 47.—John 5: 40.—John 10: 27.

Now for a season, if need be, ye are in heaviness through manifold temptations.

Bᴇʟᴏᴠᴇᴅ, think it not strange concerning the fiery trial which is to try you, as though some strange thing happened unto you: but rejoice, inasmuch as ye are partakers of Christ's sufferings; that, when his glory shall be revealed, ye may be glad also with exceeding joy.——The exhortation . . . speaketh unto you as unto children. My son, despise not thou the chastening of the Lord, nor faint when thou art rebuked of him.—Now no chastening for the present seemeth to be joyous, but grievous: nevertheless afterward it yieldeth the peaceable fruit of righteousness unto them which are exercised thereby.

We have not a high priest which cannot be touched with the feeling of our infirmities; but was in all points tempted like as we are, yet without sin.—For in that he himself hath suffered being tempted, he is able to succor them that are tempted.—God is faithful, who will not suffer you to be tempted above that ye are able.

I PETER 1: 6. I Peter 4: 12, 13.—Hebrews 12: 5.— Hebrews 12: 11. Hebrews 4: 15.—Hebrews 2: 18.—I Corinthians 10: 13.

NOVEMBER 5

Take thou also unto thee principal spices, and thou shalt make it an oil of holy ointment.

Upon man's flesh shall it not be poured, neither shall ye make any other like it, after the composition of it: it is holy, and it shall be holy unto you.—One Spirit.—Diversities of gifts, but the same Spirit.

Thy God hath anointed thee with the oil of gladness above thy fellows.—God anointed Jesus of Nazareth with the Holy Ghost and with power.—God giveth not the Spirit by measure unto him.

Of his fulness have all we received.—As the same anointing teacheth you of all things, and is truth, and is no lie, and even as it hath taught you, ye shall abide in him.—He which . . . hath anointed us, is God; who hath also sealed us, and given the earnest of the Spirit in our hearts.

The fruit of the Spirit is love, joy, peace, long-suffering, gentleness, goodness, faith, meekness, temperance: against such there is no law.

EXODUS 30: 23, 25. Exodus 30: 32.—Ephesians 4: 4.—I Corinthians 12: 4. Psalms 45: 7.—Acts 10: 38.—John 3: 34. John 1: 16.—I John 2: 27.—II Corinthians 1: 21, 22. Galatians 5: 22, 23.

When Christ, who is our life, shall appear, then shall ye also appear with him in glory.

I AM the resurrection, and the life: he that believeth in me, though he were dead, yet shall he live.—God hath given to us eternal life, and this life is in his Son. He that hath the Son hath life: and he that hath not the Son of God hath not life.

The Lord himself shall descend from heaven with a shout, with the voice of the archangel, and with the trump of God: and the dead in Christ shall rise first: then we which are alive and remain shall be caught up together with them in the clouds, to meet the Lord in the air: and so shall we ever be with the Lord. Wherefore comfort one another with these words.—When he shall appear, we shall be like him; for we shall see him as he is.—It is sown in dishonor; it is raised in glory: it is sown in weakness; it is raised in power.

If I go and prepare a place for you, I will come again, and receive you unto myself; that where I am, there ye may be also.

COLOSSIANS 3: 4. John 11: 25.—I John 5: 11, 12. I Thessalonians 4: 16-18.—I John 3: 2.—I Corinthians 15: 43. John 14: 3.

NOVEMBER 7

Oh that men would praise the Lord for his goodness, and for his wonderful works to the children of men.

O TASTE and see that the LORD is good: blessed is the man that trusteth in him.—How great is thy goodness, which thou hast laid up for them that fear thee!

This people have I formed for myself; they shall show forth my praise.—Having predestinated us unto the adoption of children by Jesus Christ to himself, according to the good pleasure of his will, to the praise of the glory of his grace, wherein he hath made us accepted in the beloved. That we should be to the praise of his glory, who first trusted in Christ.

How great is his goodness and how great is his beauty!—The LORD is good to all: and his tender mercies are over all his works. All thy works shall praise thee, O LORD; and thy saints shall bless thee. They shall speak of the glory of thy kingdom, and talk of thy power; to make known to the sons of men his mighty acts, and the glorious majesty of his kingdom.

PSALMS 107: 8. Psalms 34: 8.—Psalms 31: 19. Isaiah 43: 21.—Ephesians 1: 5, 6, 12. Zechariah 9: 17.—Psalms 145: 9-12.

NOVEMBER 8

Let us, who are of the day, be sober, putting on the breastplate of faith and love; and for a helmet, the hope of salvation.

GIRD up the loins of your mind, be sober, and hope to the end for the grace that is to be brought unto you at the revelation of Jesus Christ.—Stand therefore, having your loins girt about with truth, and having on the breastplate of righteousness: above all, taking the shield of faith, wherewith ye shall be able to quench all the fiery darts of the wicked. And take the helmet of salvation, and the sword of the Spirit, which is the word of God.

He will swallow up death in victory; and the Lord God will wipe away tears from off all faces; and the rebuke of his people shall he take away from off all the earth. And it shall be said in that day, Lo, this is our God: we have waited for him, and he will save us: this is the LORD; we have waited for him, we will be glad and rejoice in his salvation.

Faith is the substance of things hoped for, the evidence of things not seen.

I THESSALONIANS 5: 8. I Peter 1: 13.—Ephesians 6: 14, 16, 17. Isaiah 25: 8, 9. Hebrews 11: 1.

NOVEMBER 9

I have laid help upon one that is mighty; I have exalted one chosen out of the people.

I, EVEN I, am the LORD; and beside me there is no saviour.—There is one God, and one mediator between God and men, the man Christ Jesus.—There is none other name under heaven given among men, whereby we must be saved.

The mighty God.—Who made himself of no reputation, and took upon him the form of a servant, and was made in the likeness of men: and being found in fashion as a man, he humbled himself, and became obedient unto death, even the death of the cross. Wherefore God also hath highly exalted him, and given him a name which is above every name.—We see Jesus, who was made a little lower than the angels for the suffering of death, crowned with glory and honor; that he by the grace of God should taste death for every man.—Forasmuch . . . as the children are partakers of flesh and blood, he also himself likewise took part of the same.

PSALMS 89: 19. Isaiah 43: 11.—I Timothy 2: 5.—Acts 4: 12. Isaiah 9: 6.—Philippians 2: 7-9.—Hebrews 2: 9.—Hebrews 2: 14.

Fruitful in every good work, and increasing in the knowledge of God.

I BESEECH you, . . . brethren, by the mercies of God, that ye present your bodies a living sacrifice, holy, acceptable unto God, which is your reasonable service. And be not conformed to this world: but be ye transformed by the renewing of your mind, that ye may prove what is that good, and acceptable, and perfect, will of God.—As ye have yielded your members servants to uncleanness and to iniquity unto iniquity; even so now yield your members servants to righteousness unto holiness.—In Christ Jesus neither circumcision availeth anything, nor uncircumcision, but a new creature. And as many as walk according to this rule, peace be on them, and mercy.

Herein is my Father glorified, that ye bear much fruit; so shall ye be my disciples.—Ye have not chosen me, but I have chosen you, and ordained you, that ye should go and bring forth fruit, and that your fruit should remain.

COLOSSIANS 1: 10. Romans 12: 1. 2 —Romans 6: 19.—
Galatians 6: 15, 16. John 15: 8.—John 15: 16.

NOVEMBER 11

He led them on safely.

I LEAD in the way of righteousness, in the midst of the paths of judgment.

Behold, I send an Angel before thee, to keep thee in the way, and to bring thee into the place which I have prepared.—In all their affliction he was afflicted, and the Angel of his presence saved them: in his love and in his pity he redeemed them; and he bare them, and carried them all the days of old.

They got not the land in possession by their own sword, neither did their own arm save them; but thy right hand, and thine arm, and the light of thy countenance, because thou hadst a favor unto them. —So didst thou lead thy people, to make thyself a glorious name.

Lead me, O LORD, in thy righteousness because of mine enemies; make thy way straight before my face. —O send out thy light and thy truth: let them lead me; let them bring me unto thy holy hill, and to thy tabernacles. Then will I go unto the altar of God, unto God my exceeding joy: yea, upon the harp will I praise thee, O God.

PSALMS 78: 53. Proverbs 8: 20. Exodus 23: 20.—Isaiah 63: 9. Psalms 44: 3.—Isaiah 63: 14. Psalms 5: 8.—Psalms 43: 3, 4.

Godly sorrow worketh repentance not to be repented of.

PETER remembered the word of Jesus, which said unto him, Before the cock crow thou shalt deny me thrice. And he went out, and wept bitterly.—If we confess our sins, he is faithful and just to forgive us our sins, and to cleanse us from all unrighteousness. —The blood of Jesus Christ his Son cleanseth us from all sin.

Mine iniquities have taken hold upon me, so that I am not able to look up; they are more than the hairs of my head: therefore my heart faileth me. Be pleased, O LORD, to deliver me: O LORD, make haste to help me.

Turn thou to thy God: keep mercy and judgment, wait on thy God continually.

The sacrifices of God are a broken spirit: a broken and a contrite heart, O God, thou wilt not despise.— He healeth the broken in heart.—He hath showed thee, O man, what is good: and what doth the LORD require of thee, but to do justly, and to love mercy, and to walk humbly with thy God?

II CORINTHIANS 7: 10. Matthew 26: 75.—I John 1: 9.— I John 1: 7. Psalms 40: 12, 13. Hosea 12: 6. Psalms 51: 17.—Psalms 147: 3.—Micah 6: 8.

NOVEMBER 13

Christ loved the church, and gave himself for it; that he might sanctify and cleanse it with the washing of water by the word.

WALK in love, as Christ also hath loved us, and hath given himself for us an offering and a sacrifice to God for a sweet-smelling savor.

Being born again, not of corruptible seed, but of incorruptible, by the word of God, which liveth and abideth forever.—Sanctify them through thy truth: thy word is truth.—Except a man be born of water and of the Spirit, he cannot enter into the kingdom of God.

Not by works of righteousness which we have done, but according to his mercy he saved us, by the washing of regeneration, and renewing of the Holy Ghost.—Thy word hath quickened me.

The law of the LORD is perfect, converting the soul: the testimony of the LORD is sure, making wise the simple. The statutes of the Lord are right, rejoicing the heart: the commandment of the LORD is pure, enlightening the eyes.

EPHESIANS 5: 25, 26. Ephesians 5: 2. I Peter 1: 23.— John 17: 17.—John 3: 5. Titus 3: 5.—Psalms 119: 59. Psalms 19: 7, 8.

Thou art my help and my deliverer; make no tarrying, O my God.

THE steps of a good man are ordered by the LORD: and he delighteth in his way. Though he fall, he shall not be utterly cast down: for the LORD upholdeth him with his hand.—In the fear of the LORD is strong confidence: and his children shall have a place of refuge.

Who art thou, that thou shouldest be afraid of a man that shall die, and of the son of man which shall be made as grass; and forgettest the LORD thy Maker?

I am with thee to deliver thee.—Be strong and of a good courage, fear not, nor be afraid of them: for the LORD thy God, he it is that doth go with thee; he will not fail thee, nor forsake thee.

I will sing of thy power; yea, I will sing aloud of thy mercy in the morning: for thou hast been my defence and refuge in the day of my trouble.—Thou art my hiding-place; thou shalt preserve me from trouble: thou shalt compass me about with songs of deliverance.

PSALMS 40: 17. Psalms 37: 23, 24.—Proverbs 14: 26. Isaiah 51: 12, 13. Jeremiah 1: 8.—Deuteronomy 31: 6. Psalms 59: 16.—Psalms 32: 7.

NOVEMBER 15

God is faithful, by whom ye were called unto the fellowship of his Son Jesus Christ our Lord.

Let us hold fast the profession of our faith without wavering; for he is faithful that promised.—God hath said, I will dwell in them, and walk in them; and I will be their God, and they shall be my people.— Truly our fellowship is with the Father, and with his Son Jesus Christ.—Rejoice, inasmuch as ye are partakers of Christ's sufferings; that, when his glory shall be revealed, ye may be glad also with exceeding joy.

That Christ may dwell in your hearts by faith; that ye, being rooted and grounded in love, may be able to comprehend with all saints what is the breadth, and length, and depth, and height; and to know the love of Christ, which passeth knowledge, that ye might be filled with all the fulness of God.

Whosoever shall confess that Jesus is the Son of God, God dwelleth in him, and he in God.—And he that keepeth his commandments dwelleth in Him, and He in him.

I CORINTHIANS 1: 9. Hebrews 10: 23.—II Corinthians 6: 16.—I John 1: 3.—I Peter 4: 13. Ephesians 3: 17-19. I John 4: 15.—I John 3: 24.

Sanctify them through thy truth: thy word is truth.

Now ye are clean through the word which I have spoken unto you.—Let the word of Christ dwell in you richly in all wisdom.

Wherewithal shall a young man cleanse his way? by taking heed thereto according to thy word. With my whole heart have I sought thee: O let me not wander from thy commandments.

When wisdom entereth into thy heart, and knowledge is pleasant unto thy soul: discretion shall preserve thee, understanding shall keep thee.

My foot hath held his steps, his way have I kept, and not declined. Neither have I gone back from the commandment of his lips; I have esteemed the words of his mouth more than my necessary food.—I have more understanding than all my teachers: for thy testimonies are my meditation.—If ye continue in my word, then are ye my disciples indeed; and ye shall know the truth, and the truth shall make you free.

JOHN 17: 17. John 15: 3.—Colossians 3: 16. Psalms 119: 9, 10. Proverbs 2: 10, 11. Job 23: 12.—Psalms 119: 99.— John 8: 31, 32.

NOVEMBER 17

Thy thoughts are very deep.

W<small>E</small> . . . do not cease to pray for you, and to desire that ye might be filled with the knowledge of his will in all wisdom and spiritual understanding.—That ye, being rooted and grounded in love, may be able to comprehend with all saints what is the breadth, and length, and depth, and height; and to know the love of Christ, which passeth knowledge, that ye might be filled with all the fulness of God.

O the depth of the riches both of the wisdom and knowledge of God! how unsearchable are his judgments, and his ways past finding out!—My thoughts are not your thoughts, neither are your ways my ways, saith the L<small>ORD</small>. For as the heavens are higher than the earth, so are my ways higher than your ways, and my thoughts than your thoughts.—Many, O L<small>ORD</small> my God, are thy wonderful works which thou hast done, and thy thoughts which are to us-ward: they cannot be reckoned up in order unto thee: if I would declare and speak of them, they are more than can be numbered.

PSALMS 92: 5. Colossians 1: 9.—Ephesians 3: 17-19. Romans 11: 33.—Isaiah 55: 8, 9.—Psalms 40: 5.

He stayeth his rough wind in the day of the east wind.

LET us fall now into the hand of the LORD; for his mercies are great.—I am with thee, saith the LORD, to save thee: . . . I will correct thee in measure, and will not leave thee altogether unpunished.—He will not always chide: neither will he keep his anger for ever. He hath not dealt with us after our sins, nor rewarded us according to our iniquities. For he knoweth our frame; he remembereth that we are dust.—I will spare them, as a man spareth his own son that serveth him.

God is faithful, who will not suffer you to be tempted above that ye are able; but will with the temptation also make a way to escape, that ye may be able to bear it.—Satan hath desired to have you, that he may sift you as wheat: but I have prayed for thee, that thy faith fail not.

Thou hast been a strength to the poor, a strength to the needy in his distress, a refuge from the storm, a shadow from the heat, when the blast of the terrible ones is as a storm against the wall.

ISAIAH 27: 8. II Samuel 24: 14.—Jeremiah 30: 11.— Psalms 103: 9, 10, 14.—Malachi 3: 17. I Corinthians 10: 13.—Luke 22: 31, 32. Isaiah 25: 4.

NOVEMBER 19

By their fruits ye shall know them.

LITTLE children, let no man deceive you: he that doeth righteousness is righteous, even as He is righteous.—Doth a fountain send forth at the same place sweet water and bitter? Can the fig-tree, my brethren, bear olive berries? either a vine, figs? so can no fountain both yield salt water and fresh. Who is a wise man and endued with knowledge among you? let him show out of a good conversation his works with meekness of wisdom.—Having your conversation honest among the Gentiles: that, whereas they speak against you as evil-doers, they may by your good works, which they shall behold, glorify God in the day of visitation.

Either make the tree good, and his fruit good; or else make the tree corrupt and his fruit corrupt: for the tree is known by his fruit.—A good man out of the good treasure of the heart bringeth forth good things: and an evil man out of the evil treasure bringeth forth evil things.

What could have been done more to my vineyard, that I have not done in it?

MATTHEW 7: 20. I John 3: 7.—James 3: 11-13.—
I Peter 2: 12. Matthew 12: 33.—Matthew 12: 35. Isaiah 5: 4.

When I sit in darkness, the Lord shall be a light unto me.

WHEN thou passest through the waters, I will be with thee; and through the rivers, they shall not overflow thee: when thou walkest through the fire, thou shalt not be burned; neither shall the flame kindle upon thee. For I am the LORD thy God, the Holy One of Israel, thy Saviour.—I will bring the blind by a way that they knew not; I will lead them in paths that they have not known: I will make darkness light before them, and crooked things straight. These things will I do unto them, and not forsake them.

Yea, though I walk through the valley of the shadow of death, I will fear no evil: for thou art with me; thy rod and thy staff they comfort me.—What time I am afraid, I will trust in thee. In God I will praise his word, in God I have put my trust; I will not fear what flesh can do unto me.—The LORD is my light and my salvation; whom shall I fear? the LORD is the strength of my life, of whom shall I be afraid?

MICAH 7: 8. Isaiah 43: 2, 3.—Isaiah 42: 16. Psalms 23: 4.—Psalms 56: 3, 4.—Psalms 27: 1.

Him that cometh to me I will in no wise cast
out.

IT shall come to pass, when he crieth unto me, that
I will hear: for I am gracious.—I will not cast them
away, neither will I abhor them, to destroy them
utterly, and to break my covenant with them: for I
am the LORD their God.—I will remember my covenant with thee in the days of thy youth, and I will
establish unto thee an everlasting covenant.

Come now, and let us reason together, saith the
LORD: though your sins be as scarlet, they shall be as
white as snow; though they be red like crimson, they
shall be as wool.—Let the wicked forsake his way, and
the unrighteous man his thoughts: and let him return
unto the Lord, and he will have mercy upon him; and
to our God, for he will abundantly pardon.—Lord,
remember me when thou comest into thy kingdom.
And Jesus said unto him, Verily I say unto thee,
To-day shalt thou be with me in paradise.

A bruised reed shall he not break, and the smoking
flax shall he not quench.

JOHN 6: 37. Exodus 22: 27.—Leviticus 26: 44.—Ezekiel
16: 60. Isaiah 1: 18.—Isaiah 55: 7.—Luke 23: 42, 43. Isaiah
42: 3.

Praying in the Holy Ghost.

G<small>OD</small> is a Spirit: and they that worship him must worship him in spirit and in truth.—We . . . have access by one Spirit unto the Father.

O my Father, if it be possible, let this cup pass from me: nevertheless, not as I will, but as thou wilt.

The Spirit . . . helpeth our infirmities: for we know not what we should pray for as we ought: but the Spirit itself maketh intercession for us with groanings which cannot be uttered. And he that searcheth the hearts knoweth what is the mind of the Spirit, because he maketh intercession for the saints according to the will of God.—This is the confidence that we have in him, that, if we ask anything according to his will, he heareth us.—When he, the Spirit of truth, is come, he will guide you into all truth.

Praying always with all prayer and supplication in the Spirit, and watching thereunto with all perseverance and supplication for all saints.

JUDE 20. John 4: 24.—Ephesians 2: 18. Matthew 26: 39. Romans 8: 26, 27.—I John 5: 14.—John 16: 13. Ephesians 6: 18.

Whoso hearkeneth unto me shall dwell safely, and shall be quiet from fear of evil.

LORD, thou hast been our dwelling-place in all generations.—He that dwelleth in the secret place of the Most High shall abide under the shadow of the Almighty.—His truth shall be thy shield and buckler.

Your life is hid with Christ in God.—He that toucheth you toucheth the apple of his eye.—Fear ye not, stand still, and see the salvation of the LORD. The LORD shall fight for you, and ye shall hold your peace. —God is our refuge and strength, a very present help in trouble.

Jesus spake unto them, saying, Be of good cheer; it is I; be not afraid.—Why are ye troubled? and why do thoughts arise in your hearts? Behold my hands and my feet, that it is I myself: handle me, and see; for a spirit hath not flesh and bones, as ye see me have.—I know whom I have believed, and am persuaded that he is able to keep that which I have committed unto him against that day.

PROVERBS 1: 33. Psalms 90: 1.—Psalms 91: 1.—Psalms 91: 4. Colossians 3: 3.—Zechariah 2: 8.—Exodus 14: 13, 14.—Psalms 46: 1. Matthew 14: 27.—Luke 24: 38, 39.— I Timothy 1: 12.

My mother and my brethren are these which
hear the word of God, and do it.

Both he that sanctifieth and they who are sanctified
are all of one: for which cause he is not ashamed to
call them brethren: saying, I will declare thy name
unto my brethren; in the midst of the church will I
sing praise unto thee.—In Jesus Christ neither circumcision availeth anything, nor uncircumcision; but
faith which worketh by love.—Ye are my friends, if
ye do whatsoever I command you.—Blessed are they
that hear the word of God, and keep it.

Not every one that saith unto me, Lord, Lord, shall
enter into the kingdom of heaven: but he that doeth
the will of my Father which is in heaven.—My meat
is to do the will of him that sent me.

If we say that we have fellowship with him, and
walk in darkness we lie, and do not the truth.—Whoso
keepeth his word, in him verily is the love of God
perfected: hereby know we that we are in him.

LUKE 8: 21. Hebrews 2: 11, 12.—Galatians 5: 6.—John
15: 14.—Luke 11: 28. Matthew 7: 21.—John 4: 34. I John
1: 6.—I John 2: 5.

NOVEMBER 25

Being made free from sin, ye became the servants of righteousness.

Ye cannot serve God and Mammon.—When ye were the servants of sin, ye were free from righteousness. What fruit had ye then in those things whereof ye are now ashamed? for the end of those things is death. But now being made free from sin, and become servants to God, ye have your fruit unto holiness, and the end everlasting life.

Christ is the end of the law for righteousness to every one that believeth.

If any man serve me, let him follow me; and where I am, there shall also my servant be: if any man serve me, him will my Father honor.—Take my yoke upon you, and learn of me: for I am meek and lowly in heart: and ye shall find rest unto your souls. For my yoke is easy, and my burden is light.

O Lord our God, other lords beside thee have had dominion over us; but by thee only will we make mention of thy name.—I will run the way of thy commandments, when thou shalt enlarge my heart.

ROMANS 6: 18. Matthew 6: 24.—Romans 6: 19-22. Romans 10: 4. John 12: 26.—Matthew 11: 29, 30. Isaiah 26: 3.—Psalms 119: 32.

The Lord delighteth in thee.

THUS saith the LORD that created thee, . . . Fear not: for I have redeemed thee, I have called thee by thy name; thou art mine.—Can a woman forget her sucking child, that she should not have compassion on the son of her womb? yea, they may forget, yet will I not forget thee. Behold, I have graven thee upon the palms of my hands: thy walls are continually before me.

The steps of a good man are ordered by the LORD: and he delighteth in his way.—My delights were with the sons of men.—The LORD taketh pleasure in them that fear him, in those that hope in his mercy.—They shall be mine, saith the LORD of hosts, in that day when I make up my jewels; and I will spare them as a man spareth his own son that serveth him.

You, that were sometime alienated and enemies in your mind by wicked works, yet now hath he reconciled in the body of his flesh through death, to present you holy and unblamable and unreprovable in his sight.

ISAIAH 62: 4. Isaiah 43: 1.—Isaiah 49: 15, 16. Psalms 37: 23.—Proverbs 8: 31.—Psalms 147: 11.—Malachi 3: 17. Colossians 1: 21, 22.

The glory which thou gavest me I have given them.

I saw . . . the Lord sitting upon a throne, high and lifted up, and his train filled the temple. Above it stood the seraphim. And one cried unto the other, and said, Holy, holy, holy, is the Lord of hosts: the whole earth is full of his glory.—These things said Esaias, when he saw his glory, and spake of him.—Upon the likeness of the throne was the likeness . . . of a man above upon it. As the appearance of the bow that is in the cloud in the day of rain, so was the appearance of the brightness round about. This was the appearance of the likeness of the glory of the Lord.

I beseech thee, show me thy glory. And he said, Thou canst not see my face: for there shall no man see me, and live.—No man hath seen God at any time; the only begotten Son, which is in the bosom of the Father, he hath declared him.—God, who commanded the light to shine out of darkness, hath shined in our hearts, to give the light of the knowledge of the glory of God in the face of Jesus Christ.

JOHN 17: 22. Isaiah 6: 1-3.—John 12: 41.—Ezekiel 1: 26, 28. Exodus 33: 18, 20.—John 1: 18.—II Corinthians 4: 6.

As the body without the spirit is dead, so faith without works is dead also.

Not every one that saith, . . . Lord, Lord, shall enter into the kingdom of heaven; but he that doeth the will of my Father which is in heaven.—Holiness, without which no man shall see the Lord.—Add to your faith virtue; and to virtue knowledge; and to knowledge temperance; and to temperance patience; and to patience godliness; and to godliness brotherly kindness; and to brotherly kindness charity. For if these things be in you, and abound, they make you that ye shall neither be barren nor unfruitful in the knowledge of our Lord Jesus Christ. But he that lacketh these things is blind, and cannot see afar off, and hath forgotten that he was purged from his old sins. Wherefore the rather, brethren, give diligence to make your calling and election sure: for if ye do these things, ye shall never fall.

By grace are ye saved through faith; and that not of yourselves; it is the gift of God.

JAMES 2: 26. Matthew 7: 21.—Hebrews 12: 14. II Peter 1: 5-9. Ephesians 2: 8.

We shall be satisfied with the goodness of thy house.

ONE thing have I desired of the Lord, that will I seek after; that I may dwell in the house of the LORD all the days of my life, to behold the beauty of the LORD, and to inquire in his temple.

Blessed are they which do hunger and thirst after righteousness: for they shall be filled.—He hath filled the hungry with good things: and the rich he hath sent empty away.

He satisfieth the longing soul, and filleth the hungry soul with goodness.—I am the bread of life: he that cometh to me shall never hunger; and he that believeth on me shall never thrist.

How excellent is thy loving-kindness, O God! therefore the children of men put their trust under the shadow of thy wings. They shall be abundantly satisfied with the fatness of thy house; and thou shalt make them drink of the river of thy pleasures. For with thee is the fountain of life: in thy light shall we see light.

PSALMS 65: 4. Psalms 27: 4. Matthew 5: 6.—Luke 1: 53. Psalms 107: 9.—John 6: 35. Psalms 36: 7-9.

The Lord of peace himself give you peace always by all means. The Lord be with you all.

Peace, from him which is, and which was, and which is to come.—The peace of God, which passeth all understanding, shall keep your hearts and minds through Christ Jesus.

Jesus himself stood in the midst of them, and saith unto them, Peace be unto you.—Peace I leave with you, my peace I give unto you: not as the world giveth, give I unto you. Let not your heart be troubled, neither let it be afraid.

The Comforter . . . even the Spirit of truth.—The fruit of the Spirit is love, joy, peace.—The Spirit itself beareth witness with our spirit, that we are the children of God.

My presence shall go with thee, and I will give thee rest. And he said unto him, If thy presence go not with me, carry us not up hence. For wherein shall it be known here that I and thy people have found grace in thy sight? is it not in that thou goest with us?

II THESSALONIANS 3: 16. Revelation 1: 4.—Philippians 4: 7. Luke 24: 36.—John 14: 27. John 15: 26.—Galatians 5: 22.—Romans 8: 16. Exodus 33: 14-16.

DECEMBER 1

A man shall be as a hiding-place from the wind, and a covert from the tempest.

FORASMUCH . . . as the children are partakers of flesh and blood, he also himself likewise took part of the same.—The Man that is my Fellow, saith the LORD of hosts.—I and my Father are one.

He that dwelleth in the secret place of the Most High shall abide under the shadow of the Almighty. —There shall be a tabernacle for a shadow in the daytime from the heat, and for a place of refuge, and for a covert from storm and from rain.—The LORD is thy shade upon thy right hand. The sun shall not smite thee by day, nor the moon by night.

When my heart is overwhelmed: lead me to the rock that is higher than I.—Thou art my hiding-place; thou shalt preserve me from trouble.—Thou hast been a strength to the poor, a strength to the needy in his distress, a refuge from the storm, a shadow from the heat.

ISAIAH 32: 2. Hebrews 2: 14.—Zechariah 13: 7.—John 10: 30. Psalms 91: 1.—Isaiah 4: 6.—Psalms 121: 5, 6. Psalms 61: 2.—Psalms 32: 7.—Isaiah 25: 4.

Ye have an unction from the Holy One, and ye
know all things.

Gᴏᴅ anointed Jesus of Nazareth with the Holy
Ghost and with power.—It pleased the Father that
in him should all fulness dwell.—Of his fulness have
all we received, and grace for grace.

Thou anointest my head with oil.—The anointing
which ye have received of him abideth in you, and
ye need not that any man teach you: but as the same
anointing teacheth you of all things, and is truth, and
is no lie, and even as it hath taught you, ye shall
abide in him.

The Comforter, which is the Holy Ghost, whom
the Father will send in my name, he shall teach you
all things, and bring all things to your remembrance,
whatsoever I have said unto you.

The Spirit also helpeth our infirmities: for we know
not what we should pray for as we ought: but the
Spirit itself maketh intercession for us with groanings
which cannot be uttered.

I JOHN 2: 20. Acts 10: 38.—Colossians 1: 19.—John
1: 16. Psalms 23: 5.—I John 2: 27. John 14: 26. Romans
8: 26.

DECEMBER 3

I would seek unto God, and unto God would I commit my cause.

Is anything too hard for the LORD?—Commit thy way unto the LORD; trust also in him; and he shall bring it to pass.—Be careful for nothing; but in everything by prayer and supplication, with thanksgiving, let your requests be made known unto God.—Casting all your care upon him, for he careth for you.

Hezekiah received the letter from the hand of the messengers, and read it: and Hezekiah went up unto the house of the LORD, and spread it before the LORD. And Hezekiah prayed unto the LORD.

It shall come to pass, that before they call I will answer; and while they are yet speaking, I will hear. —The effectual fervent prayer of a righteous man availeth much.

I love the LORD, because he hath heard my voice and my supplications. Because he hath inclined his ear unto me, therefore will I call upon him as long as I live.

JOB 5: 8. Genesis 18: 14.—Psalms 37: 5.—Philippians 4: 6.—I Peter 5: 7. Isaiah 37: 14, 15. Isaiah 65: 24.—James 5: 16. Psalms 161: 1, 2.

Where shall wisdom be found?

IF any of you lack wisdom, let him ask of God, that giveth to all men liberally, and upbraideth not: and it shall be given him. But let him ask in faith, nothing wavering.—Trust in the LORD with all thy heart; and lean not unto thine own understanding. In all thy ways acknowledge him, and he shall direct thy paths. —The only wise God.—Be not wise in thine own eyes; fear the Lord and depart from evil.

Ah, Lord God! behold, I cannot speak; for I am a child. But the LORD said unto me, Say not, I am a child: for thou shalt go to all that I shall send thee, and whatsoever I command thee thou shalt speak. Be not afraid of their faces: for I am with thee to deliver thee, saith the Lord.

Whatsover ye shall ask the Father in my name, he will give it you. Hitherto have ye asked nothing in my name: ask, and ye shall receive, that your joy may be full.—All things whatsoever ye shall ask in prayer, believing, ye shall receive.

JOB 28: 12. James 1: 5, 6.—Proverbs 3: 5, 6.—I Timothy 1: 17.—Proverbs 3: 7. Jeremiah 1· 6-8. John 16: 23, 24.— Matthew 21: 24.

DECEMBER 5

It is good for me that I have been afflicted; that I might learn thy statutes.

Though he were a Son, yet learned he obedience by the things which he suffered.—We suffer with him, that we may be also glorified together. For I reckon that the sufferings of this present time are not worthy to be compared with the glory which shall be revealed in us.

He knoweth the way that I take: when he hath tried me, I shall come forth as gold. My foot hath held his steps, his way have I kept, and not declined.

Thou shalt remember all the way which the Lord thy God led thee these forty years in the wilderness, to humble thee, and to prove thee, to know what was in thy heart, whether thou wouldest keep his commandment, or no. Thou shalt also consider in thy heart, that, as a man chasteneth his son, so the Lord thy God chasteneth thee. Therefore thou shalt keep the commandments of the Lord thy God, to walk in his ways, and to fear him.

PSALMS 119: 71. Hebrews 5: 8.—Romans 8: 17, 18. Job 23: 10, 11. Deuteronomy 8: 2, 5, 6.

DECEMBER 6

It is God which worketh in you.

Not that we are sufficient of ourselves to think anything as of ourselves; but our sufficiency is of God.—A man can receive nothing, except it be given him from heaven.—No man can come to me, except the Father which hath sent me draw him: and I will raise him up at the last day.—And I will give them one heart, and one way, that they may fear me for ever.

Do not err, my beloved brethren. Every good gift and every perfect gift is from above, and cometh down from the Father of lights, with whom is no variableness, neither shadow of turning. Of his own will begat he us with the word of truth, that we should be a kind of first-fruits of his creatures.

For we are his workmanship, created in Christ Jesus unto good works, which God hath before ordained that we should walk in them.

Lord, thou wilt ordain peace for us: for thou also hast wrought all our works in us.

PHILIPPIANS 2: 13. II Corinthians 3: 5.—John 3: 27.—John 6: 44.—Jeremiah 32: 39. James 1: 16-18. Ephesians 2: 10. Isaiah 26: 12.

DECEMBER 7

> He hath made him to be sin for us, who knew
> no sin; that we might be made the righteous-
> ness of God in him.

THE LORD hath laid on him the iniquity of us all.—
Who his own self bare our sins in his own body on
the tree, that we, being dead to sins, should live unto
righteousness: by whose stripes ye were healed.—As
by one man's disobedience many were made sinners,
so by the obedience of one shall many be made
righteous.

After that the kindness and love of God our
Saviour toward man appeared, not by works of righteousness which we have done, but according to his
mercy he saved us, by the washing of regeneration,
and renewing of the Holy Ghost; which he shed on
us abundantly through Jesus Christ our Saviour; that
being justified by his grace, we should be made heirs
according to the hope of eternal life.—There is therefore now no condemnation to them which are in
Christ Jesus, who walk not after the flesh, but after
the Spirit.

The LORD our Righteousness.

II CORINTHIANS 5: 21. Isaiah 53: 6.—I Peter 2: 24.—
Romans 5: 19. Titus 3: 4-7.—Romans 8: 1. Jeremiah 23: 6.

By love serve one another.

Brethren, if a man be overtaken in a fault, ye which are spiritual, restore such a one in the spirit of meekness; considering thyself, lest thou also be tempted. Bear ye one another's burdens, and so fulfil the law of Christ.

Brethren, if any of you do err from the truth, and one convert him; let him know, that he which converteth the sinner from the error of his way shall save a soul from death, and shall hide a multitude of sins.—Seeing ye have purified your souls in obeying the truth through the Spirit unto unfeigned love of the brethren, see that ye love one another with a pure heart fervently.—Owe no man anything, but to love one another: for he that loveth another hath fulfilled the law.—Be kindly affectioned one to another in brotherly love; in honor preferring one another.—Yea, all of you be subject one to another, and be clothed with humility: for God resisteth the proud, and giveth grace to the humble.

We . . . that are strong ought to bear the infirmities of the weak, and not to please ourselves.

GALATIANS 5: 13. Galatians 6: 1, 2. James 5: 19, 20.—
I Peter 1: 22.—Romans 13: 8.—Romans 12: 10.—I Peter
5: 5. Romans 15: 1.

DECEMBER 9

To do justice and judgment is more acceptable
to the Lord than sacrifice.

He hath showed thee, O man, what is good; and
what doth the Lord require of thee, but to do justly,
and to love mercy, and to walk humbly with thy
God?—Hath the Lord as great delight in burnt
offerings and sacrifices, as in obeying the voice of the
Lord? Behold, to obey is better than sacrifice, and
to hearken than the fat of rams.—To love him with
all the heart, and with all the understanding, and
with all the soul, and with all the strength, and to
love his neighbor as himself, is more than all whole
burnt offerings and sacrifices.

Therefore turn thou to thy God: keep mercy and
judgment, and wait on thy God continually.—Mary
. . . sat at Jesus' feet, and heard his word. One thing
is needful: and Mary hath chosen that good part
which shall not be taken away from her.

It is God which worketh in you both to will and
to do of his good pleasure.

PROVERBS 21: 3. Micah 6: 8.—I Samuel 15: 22.—Mark
12: 33. Hosea 12: 6.—Luke 10: 39, 42. Philippians 2: 13.

No man is able to pluck them out of my Father's hand.

I KNOW whom I have believed, and am persuaded that he is able to keep that which I have committed unto him against that day.—The Lord shall deliver me from every evil work, and will preserve me unto his heavenly kingdom.—We are more than conquerors through him that loved us. For I am persuaded, that neither death, nor life, nor angels, nor principalities, nor powers, nor things present, nor things to come, nor height, nor depth, nor any other creature, shall be able to separate us from the love of God, which is in Christ Jesus our Lord.—Your life is hid with Christ in God.

Hath not God chosen the poor of this world rich in faith, and heirs of the kingdom which he hath promised to them that love him?

Our Lord Jesus Christ himself, and God, even our Father, which hath loved us, and hath given us everlasting consolation and good hope through grace, comfort your hearts, and stablish you in every good word and work.

JOHN 10: 29. II Timothy 1: 12.—II Timothy 4: 18.—Romans 8: 38, 39.—Colossians 3: 3. James 2: 5. II Thessalonians 2: 16, 17.

DECEMBER 11

Let not your good be evil spoken of.

ABSTAIN from all appearance of evil.—Providing for honest things, not only in the sight of the Lord, but also in the sight of men.—For so is the will of God, that with well-doing ye may put to silence the ignorance of foolish men.

But let none of you suffer as a murderer, or as a thief, or as an evil-doer, or as a busybody in other men's matters. Yet if any man suffer as a Christian, let him not be ashamed; but let him glorify God on this behalf.

Brethren, ye have been called unto liberty; only use not liberty for an occasion to the flesh, but by love serve one another.—Take heed lest by any means this liberty of yours become a stumbling-block to them that are weak.—Whoso shall offend one of these little ones which believe in me, it were better for him that a millstone were hanged about his neck, and that he were drowned in the depth of the sea.—Inasmuch as ye have done it unto one of the least of these my brethren, ye have done it unto me.

ROMANS 14: 16. I Thessalonians 5: 22.—II Corinthians 8: 21.—I Peter 2: 15. I Peter 4: 15, 16. Galatians 5: 13.—I Corinthians 8: 9.—Matthew 18: 6.—Matthew 25: 40.

The Lord is in the midst of thee.

FEAR thou not: for I am with thee: be not dismayed; for I am thy God: I will strengthen thee; yea, I will help thee; yea, I will uphold thee with the right hand of my righteousness.—Strengthen ye the weak hands, and confirm the feeble knees. Say to them that are of a fearful heart, Be strong, fear not: behold, your God will come with vengeance, even God with a recompense; he will come and save you.—The LORD thy God in the midst of thee is mighty; he will save, he will rejoice over thee with joy; he will rest in his love, he will joy over thee with singing.—Wait on the LORD: be of good courage, and he shall strengthen thy heart.

I heard a great voice out of heaven, saying, Behold, the tabernacle of God is with men, and he will dwell with them, and they shall be his people, and God himself shall be with them, and be their God. And God shall wipe away all tears from their eyes; and there shall be no more death, neither sorrow, nor crying, neither shall there be any more pain.

ZEPHANIAH 3: 15. Isaiah 41: 10.—Isaiah 35: 3, 4.—
Zephaniah 8: 17.—Psalms 27: 14. Revelation 21: 3, 4.

DECEMBER 13

Be strong in the grace that is in Christ Jesus.

S TRENGTHENED with all might, according to his glorious power.—As ye have therefore received Christ Jesus the Lord, so walk ye in him: rooted and built up in him, and stablished in the faith, as ye have been taught, abounding therein with thanksgiving.—Trees of righteousness, the planting of the LORD, that he might be glorified.—Built upon the foundation of the apostles and prophets, Jesus Christ himself being the chief corner-stone; in whom all the building fitly framed together groweth unto a holy temple in the LORD: in whom ye also are builded together for a habitation of God through the Spirit.

I commend you to God, and to the word of his grace, which is able to build you up, and to give you an inheritance among all them which are sanctified.—Being filled with the fruits of righteousness, which are by Jesus Christ, unto the glory and praise of God.

Fight the good fight of faith—In nothing terrified by your adversaries.

II TIMOTHY 2: 1. Colossians 1: 11.—Colossians 2: 6, 7.—Isaiah 61: 3.—Ephesians 2: 20-22. Acts 20: 32.—Philippians 1: 11. I Timothy 6: 12.—Philippians 1: 28.

Make his praise glorious.

This people have I formed for myself; they shall show forth my praise.—I will cleanse them from all their iniquity, whereby they have sinned against me: and I will pardon all their iniquities, whereby they have sinned, and whereby they have transgressed against me. And it shall be to me a name of joy, a praise and an honor before all the nations of the earth.—By him therefore let us offer the sacrifice of praise to God continually, that is, the fruit of our lips giving thanks to his name.

I will praise thee, O Lord my God, with all my heart: and I will glorify thy name for evermore. For great is thy mercy toward me: and thou hast delivered my soul from the lowest hell.—Who is like unto thee, O Lord, . . . glorious in holiness, fearful in praises, doing wonders?—I will praise the name of God with a song, and will magnify him with thanksgiving.— They sing the song of Moses the servant of God, and the song of the Lamb, saying, Great and marvellous are thy works, Lord God Almighty.

PSALMS 66: 2. Isaiah 43: 21.—Isaiah 33: 8, 9.—Hebrews 13: 15. Psalms 86: 12, 13.—Exodus 15: 11.—Psalms 69: 30.— Revelation 15: 3.

DECEMBER 15

Bear ye one another's burdens, and so fulfil the law of Christ.

Look not every man on his own things, but every man also on the things of others. Let this mind be in you, which was also in Christ Jesus: who . . . took upon him the form of a servant.—Even the Son of man came not to be ministered unto, but to minister, and to give his life a ransom for many.—He died for all, that they which live should not henceforth live unto themselves, but unto him which died for them, and rose again.

When Jesus . . . saw her weeping, and the Jews also weeping which came with her, he groaned in the Spirit, and was troubled. Jesus wept,—Rejoice with them that do rejoice, and weep with them that weep.

Be ye all of one mind, having compassion one of another, love as brethren, be pitiful, be courteous: not rendering evil for evil, or railing for railing: but contrariwise blessing; knowing that ye are thereunto called, that ye should inherit a blessing.

GALATIANS 6: 2. Philippians 2: 4, 5, 7.—Mark 10: 45.—II Corinthians 5: 15. John 11: 33. Romans 12: 15. I Peter 3: 8, 9.

Having loved his own which were in the world, he loved them unto the end.

I PRAY for them: I pray not for the world, but for them which thou hast given me; for they are thine. And all mine are thine, and thine are mine; and I am glorified in them. I pray not that thou shouldest take them out of the world, but that thou shouldest keep them from the evil. They are not of the world, even as I am not of the world.

As the Father hath loved me, so have I loved you: continue ye in my love.—Greater love hath no man than this, that a man lay down his life for his friends. Ye are my friends, if ye do whatsoever I command you.—A new commandment I give unto you, That ye love one another; as I have loved you, that ye also love one another.

He which hath begun a good work in you will perform it until the day of Jesus Christ.—Christ . . . loved the church, and gave himself for it; that he might sanctify and cleanse it by the washing of water by the word.

JOHN 13: 1. John 17: 9, 10, 15, 16. John 15: 9.— John 15: 13, 14.—John 13: 34. Philippians 1: 6.—Ephesians 5: 25, 26.

DECEMBER 17

Quicken us, and we will call upon thy name.

I T is the Spirit that quickeneth.—The Spirit also helpeth our infirmities: for we know not what we should pray for as we ought: but the Spirit itself maketh intercession for us with groanings which cannot be uttered. And he that searcheth the hearts knoweth what is the mind of the Spirit, because he maketh intercession for the saints according to the will of God.—Praying always with all prayer and supplication in the Spirit, and watching thereunto with all perseverance.

I will never forget thy precepts: for with them thou hast quickened me.—The words that I speak unto you, they are spirit, and they are life.—The letter killeth, but the spirit giveth life.—If ye abide in me, and my words abide in you, ye shall ask what ye will, and it shall be done unto you.—This is the confidence that we have in him, that, if we ask anything according to his will, he heareth us.

No man can say that Jesus is the Lord, but by the Holy Ghost.

PSALMS 80: 18. John 6: 63.—Romans 8: 26, 27.—Ephesians 6: 18. Psalms 119: 93.—John 6: 63.—II Corinthians 3: 6.—John 15: 7.—I John 5: 14. I Corinthians 12: 3.

DECEMBER 18

Let us come boldly unto the throne of grace, that we may obtain mercy, and find grace to help in time of need.

B<small>E</small> careful for nothing; but in everything by prayer and supplication with thanksgiving let your requests be made known unto God. And the peace of God, which passeth all understanding, shall keep your hearts and minds through Christ Jesus.—Ye have not received the spirit of bondage again to fear; but ye have received the Spirit of adoption, whereby we cry, Abba, Father.

I said not unto the seed of Jacob, Seek ye me in vain.—Having therefore . . . boldness to enter into the holiest by the blood of Jesus, by a new and living way, which he hath consecrated for us, through the veil, that is to say, his flesh; and having a high-priest over the house of God; let us draw near with a true heart in full assurance of faith, having our hearts sprinkled from an evil conscience, and our bodies washed with pure water.—We may boldly say, The Lord is my helper, and I will not fear what man shall do unto me.

HEBREWS 4: 16. Philippians 4: 6, 7.—Romans 8: 15. Isaiah 45: 19.—Hebrews 10: 19-21.—Hebrews 13: 6.

DECEMBER 19

Unto the upright there ariseth light in the darkness.

Who is among you that feareth the Lord, that obeyeth the voice of his servant, that walketh in darkness, and hath no light? let him trust in the name of the Lord, and stay upon his God.—Though he fall, he shall not be utterly cast down: for the Lord upholdeth him with his hand.—The commandment is a lamp, and the law is light.

Rejoice not against me, O mine enemy: when I fall, I shall arise; when I sit in darkness, the Lord shall be a light unto me. I will bear the indignation of the Lord, because I sinned against him, until he plead my cause, and execute judgment for me: he will bring me forth to the light, and I shall behold his righteousness.

The light of the body is the eye: if therefore thine eye be single, thy whole body shall be full of light. But if thine eye be evil, thy whole body shall be full of darkness. If therefore the light that is in thee be darkness, how great is that darkness!

PSALMS 112: 4. Isaiah 50: 10.—Psalms 37: 29.—Proverbs 6: 23. Micah 7: 8, 9. Matthew 6: 22, 23.

He hath chosen us in Him before the foundation of the world.

THAT we should be holy and without blame before him in love.

God hath from the beginning chosen you to salvation through sanctification of the Spirit and belief of the truth: whereunto he called you, . . . to the obtaining of the glory of our Lord Jesus Christ.—Whom he did foreknow, he also did predestinate to be conformed to the image of his Son, that he might be the first-born among many brethren. Moreover whom he did predestinate, them he also called: and whom he called, them he also justified: and whom he justified, them he also glorified.—Elect according to the foreknowledge of God the Father, through sanctification of the Spirit, unto obedience and sprinkling of the blood of Jesus Christ.

A new heart also will I give you, and a new spirit will I put within you: and I will take away the stony heart out of your flesh, and I will give you a heart of flesh.—God hath not called us unto uncleanness, but unto holiness.

EPHESIANS 1: 4. Ephesians 1: 4. II Thessalonians 2: 13, 14.—Romans 8: 29, 30.—I Peter 1, 2. Ezekiel 36: 26.— I Thessalonians 4: 7.

DECEMBER 21

The days of thy mourning shall be ended.

THE whole creation groaneth and traveleth in pain together until now. And not only they, but ourselves also, which have the first-fruits of the Spirit, even we ourselves groan within ourselves, waiting for the adoption, to wit, the redemption of our body.—We that are in this tabernacle do groan, being burdened: not for that we would be unclothed, but clothed upon, that mortality might be swallowed up of life.

These are they which came out of great tribulation, and have washed their robes, and made them white in the blood of the Lamb. Therefore are they before the throne of God, and serve him day and night in his temple: and he that sitteth on the throne shall dwell among them. They shall hunger no more, neither thirst any more; neither shall the sun light on them, nor any heat. For the Lamb which is in the midst of the throne shall feed them, and shall lead them into living fountains of water; and God shall wipe away all tears from their eyes.

ISAIAH 60: 20. Romans 8: 22, 23.—II Corinthians 5: 4. Revelation 7: 14-17.

Your work of faith.

THIS is the work of God, that ye believe on him whom he hath sent.

Faith, if it hath not works, is dead, being alone.— Faith worketh by love.—He that soweth to his flesh, shall of the flesh reap corruption; but he that soweth to the Spirit shall of the Spirit reap life everlasting.— We are his workmanship, created in Christ Jesus unto good works, which God hath before ordained that we should walk in them.—Who gave himself for us, that he might redeem us from all iniquity, and purify unto himself a peculiar people, zealous of good works.

We are bound to thank God always for you, brethren, as it is meet, because that your faith groweth exceedingly, and the charity of every one of you all toward each other aboundeth. Wherefore also we pray always for you, that our God would count you worthy of this calling, and fulfil all the good pleasure of his goodness, and the work of faith with power.—It is God which worketh in you both to will and to do of his good pleasure.

I THESSALONIANS 1: 3. John 6: 29. James 2: 17.— Galatians 5: 6.—Galatians 6: 8.—Ephesians 2: 10.—Titus 2: 14. II Thessalonians 1: 3, 11.—Philippians 2: 13.

DECEMBER 23

Let him take hold of my strength, that he may make peace with me.

I KNOW the thoughts that I think toward you, saith the LORD, thoughts of peace, and not of evil.—There is no peace, saith the LORD, unto the wicked.

In Christ Jesus ye who sometime were far off are made nigh by the blood of Christ. For he is our peace.

It pleased the Father that in him should all fulness dwell: and having made peace through the blood of his cross, by him to reconcile all things unto himself. —Christ Jesus: whom God hath set forth to be a propitiation through faith in his blood, to declare his righteousness for the remission of sins that are past: . . . that he might be just, and the justifier of him which believeth in Jesus.—If we confess our sins, he is faithful and just to forgive us our sins, and to cleanse us from all unrighteousness.

Trust ye in the LORD for ever, for in the LORD JEHOVAH is everlasting strength.

ISAIAH 27: 5. Jeremiah 29: 11.—Isaiah 48: 22. Ephesians 2: 13, 14. Colossians 1: 19, 20.—Romans 3: 24-26.—I John 1: 9. Isaiah 26: 4.

If ye live after the flesh, ye shall die: but if ye through the Spirit do mortify the deeds of the body, ye shall live.

Now the works of the flesh are manifest, which are these; Adultery, fornication, . . . and such like: of which I tell you before, as I have also told you in time past, that they which do such things shall not inherit the kingdom of God. But the fruit of the Spirit is love, joy, peace, long-suffering, gentleness, goodness, faith, meekness, temperance: against such there is no law. And they that are Christ's have crucified the flesh with the affections and lusts. If we live in the Spirit, let us also walk in the Spirit.

The grace of God that bringeth salvation hath appeared to all men, teaching us that, denying ungodliness and worldly lusts, we should live soberly, righteously, and godly, in this present world; looking for that blessed hope, and the glorious appearing of the great God and our Saviour Jesus Christ; who gave himself for us, that he might redeem us from all iniquity.

ROMANS 8: 13. Galatians 5: 19, 21, 25. Titus 2: 11-14.

DECEMBER 25

The kindness and love of God our Saviour toward man appeared.

I HAVE loved thee with an everlasting love.

In this was manifested the love of God toward us, because that God sent his only begotten Son into the world, that we might live through him. Herein is love, not that we loved God, but that he loved us, and sent his Son to be the propitiation for our sins.

When the fulness of the time was come, God sent forth his Son, made of a woman, made under the law, to redeem them that were under the law, that we might receive the adoption of sons.—The Word was made flesh, and dwelt among us, and we beheld his glory, the glory as of the only begotten of the Father full of grace and truth.—Great is the mystery of godliness: God was manifest in the flesh.

As the children are partakers of flesh and blood, he also himself likewise took part of the same; that through death he might destroy him that had the power of death, that is, the devil.

TITUS 3: 4. Jeremiah 31: 3. I John 4: 9, 10. Galatians 4: 5.—John 1: 14.—I Timothy 3: 16. Hebrews 2: 14.

DECEMBER 26

Be ye steadfast, unmoveable, always abounding in the work of the Lord.

Y<small>E</small> know that your labor is not in vain in the Lord. —As ye have . . . received Christ Jesus the Lord, so walk ye in him: rooted and built up in him, and stablished in the faith, as ye have been taught, abounding therein with thanksgiving.—He that shall endure unto the end, the same shall be saved.—That on the good ground are they, which in an honest and good heart, having heard the word, keep it, and bring forth fruit with patience.—By faith ye stand.

I must work the works of him that sent me, while it is day: the night cometh, when no man can work.

He that soweth to his flesh shall of the flesh reap corruption; but he that soweth to the Spirit shall of the Spirit reap life everlasting. And let us not be weary in well-doing: for in due season we shall reap, if we faint not. As we have therefore opportunity, let us do good unto all men, especially unto them who are of the household of faith.

I CORINTHIANS 15: 58. I Corinthians 15: 58.—Colossians 2: 6, 7.—Matthew 24: 13.—Luke 8: 15.—II Corinthians 1: 24. John 9: 4. Galatians 6: 8-10.

DECEMBER 27

We look not at the things which are seen: . . .
for the things which are seen are temporal; but
the things which are not seen are eternal.

HERE have we no continuing city.—Ye have in
heaven a better and an enduring substance.

Fear not, little flock: for it is your Father's good
pleasure to give you the kingdom.

Now for a season, if need be, ye are in heaviness
through manifold temptations. There the wicked
cease from troubling; and there the weary be at rest.

We that are in this tabernacle do groan, being
burdened.—God shall wipe away all tears from their
eyes; and there shall be no more death, neither sorrow, nor crying, neither shall there be any more pain:
for the former things are passed away.

The sufferings of this present time are not worthy
to be compared with the glory which shall be revealed in us.—Our light affliction . . . worketh for us
a far more exceeding and eternal weight of glory.

II CORINTHIANS 4: 18. Hebrews 13: 14.—Hebrews 10:
34. Luke 12: 32. I Peter 1: 6.—Job 3: 17. II Corinthians
5: 4.—Revelation 21: 4. Romans 8: 18.—II Corinthians
4: 17.

Thy sins be forgiven thee.

I WILL forgive their iniquity, and I will remember their sin no more.—Who can forgive sins but God only?

I, even I, am he that blotteth out thy transgressions for mine own sake, and will not remember thy sins. —Blessed is he whose transgression is forgiven, whose sin is covered. Blessed is the man unto whom the LORD imputeth not iniquity.—Who is a God like unto thee, that pardoneth iniquity?

God for Christ's sake hath forgiven you.—The blood of Jesus Christ his Son cleanseth us from all sin. If we say that we have no sin, we deceive ourselves, and the truth is not in us. If we confess our sins, he is faithful and just to forgive us our sins, and to cleanse us from all unrighteousness.

As far as the east is from the west, so far hath he removed our transgressions from us.—Sin shall not have dominion over you: for ye are not under the law, but under grace. Being then made free from sin, ye became the servants of righteousness.

MARK 2: 5. Jeremiah 31: 34.—Mark 2: 7. Isaiah 43: 25.— Psalms 32: 1, 2.—Micah 7: 18. Ephesians 4: 32.—I John 1: 7-9. Psalms 103: 12.—Romans 6: 14, 18.

DECEMBER 29

Understanding what the will of the Lord is.

This is the will of God, even your sanctification.—Acquaint now thyself with him, and be at peace: thereby good shall come unto thee.—This is life eternal, that they might know thee the only true God, and Jesus Christ, whom thou hast sent.

We know that the Son of God is come, and hath given us an understanding, that we may know him that is true, and we are in him that is true, even in his Son Jesus Christ.

We . . . do not cease to pray for you, and to desire that ye might be filled with the knowledge of his will in all wisdom and spiritual understanding.—The God of our Lord Jesus Christ, the Father of glory, . . . give unto you the spirit of wisdom and revelation in the knowledge of him: the eyes of your understanding being enlightened; that ye may know what is the hope of his calling, and what the riches of the glory of his inheritance in the saints; and what is the exceeding greatness of his power to us-ward who believe.

EPHESIANS 5: 17. I Thessalonians 4: 3.—Job 22: 21.—John 17: 3. I John 5: 20. Colossians 1: 19.—Ephesians 1: 17, 18.

Blameless in the day of our Lord Jesus Christ.

You, that were sometime alienated and enemies in your mind by wicked works, yet now hath he reconciled in the body of his flesh through death, to present you holy and unblamable and unreprovable in his sight: if ye continue in the faith grounded and settled, and be not moved away from the hope of the gospel. —That ye may be blameless and harmless, the sons of God, without rebuke, in the midst of a crooked and perverse nation, among whom ye shine as lights in the world.

Wherefore, beloved, seeing that ye look for such things, be diligent, that ye may be found of him in peace, without spot, and blameless.—That ye may be sincere and without offence till the day of Christ.

Now unto him that is able to keep you from falling, and to present you faultless before the presence of his glory with exceeding joy, to the only wise God our Saviour, be glory and majesty, dominion and power, both now and ever.

I CORINTHIANS 1: 8. Colossians 1: 21-23.—Philippians 2: 15. II Peter 3: 14.—Philippians 1: 10. Jude 24, 25.

DECEMBER 31

The Lord thy God bare thee, as a man doth bear his son, in all the way . . . until ye came into this place.

I BARE you on eagles' wings, and brought you unto myself.—In his love and in his pity he redeemed them; and he bare them, and carried them all the days of old.—As an eagle stirreth up her nest, fluttereth over her young, spreadeth abroad her wings, taketh them, beareth them on her wings, so the LORD alone did lead him.

Even to your old age I am he; and even to hoar hairs will I carry you.—This God is our God for ever and ever; he will be our guide even unto death.

Cast thy burden upon the LORD, and he shall sustain thee.—Take no thought for your life, what ye shall eat, or what ye shall drink; nor yet for your body, what ye shall put on. For your heavenly Father knoweth that ye have need of all these things.

Hitherto hath the LORD helped us.

DEUTERONOMY 1: 31. Exodus 19: 4.—Isaiah 63: 9.—
Deuteronomy 32: 11, 12. Isaiah 46: 4.—Psalms 48: 14.
Psalms 55: 22.—Matthew 6: 25, 32. I Samuel 7: 12.

THOUGHTS FOR
SPECIAL OCCASIONS

THANKSGIVING

They cry unto the Lord in their trouble, and he saveth them out of their distresses. Oh, that men would praise the Lord for his goodness and for his wonderful works to the children of men!

WERE there not ten cleansed? but where are the nine?—Forget not all his benefits.—God, who answered me in the day of my distress.

I sought the LORD, and he heard me and delivered me from all my fears.—I love the LORD, because he hath heard my voice and my supplications. Because he hath inclined his ear unto me, therefore will I call upon him as long as I live.—My heart trusted in him and I am helped; therefore my heart greatly rejoiceth, and with my song will I praise him.

Call upon me in the day of trouble: I will deliver thee, and thou shalt glorify me.—Whoso offereth praise glorifieth me.

Giving thanks always for all things unto God and the Father in the name of our Lord Jesus Christ.

PSALMS 107: 19, 21. Luke 17: 17.—Psalms 103: 2.— Genesis 35: 3. Psalms 34: 4.—Psalms 116: 1, 2.—Psalms 28: 7. Psalms 50: 15.—Psalms 50: 23. Ephesians 5: 20.

FOR A BIRTHDAY

The Lord bless thee and keep thee.

THE LORD that made heaven and earth bless thee.
—God, even our Father.—The living God, who giveth
us richly all things to enjoy.

Your heavenly Father knoweth that ye have need
of all these things.—For the Father himself loveth you.

No good thing will he withhold from them that
walk uprightly.—He layeth up sound wisdom for the
righteous: he is a buckler to them that walk uprightly.—Blessed are they that keep his testimonies
and that seek him with the whole heart.

He that keepeth thee will not slumber. Behold, he
that keepeth Israel shall neither slumber nor sleep.—
The LORD shall be thy confidence and shall keep thy
foot from being taken.—Thou wilt keep him in perfect peace whose mind is stayed on thee, because he
trusteth in thee.

The LORD of peace himself give you peace always by
all means.

NUMBERS 6: 24. Psalms 134: 3.—II Thessalonians 2:
16.—I Timothy 6: 17. Matthew 6: 32.—John 16: 27. Psalms
84: 11.—Proverbs 2: 7.—Psalms 119: 2. Psalms 121: 3, 4.
Proverbs 3: 26.—Isaiah 26: 3.—II Thessalonians 3: 16.

FOR A BIRTHDAY

Oh, send out thy light and thy truth: let them lead me!

Where is the way where light dwelleth?—The Lord shall be unto thee an everlasting light.—God is light, and in him is no darkness at all. If we walk in the light, as he is in the light, we have fellowship one with another, and the blood of Jesus Christ his Son cleanseth us from all sin.

Show me thy ways, O Lord. . . . Lead me in thy truth and teach me: for thou art the God of my salvation; on thee do I wait all the day.—Thy word is a lamp unto my feet and a light unto my path.—Thy word is truth.

The Lord is my light and my salvation: whom shall I fear?—He leadeth me in the paths of righteousness for his name's sake. Surely goodness and mercy shall follow me all the days of my life; and I will dwell in the house of the Lord for ever.

PSALMS 43: 3. Job 38: 19.—Isaiah 60: 19.—I John 1: 5, 7. Psalms 25: 4, 5.—Psalms 119: 105.—John 17: 17. Psalms 27: 1.—Psalms 23: 3, 6.

MARRIAGE

Jesus was called, and his disciples, to the marriage.

M ARRIAGE is honorable in all.—The Lord God said, It is not good that man should be alone.—Every creature of God is good, and nothing to be refused, if it be received with thanksgiving; for it is sanctified by the word of God and prayer.

The blessing of the LORD, it maketh rich, and he addeth no sorrow with it.—The living God giveth us richly all things to enjoy.—Who crowneth thee with loving-kindness and tender mercies, who satisfieth thy mouth with good things.

Christ loved the church and gave himself for it.— Ye are not your own.

Brethren, the time is short: it remaineth that both they that have wives be as though they had none, and they that rejoice as though they rejoiced not, and they that use this world as not abusing it: for the fashion of this world passeth away.—Set your affection on things above.

JOHN 2: 2. Hebrews 13: 4.—Genesis 2: 18.—I Timothy 4: 4, 5. Proverbs 10: 22.—I Timothy 6: 17.—Psalms 103: 4, 5. Ephesians 5: 25.—I Corinthians 6: 19. I Corinthians 7: 29, 31.—Colossians 3: 2.

FOR TIMES OF ANXIETY

Neither know we what to do, but our eyes are upon thee.

O God, thou knowest my foolishness, and my sins are not hid from thee.—Teach me to do thy will; for thou art my God.—Lead me, O Lord, in thy righteousness: make thy way straight before my face.—My times are in thy hand.

If any of you lack wisdom, let him ask of God, that giveth to all men liberally and upbraideth not, and it shall be given him. But let him ask in faith, nothing wavering.—Who is among you that feareth the Lord, that walketh in darkness, and hath no light? let him trust in the name of the Lord and stay upon his God.

In the multitude of my thoughts within me thy comforts delight my soul.—Why art thou cast down, O my soul, and why art thou disquieted within me? Hope thou in God.

Jesus . . . said unto them, Why are ye so fearful? How is it that ye have no faith?—Now faith is the evidence of things not seen.

II CHRONICLES 20: 12. Psalms 69: 5.—Psalms 143: 10.—Psalms 5: 8.—Psalms 31: 15. James 1: 5, 6.—Isaiah 50: 10. Psalms 94: 19.—Psalms 42: 5. Mark 4: 40.—Revelation 11: 1.

FOR SICKNESS

Lord, behold, he whom thou lovest is sick.

Surely he hath borne our griefs and carried our sorrows.—Himself took our infirmities and bare our sicknesses.—He, being full of compassion.—Like as a father pitieth his children, so the Lord pitieth them that fear him. For he knoweth our frame.

Who shall separate us from the love of Christ? Shall tribulation or distress?—Whom the Lord loveth he chasteneth.—Now no chastening for the present seemeth to be joyous, but grievous: nevertheless afterward it yieldeth the peaceable fruit of righteousness unto them which are exercised thereby.—We know that all things work together for good to them that love God.

The Lord said unto me, My grace is sufficient for thee, for my strength is made perfect in weakness. Most gladly therefore will I rather glory in my infirmities, that the power of Christ may rest upon me.

JOHN 11: 3. Isaiah 53: 4.—Matthew 8: 17.—Psalms 78: 38.—Psalms 103: 13, 14. Romans 8: 35.—Hebrews 12: 6.—Hebrews 12: 11.—Romans 8: 28. II Corinthians 12: 9.

AFFLICTION

Save me, O God, for the waters are come in unto my soul.

O my Father, if it be possible, let this cup pass from me: nevertheless, not as I will, but as thou wilt. —Being in an agony.—Jesus wept.

Surely he hath borne our griefs and carried our sorrows.—We have not a high priest which cannot be touched with the feeling of our infirmities, but was in all points tempted like as we are, yet without sin. Let us therefore come boldly unto the throne of grace, that we may . . . find grace to help in time of need.

He careth for you.—I have called thee by thy name; thou art mine.—When thou passest through the waters, I will be with thee, and through the rivers, they shall not overflow thee.—I will never leave thee nor forsake thee.

Though he slay me, yet will I trust in him.—My flesh and my heart faileth; but God is the strength of my heart and my portion for ever.

PSALMS 69: 1. Matthew 26: 39.—Luke 22: 44.—John 11: 35. Isaiah 53: 4.—Hebrews 4: 1, 16. I Peter 5: 7.—Isaiah 43: 1.—Isaiah 43: 2.—Hebrews 13: 5. Job 13: 15.—Psalms 73: 26.

BEREAVEMENT

Father, I will that they also whom thou hast given me be with me where I am.

H<small>E</small> shall return no more to his house, neither shall his place know him any more.

While we are at home in the body we are absent from the Lord; we are willing rather to be absent from the body and to be present with the Lord.—I am in a strait betwixt two, having a desire to depart and to be with Christ, which is far better.—Whether we live or die, we are the Lord's.

Ye have in heaven a better and an enduring substance.—It doth not yet appear what we shall be; but we know that, when he shall appear, we shall be like him, for we shall see him as he is.—Now we see through a glass, darkly, but then face to face.—I will behold thy face in righteousness: I shall be satisfied, when I awake, with thy likeness.

So shall we ever be with the Lord. Wherefore comfort one another with these words.

JOHN 17: 24. Job 7: 10. II Corinthians 5: 6-8.—I Corinthians 1: 23.—Romans 14: 8. Hebrews 10: 34.—I John 3: 2.—I Corinthians 13: 12.—Psalms 17: 15. I Thessalonians 4: 17, 18.